INTERPERSONAL

PSYCHOTHERAPY

OF DEPRESSION

INTERPERSONAL PSYCHOTHERAPY OF DEPRESSION

Gerald L. Klerman, M.D.
Myrna M. Weissman, Ph.D.
Bruce J. Rounsaville, M.D.
Eve S. Chevron, M.S.

JASON ARONSON INC.
Northvale, New Jersey
London

THE MASTER WORK SERIES

First softcover edition 1994

ISBN: 1-56821-350-6
Library of Congress Catalog Card Number: 94-72437

Manufactured in the United States of America. Jason Aronson Inc. offers books and cassettes. For information and catalog write to Jason Aronson Inc., 230 Livingston Street, Northvale, New Jersey 07647.

The field of psychiatry is the field of interpersonal relations, under any and all circumstances in which these relations exist . . . a personality can never be isolated from the complex of interpersonal relations in which the person lives and has his being.

Harry Stack Sullivan
Conceptions of Modern Psychiatry

Contents

PART III

SELECTED ASPECTS OF IPT

Preface

Interpersonal Psychotherapy of Depression describes the theoretical and empirical basis for interpersonal psychotherapy of depression and offers a guide to the planning and conduct of the therapy. IPT is a new and, we believe, effective therapy developed specifically for the treatment of depression. The book is therefore intended for mental health professionals who are interested in learning the principles of IPT of depression.

IPT of depression has evolved over the past fifteen years from the experiences of the New Haven–Boston Collaborative Depression Research Project in the treatment of ambulatory depressed, nonpsychotic, nonbipolar patients (Bipolar depression refers to patients who were previously called manic-depressive because they have episodes of both depression and mania). Variants of IPT have been tested in several clinical trials of depressed patients: one of maintenance (Klerman et al., 1974; Weissman et al., 1974); the second of acute treatment (Weissman et al., 1979; DiMascio et al., 1979); and the third a multisite collaborative study sponsored by the National Institute of Mental Health, which is currently underway (Waskow and Parloff). At least three other smaller clinical trials of IPT on ambulatory depressives are underway as of early 1984 (Weissman, 1984).

We believe that many types of treatment are suitable for depression, depending on the needs of the particular patient. Many psychological and pharmacologic treatments are available for use alone or in combination, and therapists will best serve each patient's needs by using a combination of research and personal empathy to settle upon a productive line of treatment for the depressed person.

This book evolved from a manual which was developed to train therapists in the concepts and techniques of IPT so that efficacy studies could be undertaken. The project, carried out by Chevron, Rounsaville, and Weissman at Yale University's Depression Research Unit, developed a program for training experienced therapists of different disciplines—psychiatrists, psychologists, social workers, and psychiatric nurses—in IPT principles.

This work has involved the efforts of many people over the years, especially the late Alberto DiMascio, Ph.D., who led the Boston portion of the project; Brigitte Prusoff, Ph.D., who was in charge of the data analysis of the two clinics;

and Carlos Neu, M.D., who helped prepare early versions of the IPT Manual.

Our work has always involved the testing of psychotherapy with and without drugs for depressed patients. We are grateful to Jerome Levine, M.D., chief of the Psychopharmacology Branch, NIMH, for his support during the early phase of these studies, when pharmacotherapy as maintenance treatment was the major research interest. Irene Elkin Waskow, Ph.D., in her role as project director of the NIMH Collaborative Study on the Treatment of Depression, which included IPT as one of the treatments, gave us the impetus to further refine the treatment and develop the training. Morris Parloff, Ph.D., was the guiding spirit and organizer of the collaborative study. The leadership provided by Morris Parloff has been carried on without interruption by John Docherty, M.D.

We especially wish to express appreciation to those who participated in our various IPT research training programs as therapists or evaluators—Lillian Comas-Diaz, Ph.D.; Cleon Cornes, M.D.; Lois Freedman, M.D.; Effie Geanakoplos, M.S.W.; Bill Glazer, M.D.; Kay Goebel, Ph.D.; Norman Harway, Ph.D.; David Joseph, M.D.; Elizabeth Keating, Ph.D.; Anthony Kowalski, M.D.; Helen Orvaschel, Ph.D.; Karen Orzack-Moore, M.S.W.; Elizabeth Rogoff, Ed.D.; Esther Rothblum, Ph.D.; Louise Schneider, M.D.; Herbert Schulberg, Ph.D.; Anne Schwartz, M.S.W.; Roger Shapiro, M.D.; Steven Shapiro, M.D.; John R. Smith, M.D.; Lester Turner, Ph.D.; and Diana Zuckerman, Ph.D.—and to the Principal Investigators of the research sites where the collaborative study is being carried out: Stanley Imber, Ph.D.; Stuart Sotsky, M.D.; and John Watkins, Ph.D. Their comments and experiences are incorporated in the many revisions of the manual and finally in this book.

We appreciate the support of the Harvard Department of Psychiatry at Massachusetts General Hospital, particularly Thomas P. Hackett, M.D., Chairman. Appreciation is also expressed to the George Harrington Trust, Boston, Massachusetts for support of Dr. Klerman and the George Harrington Program.

We also appreciate the support of the Yale faculty, particularly Morton Reiser, M.D., Chairman of the Department of Psychiatry and Boris Astrachan, M.D., Vice-Chairman of the Department and Director of the Connecticut Mental Health Service.

We also thank Joan Smolka, Grace Pauls, and Jerri Levchuk for their patient typing of the many versions of this manuscript.

Development and testing of IPT have been supported over the years by grants MH137838, MH15650, MH26466, and MH26467 from the Psychopharmacology Research Branch and the Clinical Research Branch, and grant MH33827-03 from the Psychosocial Treatments Research Branch of the National Institute of Mental Health, Alcohol, Drug Abuse, and Mental Health Administration.

Most important, we thank the many depressed patients who have participated in our studies of IPT through the years. Without their willingness to discuss their treatment with us, and at times to allow us to videotape actual psychotherapy sessions, we would have been unable to develop this therapy. All case material has been substantially altered so that it is not possible to relate any case material presented to the actual patients treated.

INTERPERSONAL

PSYCHOTHERAPY

OF DEPRESSION

"I *do* like you. *You* don't like you!"
Drawing by Weber; © 1965
The New Yorker Magazine, Inc.

Overview of IPT

The cartoon from the *New Yorker* illustrates many of the clinical features of depression. It is immediately apparent that the woman is depressed. How do we know this? The nonverbal and behavioral features convey her depressed state. She has a downcast gaze and a flattening of the nasal labial folds reflecting the facial changes first described by Darwin. She is slumped in the chair, a sign of "slowing down," or psychomotor retardation. She looks dowdy, which indicates the scant attention that depressed individuals give to their dress and grooming. And the fact that the depressed person is a woman is more than fortuitous: epidemiologic studies indicate that depression occurs more frequently in women than in men (Weissman and Klerman, 1977a). In addition, this woman is middle-aged, and depression occurs increasingly after puberty, peaking during the ages twenty-five to forty-four and declining somewhat in later years (Weissman, Myers, and Thompson, 1981). More recent studies in the U.S., Canada, and western Europe indicate a younger onset for women (Murphy, unpublished).

But we see that, although it is the woman who is depressed, the problem is a family affair. The man in the cartoon (we assume it is her husband, since couples of this generation are less likely to be merely living together) is irritated and frustrated. He has a sense of futility as he says, "I *do* like you. *You* don't like you." In this he captures an important aspect of the clinical phenomenology of depression, the fall in self-esteem and the self-depreciating sense of worthlessness and helplessness.

While the wife is depressed and sullen, the husband is out of patience and even hostile. This precisely illustrates the effect of protracted clinical depression on interpersonal relationships. In the early stages of a depressive episode, sympathy, nurturance, and reassurance are elicited from "significant others"—significant people in the person's life, such as family members, friends and acquaintances. But if the depression is not resolved by what we may call "psychotherapy of everyday life," the response of those in the immediate environment tends to shift from support and encouragement to increasing irritation and frustration, if not outright anger. At this point the patient is likely to be accused of "not really trying," of wanting to "make everybody miserable," or "doing it to us on purpose." These pseudopsychological insights are usually expressed in a pejorative way, reflecting the frustration of those around the depressed person rather than any scientific understanding of the complexities of depression.

It is possible to reconstruct what probably happened to this funny but sad couple. Over a number of months, the woman has slowly become depressed, perhaps after the oldest children have left home and the "nest is empty." As part of the psychotherapy of everyday life, the husband has tried to reassure her and to be optimistic about the future. He has said, "I love you as much as when we courted in college" or "You are just as beautiful as ever." These reassurances have evidently been of little avail. His wife continues to feel discouraged and worthless —depressed.

Thus far there would be almost complete agreement among most clinicians and theorists. However, depending upon the theoretical orientation and training of the psychotherapist, a variety of responses and recommendations would be likely.

A *biological psychiatrist* would interpret this picture as reflecting a decrease in brain catecholamines at subcortical centers and say that the woman's fall in self-esteem and feelings of worthlessness reflect not psychological difficulty but the altered pathophysiology (Klerman, unpublished). The biological psychiatrist would invoke the medical model to label the patient as having a major depressive disorder and might recommend treatment with a tricyclic antidepressant; if that failed after six to eight weeks at adequate dosage, perhaps monitored by blood level determinations, then a stronger drug or electroconvulsive therapy might be considered.

A *psychoanalyst* would interpret the patient's current situation as a reactivation of unresolved childhood difficulties and ambivalent identifications with the mother. Feelings of helplessness and hopelessness would be seen as the response to inadequate mothering, most likely during the oral phases of psychosexual development. With the coming of menopause and the departure of the children, the patient experiences a loss of gratification from identification with the maternal role and regresses to early oral narcissistic stages of fixation. Perhaps psychoanalysis would be directed at uncovering the childhood antecedents, particularly in the mothering relationship at the preoedipal phase and in working through the unresolved ambivalence toward the lost image of the idealized mother.

A *family therapist* would see this as a problem in communication between husband and wife. Couples therapy would be recommended with the aim of improving communications between them and helping both of them express their mutual frustrations and hostilities, in the hope that a new relationship would emerge.

A *radical feminist therapist* might say that the patient is not depressed but rather oppressed. Rather than being seen as ill, she should be encouraged to see her psychological state as reflective of the true social position of women in a society dominated by male-chauvinism. If she feels worthless and helpless it is not a neurotic distortion of reality, the radical feminist would say, but rather a true perception of the low status of women. Without the childbearing role, she has no legitimate place in the society; lacking any marketable skills, she is in fact worthless, and her feelings of helplessness are reflections of her inability to alter the power relationship between herself and her husband. Rather than needing drugs or psychotherapy, she needs to be politically activated and to have her consciousness raised, perhaps by participating in a consciousness-raising group and in political action.

These varied responses to the same clinical picture show the current diversity of American psychiatry. There is no one, dominant American school of psychiatry, and there is no consensus as to how best regard the causes, prevention, and treatment of mental illnesses.

Given this situation, how should the mental health field proceed? The authors believe that progress will be furthered by a pluralistic, undoctrinaire, and empirical approach that builds upon clinical experience and research evidence. Since we are pluralistic, we acknowledge these multiple theoretical and clinical points of view; indeed our work has been nurtured by them. We are convinced, however, that all theories and schools require testing against the evidence, and that the most powerful evidence comes from carefully designed and well-controlled investigations. In the area of treatment, the most powerful evidence comes from controlled clinical trials, and we have subjected IPT to trials and other investigations, including a large-scale NIMH Collaborative Study of Psychotherapy of Depression.

Although many of its principles derive from the broader school of interpersonal psychiatry, IPT of depression is a psychological treatment designed specifically for the needs of depressed patients. It is a focused, short-term, time-limited therapy that emphasizes the current interpersonal relations of the depressed patient while recognizing the role of genetic, biochemical, developmental, and personality factors in causation of and vulnerability to depression. We are convinced from clinical experience and research evidence that clinical depression occurs in an interpersonal context and that psychotherapeutic interventions directed at this interpersonal context will facilitate the patients' recovery from the acute episode and possibly have preventive effects against relapse and recurrence. Part One of the book—the first three chapters—presents the rationale for IPT of depression.

The first step in using IPT successfully is to recognize just what depression is: the distinction between normal and clinical depression; the social, biological, and medical antecedents of clinical depression as diagnosed through the use of a medical model. These aspects, as well as the prevalence of depression in human society, are discussed in Chapter 1, "The Nature of Depressions—Normal and Clinical." In addition to theoretical formulations, Chapter 1 describes the empirical basis for treating depression with an interpersonal approach, including cultural research and studies of animals, children, and adults. The importance of attachment bonding, stress, and marital and other interpersonal disputes in the development of depression is emphasized.

Chapter 2 describes the theoretical basis for IPT of depression, which derives from the interpersonal school of psychotherapy, one of the distinctive contributions the United States has made to psychiatry and mental health. Adolf Meyer of Johns Hopkins may justly be called the founder of this school, and his associate, Harry Stack Sullivan, became its leading proponent. Meyer's psychobiological approach to understanding psychiatric disorders placed great emphasis on the patient's current psychosocial and interpersonal experiences; Sullivan, who linked clinical psychiatry to anthropology, sociology, and social psychology, viewed psychiatry as the scientific study of people and the processes that go on among them, rather than the exclusive study of the mind or of society.

The IPT emphasis on interpersonal and social factors in the understanding and treatment of depression also draws upon the work of many other clinicians, especially Fromm-Reichmann (1960) and Cohen et al. (1954), and more recently Arieti and Bemporad (1978). Becker (1974) and Chodoff (1970) have also emphasized the social roots of depression and the need to attend to the interpersonal aspects of the disorder. An interpersonal conceptualization has been applied to psychotherapy in the writings of Frank (1973), who stressed mastery of current interpersonal situations as an important component of psychotherapy.

In Chapter 3, the interpersonal approach is applied specifically to the understanding of clinical depression, which is considered to have three component processes:

1. *symptom function,* which involves the development of depressive affect and the negative signs and symptoms, and may derive from psychobiological and/or psychodynamic mechanisms;

2. *social and interpersonal relations,* which involve interactions in social roles with other persons and derive from learning based on childhood experi-

ences, concurrent social reinforcement, and/or personal mastery and competence; and

3. *personality and character problems,* which involve enduring traits such as inhibited expression of anger or guilt, poor psychological communication with significant others, and/or difficulty with self-esteem. These traits determine a person's reactions to interpersonal experience. Personality patterns form part of the person's predisposition to depressive symptom episodes.

IPT intervenes in the first two of these three processes: symptom function and social and interpersonal relations. Because of its relatively brief duration and its low level of psychotherapeutic intensity, there is little expectation that this treatment will have marked impact upon enduring aspects of personality structure, although personality functioning is assessed.

IPT facilitates recovery of the acute depression: 1) by relieving the depressive symptoms; and 2) by helping the patient develop more effective strategies for dealing with current interpersonal problems associated with the onset of symptoms. In Part Two, "Conducting Interpersonal Therapy of Depression," Chapters 4 and 5 discuss diagnostic techniques for depression and ways of achieving these two goals. Chapters 6 through 9 explore the four common problems—grief and loss, role disputes, role transition, and interpersonal deficits—that are associated with the onset of depression, so that patient and therapist can focus on those of most concern to each patient.

In our experience, insufficient attention has been paid in the psychotherapy of depressed patients to techniques directed at symptom reduction and facilitation of the patient's current social adjustment and interpersonal relations. With the psychotherapy undertaken in IPT, personality reconstruction is not attempted. Reliance is upon well-established techniques such as reassurance, clarification of emotional states, improvement of interpersonal communication, and testing of perceptions and performance through interpersonal contact.

These techniques are conventionally grouped under the rubric of "supportive" psychotherapy. However, in our view the term is a misnomer. Most of what is called "supportive" psychotherapy tries to help patients modify their interpersonal relationships and change their perceptions and cognitions. IPT, on the other hand, intervenes with symptom formation and social adjustment/interpersonal relations, working predominantly on *current* problems and at conscious and preconscious levels. Although unconscious factors are recognized, they are not given direct attention in IPT. The emphasis is upon current disputes, frustrations, anxieties, and wishes as defined in the interpersonal context. The influence of early childhood experiences is recognized as significant but is not emphasized in the therapy. Rather, the work focuses on the "here-and-now." Overall goals of treatment are to encourage mastery of current social roles and adaptation to interpersonal situations.

IPT strategies and techniques are of course embedded in all of this book, especially its case histories, but they are described most concretely in Chapters 10, "Termination," 11, "Specific Techniques," 12, "An Integrative Case Example," and 14, "Problems Occasionally Encountered in the Therapy." Chapter 13, "Combining Psychotherapy with Pharmacotherapy," offers guidelines for combined treatment with one therapist or two. The last chapter describes the professional background, role, and training of the IPT therapist.

Before proceeding first to the general and then to the practical chapters describing IPT of depression, a survey of other forms of psychotherapy for depression and a report on recent research comparing it with other therapies may help readers put the IPT treatment in perspective.

Other Forms of Psychotherapy for Depression

Psychotherapy has been a stunning success in the marketplace. Practitioners, consumers (patients and clients), and therapies themselves have multiplied, so that some two hundred and fifty therapies have been identified. These are administered by psychiatrists, psychologists, psychiatric social workers, nurses, clergy, counselors, and so on, for a variety of conditions, including schizophrenia, alcoholism, phobias, distress, despair, and lack of social interest. Comprehensive reviews of these therapies have recently been provided by Parloff et al. (1978) and Glass, Smith, and Miller (1981).

Alternative psychotherapeutic approaches specifically to depression are described by Beck (1976); Hersen (1976); Lewisohn, Biglan, and Zeiss (1976); McLean, Ogston, and Grauer (1973); and Rehm (1976). There is much debate about the relative therapeutic efficacy of social reorganization, as typified by women's consciousness groups, and of intrapsychic reorganization, as used in psychoanalysis and other intensive psychotherapies and medication. Several recently developed psychotherapies for depression are of special interest for practitioners of IPT.

BRIEF PSYCHOTHERAPIES BASED ON PSYCHODYNAMIC PRINCIPLES

A number of excellent brief treatments for a variety of conditions including no specific psychiatric disorder have been described by, among others, Malan (1963); Sifneos (1979); Mann (1973); Strupp (1982); Davenloo (1982); and Luborsky et al. (1975).

Malan's intensive brief psychotherapy is an anxiety-provoking therapy based on psychoanalytic techniques. The aim is to resolve either the patient's central problem or some important aspect of his psychopathology. First, there is a thoroughgoing psychodynamic assessment and psychiatric history, in order to understand the patient's illness as deeply as possible, predict the course of treatment, to decide what behavior is unsuitable, and to make a therapeutic plan. The plan is central to this brief treatment. The time-limited nature of the therapy is stated at the beginning. The average time seems to be twenty sessions, although this can vary up to one year. High motivation for insight is important in selecting patients and a thorough interpretation of transference is done. Therapist and patient must be willing to become deeply involved, and there is an early development of transference which shows the capacity to be a patient and to get help. Feelings about interpersonal situations are explored and interpreted. This therapy is not designed for any specific diagnoses. To our knowledge there are no clinical trials assessing efficacy.

Sifneos' short-term psychotherapy is similar to the treatment Malan describes and has some similarities to IPT. A therapeutic alliance is reached early and there is some agreement between patient and therapist on the symptoms and/or interpersonal conflict to be worked on. Clarification is used frequently. A history of current and past interpersonal relationships is obtained, and the change that is expected is in this area. Character traits are not the main focus of treatment. Like Malan's, this therapy differs from IPT in that it is not specific for any one psychiatric diagnosis. Psychodynamic formulations and developmental history are essential. The therapy is deliberately anxiety provoking in order to maintain the therapeutic alliance. Formulations of a patient's emotional conflict, resistance, ambivalences, and negative transference are undertaken early and repeatedly, and the focus is on circumscribed areas of unresolved conflict. The patient is taught to become aware of these conflicts and to obtain objectivity and work through the problems. Confrontation is used as a way of helping the patient experience transference. Anxiety-provoking questions and transference are used to understand the conflict in the current interpersonal relationship. The change the patient undergoes during treatment is considered intrapsychic. The intensity is somewhat similar to that of IPT, in that sessions are held once a week, but the Sifneos therapy does not specify the duration of treatment. There has been no testing of the efficacy of this treatment in randomized clinical trials.

Horowitz has described a brief psychotherapy of stress response syndrome, personal reactions to sudden serious life events that trigger internal responses with symptomatic patterns that reach a level of painful neurotic symptomatology. The therapeutic strategy is based on a pattern of phases, including denial and intrusiveness, which are modified according to individual character style. There are three goals: 1) acceptance of unalterable limitation without loss of hope or meaning in life; 2) maintenance of available relationships and development of useful new ones; and 3) working through reaction of the life event toward some type of growth. The therapy depends upon establishing a safe relationship and then reappraising the event and its meaning. A therapeutic alliance with some transference is established. Support, structuring of time and events, medication (if indicated), and permission to work on feelings around the event are offered. Twelve therapy hours are typical and the focus is on the stressful events. Whether or not changes in personality structure occurs is left open by the author.

A number of other psychodynamically oriented psychotherapies have developed forms of short-term psychotherapy. Mann (1973) and Davenloo (1982) have described the conceptual basis for their psychotherapies and provided illustrative case material, but no manuals are available and no systematic evidence (either naturalistic methods or controlled trials) for efficacy has been reported.

Very recently Strupp (1982) and Luborsky (1975) have produced manuals, Strupp for "Time Limited Dynamic Psychotherapy" and Luborsky for "Dynamic Supportive-Expressive Psychotherapy." Although these treatments were not specifically designed for depression, they have been used in systematic studies in which many of the patients probably were depressed.

BRIEF PSYCHOTHERAPIES SPECIFICALLY FOR DEPRESSION

Several psychotherapies have been designed specifically for depressive disorder. Two of these, the cognitive and the behavioral approaches, have been tested for efficacy in controlled clinical trials.

Cognitive Therapy.

Cognitive therapy is a brief treatment, usually twelve to sixteen sessions, developed by Aaron Beck. It is based on the assumption that the affective response in depression is determined by the way the individual perceives experience as a result of an emergence of maladaptive cognitive themes. Depressed patients tend to regard themselves and their future negatively, and correction of negative concepts is expected to alleviate the depressed symptoms. For example, an extremely low self-concept can be treated by presenting a hierarchy of cognitive tasks and through these tasks demonstrating the invalidity of the patients' self-perception. At least seven randomized clinical trials have tested the efficacy of cognitive therapy, and it has been compared with imipramine in at least three clinical trials. Two trials found cognitive therapy more efficacious than imipramine in the reduction of the symptoms of depression. The third found it about equal to pharmacotherapy.

Behavioral Approaches.

A number of short-term (usually around twelve sessions) behavioral approaches have been developed specifically for depressed patients. Many of them have procedural manuals to facilitate training. Behavior therapy explains the occurrence of depression in stimulus and response terms (Lewisohn, 1976). A low rate of positive reinforcement is presumed to elicit certain aspects of the depressive syndrome and be predictable by negative reinforcing events in the environment and lack of available positive reinforcement, as well as by how the individual behaves. A number of techniques based on behavioral concepts have been developed for treating depressed patients. These include social skills therapy, which emphasizes increasing assertiveness, verbal skills, and social functioning; pleasant events therapy, which focuses on increasing pleasant and rewarding experiences; and self-control therapy, which emphasizes self-monitoring, self-evaluation, and self-reinforcement, to correct problems with self-control in monitoring negative events and in making internal attributions of responsibilities and self-punishment. Such behavioral approaches have been tested in at least nine randomized clinical trials (Weissman, 1984). In all these trials behavioral therapy has been shown to be more effective than either a waiting list or a no-treatment control group. In one study, behavior therapy was found to be more effective than amitriptyline (McLean, 1973). Both the cognitive and the behavioral approaches are similar to IPT in that they were developed specifically for depression, have been tested, and have been shown to be efficacious in several randomized clinical trials. A large-scale clinical trial was begun in 1980 by the National Institute of Mental Health to test the efficacy of cognitive and interpersonal psychotherapy as compared to imipramine and a clinical management placebo control group in depressed outpatients.

BRIEF PSYCHOTHERAPIES BASED ON INTERPERSONAL CONCEPTS

A comprehensive description of a variety of interpersonal psychotherapies can be found in a book edited by Anchin and Kiesler (1982).
Interactional Individual Therapy.

Developed by Cashdan (1982), this therapy is similar to IPT in that immediate interpersonal relationships are the focus of therapy It differs in that maladaptive strategies, not clinical diagnoses, are the target for treatment. Interactional psychotherapy deals with maladaptive strategies as they present themselves in the course of treatment. The goal is to guide the patient through a series of sequential learning experiences in order to replace maladaptive patterns with more productive ways of relating. The therapy process begins with the therapy establishing a relationship in which the therapist takes on the characteristics of a significant figure, one potentially capable of satisfying the patient. After this happens, maladaptive strategies emerge spontaneously as the patient attempts to bind the therapist in an intimate and extended relationship. The therapist manipulates exchanges so that the patient is forced to relinquish the strategy to maintain the relationship. The conclusion is the development of new ways of relating, as reflected in more mature and adaptive patient and therapist exchanges. Although five stages are described, the length of treatment time is not given, and as far as we know there are no clinical trials testing its efficacy.

Communication Analytic Therapy.

A form of interpersonal therapy developed by Beier and Young (1980), this therapy is based on analysis of communication patterns, with the premise that patients in psychological distress feel they cannot accept full responsibility for their conduct. The conflict and distress are based on two mutually exclusive motivations: the desire for individual freedom and integrity, and the need for social control. The patient's pain is viewed as a message to self and others. It is assumed that the patient's characteristic style of behaving will occur within the therapeutic hour, and it is the therapist's job to point out how the patient is using this with the therapist. Understanding the communications is an important part of the therapy. Communication analysis is interpersonal in that it deals with communication patterns in the current interpersonal situation, but it is not specifically for any type of disorder. The length of treatment is unspecified and it has not been tested in clinical trials.

Brief Interactional Psychotherapy, developed by Coyne and Segal (1982), focuses on current interpersonal relations and is based on the assumption that the therapist is in a position to disregard the relationship of the patient to other people. The clinical problem presented by the patient is seen as an aspect of ongoing interpersonal systems, and the patient's distress and symptoms are believed to arise from the mismanagement of a life transition, such as marriage or divorce, or from the mishandling of everyday difficulties. Severe symptomatology may reflect the exacerbation of internal difficulties through repetition of unreasonable and inappropriate problem-solving efforts by patients and those around them. This therapy has not been tested in clinical trials and is not specifically designed for depression.

LONG-TERM INTERPERSONAL PSYCHOTHERAPY FOR DEPRESSION

The earliest expositions of interpersonal psychotherapy were of long-term treatments, notably in the writings of Sullivan and Fromm-Reichmann. These new ideas were first applied to the hospital-based treatment of schizophrenia at Chestnut Lodge in Maryland and at Austen Rggs in Massachusetts, and later to manic-depressive patients in a series of twelve cases in intensive individual psychotherapy reported by Mabel Blake-Cohen et al. in their classic report (1954).

Arieti and Bemporad (1978) have extended this approach in a comprehensive report that considers mild and severe depression separately. Mild depression is described as being constant or characterological, so that the depressed mood becomes an important feature of the character. This condition may occur after an unpleasant or adverse event and is often accompanied by anxiety or by obsessive compulsive symptoms.

Severe depression is differentiated in that the features are clearly pronounced, easily recognizable, and more easily defined. It is characterized by a pervasive feeling of melancholy, psychomotor retardation, gloomy and morbid ideas, and vegetative symptoms such as constipation, backache, skin dryness, and impotence. According to Arieti and Bemorad, psychotherapy is indicated for every case of primary severe depression, and the intensity of the depression should not deter the therapist. Although psychotropic drugs may also be essential, an immediate and intense rapport at the beginning of treatment is developed. The psychotherapist should be active and compassionate, but not so much as to make the patient feel helpless. The psychotherapist searches with the patient to understand the cause of the depression. When the therapist establishes rapport and proves a desire to nourish and offer hope, the patient often accepts the therapist but only as a dominant third. The procedure of leaning on a dominant third may arouse objection on theoretical grounds, but Arieti and Bemporad see it as necessary in obtaining initial rapport. The object of the initial stages of the therapy is to change the therapist's role from dominant third to significant third, a third person with a firm, sincere, and unambiguous personality who wants to help the patient without making demands. The only demand the therapist does make is that patient and therapist become a search team committed to finding the cause of the depression, and to altering the depression and making it less harmful. The therapist must determine the major psychodynamic pattern of living that has led to the depressive episode and offer therapeutic alternatives that allow the patient to do successful work.

As in IPT, one of the first therapeutic tasks consists of ascertaining the person with whom the patient is most involved, the dominant other. Once the therapist has gathered enough information, the relationship with the dominant other must be interpreted to the patient. The therapist also clarifies the need to live for oneself rather than conforming to the wishes of others by denying one's own wishes. Treatment of the severely depressed patient requires a change in the patient's psychological makeup that is substantial and difficult to implement. The patient is not asked to give up his identity, but whatever lie or impossible value has become connected with an inauthentic identity.

The treatment of mild depression is based on the premise that the problem often recurs and that the goals should not aim simply at recovery from the present condition but at protecting the patient from future depressions in normal life circumstances. According to the authors, patients with mild depression are caught in a network of pathological relationships with others who will attempt to prevent personality changes. The psychotherapeutic approach to mild depression centers on three basic issues: 1) the characterological defenses; 2) the underlying unconscious cognitive structures in terms of evaluation of self and others; and 3) the transference situation, which is the major therapeutic force.

The psychotherapist must be careful not to become a new dominant other on whom the patient will depend for gratification. The subtle manipulativeness of mildly depressed patients must not be allowed to elicit false assurances. These patients are often difficult, anger-provoking, and even boring. It is important for the patient to come to terms with "ghosts of the past" and with either overestimations of past dominant others or angry incriminations against them. Before termination of therapy the past must be accepted without excessive rancor and the relationship with the therapist should take on the characteristics of friendship.

The therapy described by Arieti and Bemporad is rich in clinical details. Although it differs from IPT in that it is not brief, it resembles IPT in that it derives from the theoretical approach of the interpersonal school. Arieti and Bemporad, however, also make extensive use of classic psychoanalytic approaches, especially in their attention to unconscious intrapsychic conflicts, long-standing characterological problems, and reconstruction of childhood developmental and family experiences.

IPT Compared with Other Psychotherapies

Like Frank (1973), we believe that the procedures and techniques of many of the schools of psychotherapy have much in common. Important common elements include attempts to help patients gain a sense of mastery, combating social isolation, restore a sense of group belonging, and find meaning in their lives. A major difference among the therapies is their conceptualization of the causes of the patient's problems as lying in the far past, the immediate past, or the present.

IPT focuses mainly on the patient's current life situations. It is time-limited; attends to current symptoms and to the interpersonal context associated with the depression; includes a systematic review of relations with current "significant others," and has been developed for the treatment of a single disorder—depression.

TIME-LIMITED, NOT LONG-TERM

Considerable research has demonstrated the usefulness of short-term, time-limited psychotherapy, usually less than nine to twelve months, in meeting the needs of most patients. Long-term treatment is required for changing personality dysfunction, particularly maladaptive interpersonal and cognitive patterns. For immediate problems and most symptomatic states, however, short-term treatment is efficacious.

Long-term treatment has the potential disadvantage of promoting dependence and reinforcing avoidance behavior. Short-term, time-limited treatment may well avoid these adverse effects.

FOCUSED, NOT OPEN-ENDED

In common with other brief psychotherapies, IPT is directed toward one or two problem areas in the patient's current interpersonal functioning, agreed upon by patient and therapist after several evaluation sessions.

CURRENT, NOT PAST INTERPERSONAL RELATIONSHIPS

The IPT therapist focuses the sessions on the patient's immediate social context, as it was before and has been since the onset of the current depressive episode. Past depressive episodes, early family relationships, previous significant relationships, and friendship patterns are assessed, to enhance understanding of the patient's patterns in interpersonal relationships, but in most cases, after a brief review of the patient's past behavior, the therapist focuses primarily on current social functioning.

INTERPERSONAL, NOT INTRAPSYCHIC

In exploring current interpersonal problems with the patient, the IPT therapist may recognize intrapsychic defense mechanisms such as projection, denial, isolation, undoing, or repression. However, the therapist does not attempt to help the patient see the current situation as a manifestation of an internal conflict. Rather, the patient's behavior is explored in terms of interpersonal relations.

Another example of the interpersonal focus is in the handling of dreams. Although dreams are not usually asked for, the patient may report dreams. In this case the therapist may work on the dream by focusing on the manifest content and associated affects, relating these to current interpersonal problems.

INTERPERSONAL, NOT COGNITIVE/BEHAVIORAL

IPT tries to change the way the patient thinks, feels, and acts in problematic interpersonal relationships. Behaviors such as lack of assertiveness, guilt, lack of social skills, emphasis on unpleasant events, and negative cognitions are not focused on for their own sake, but only in relationship to significant persons in the patient's life and to the way these behaviors or cognitions impinge upon the interpersonal relationships.

In common with cognitive-behavioral therapy, IPT is concerned with patients' distorted thinking about themselves and others, and about the options open to them. The IPT therapist may work with a patient on distorted thinking by calling attention to discrepancies between what the patient is saying and doing, or between the patient's standards and those of society in general. Unlike cognitive-behavioral therapies, IPT makes no attempt to uncover such distorted thoughts systematically, by giving "homework" or other assignments, nor is there an attempt to help the patient develop alternative thought patterns through prescribed practice. Rather, when evidence arises during the course of therapy, the therapist calls the patient's attention to distorted thinking in relation to significant others. From there, the therapist insists that the patient explore the effect of this maladaptive thinking on interpersonal relationships.

PERSONALITY IS RECOGNIZED BUT NOT FOCUSED ON

The patient's personality is often the major psychic-therapeutic focus, but, since IPT does not expect to make an impact on personality, this therapy recognizes but does not focus on the patient's personality characteristics. Moreover, IPT does not assume that persons who become depressed have unique personality traits. Whether they do or not is an empirical question that requires testing, and thus far research has not yielded any conclusive answers (Hirshfield and Cross, 1983).

Personality is, however, considered an important aspect of IPT therapy, as it is in all therapies. In IPT it is believed to affect several aspects of treatment.

1. Personality may predict psychotherapy outcome. Patients with personality disorders may be less able to make effective use of short-term psychotherapy than those with mild or absent personality pathology. (This too is an empirical question.)
2. Personality may alter the patient-therapist relationship.
3. Personality may be a determinant of the patient's recurrent interpersonal problems. Although IPT therapists may make no attempt to explore the antecedents of personality functioning, or to change personality, they may help patients recognize maladaptive personality features. For instance, for a patient with mild paranoid tendencies, the therapist may point out a tendency to be "touchy" with certain people under certain conditions, and help explore the interpersonal consequences. In trials of IPT, personality has not so far been found to be an important determinant of short-term outcome (Zuckerman et al., 1980).

These similarities and differences between IPT and other psychotherapies are summarized in Table I.1.

TABLE I.1
Comparison of IPT With Other Psychotherapies

IPT	Non-IPT Psychotherapies
What has contributed to this patient's depression right now?	Why did the patient become what he/she is and/or where is the patient going?
What are the current stresses?	What was the patient's childhood like?
Who are the key persons involved in the current stress? What are the current disputes and disappointments?	What is the patient's character?
Is the patient learning how to cope with the problem?	Is the patient cured?
What are the patient's assets?	What are the patient's defenses?
How can I help the patient ventilate painful emotions—talk about situations that evoke guilt, shame, resentment?	How can I find out why this patient feels guilty, ashamed, or resentful?
How can I help the patient clarify his or her wishes and have more satisfying relationships with others?	How can I understand the patient's fantasy life and help him/her get insight into the origins of present behavior?
How can I correct misinformation and suggest alternatives?	How can I help the patient discover false or incorrect ideas?

Relationship of IPT to Dynamic Psychotherapies

In training IPT psychotherapists and in discussions with clinical and research colleagues, we find a close relationship between IPT and dynamic psychotherapies. Many experienced, dynamically trained and psychoanalytically oriented psychotherapists report that the concepts and techniques of IPT are already part of their standard approach. In developing IPT, our goal was not to create a new psychotherapy but to make explicit and operational a systematic approach to depression based on theory and empirical evidence. The fact that much of IPT is part of what many, perhaps most, psychotherapists do in brief treatment is a reflection of the extent to which the interpersonal approach has permeated the mental health field and psychotherapeutic practice in the United States.

This development is probably due to two historical trends. First, most of the earlier theorists and practitioners of the interpersonal approach were trained in Freudian psychoanalysis, so that the role of early childhood experiences and of unconscious mental processes were not sources of disagreement. Disagreement arose over the existence of libido, the dual-instinct (eros and death) theory, and the relative importance of biological-instinctive forces in relation to social and cultural influences on personality development and current functioning. Second, the expansion of psychotherapy after World War II coincided with general concerns about social change, racial and sexual equality, personal well-being and the enhancement of personal potential and individual happiness—and all these cultural values were highly compatible with a scientific and professional focus on interpersonal relations and personal development throughout the whole of the life cycle.

For purposes of theoretical clarification and of research design and methodology, we often find it useful to emphasize the differences between interpersonal and psychodynamic approaches to human behavior and mental illness. The essential feature of a "pure" psychodynamic approach is a focus on unconscious mental processes and on the role of intrapsychic memories, wishes, fantasies, and conflicts in determining behavior and psychotherapy. The essential feature of a purely interpersonal approach is a focus on the social roles and interpersonal interactions in the individual's past and current life experiences. Both interpersonal and psychodynamic approaches are concerned with the whole life span, and both consider early experience and persistent personality patterns important. In understanding human transactions, however, the psychodynamic therapist is concerned with object relations while the interpersonal therapist focuses on interpersonal relations. The psychodynamic therapist listens for the patient's intrapsychic wishes and conflicts; the interpersonal therapist listens for the patient's role expectations and disputes.

Ideally, a comprehensive theory would incorporate both these approaches along with biological, behavioral, and other views. However, given the current state of science and health care, we believe it is valuable to focus on one approach and to explore its validity and utility.

Efficacy of IPT

IPT has been designed for ambulatory patients who meet the medical criteria for major depression (see Chapter 1). Two controlled clinical trials of the treatment, one for acute and one for maintenance outpatient treatment, have been completed and four are underway.

Current efficacy data are for ambulatory, nonpsychotic, and nonbipolar patients of either sex, and of various racial groups and educational levels. Although the earliest trial of IPT was conducted before the RDC and DSM-III diagnostic criteria were available, the patients included meet these criteria. Mentally retarded and chronic alcoholic patients have been excluded from these studies. However, persons with personality disorders as defined by the DSM-III or the RDC have not been excluded.

There has been one trial among opiate-addicted patients, with IPT added to a standard drug-abuse program vs. the drug-abuse program alone (Rounsaville, 1983). The results indicated that IPT offered no advantage over standard program in opiate-addicted populations. The value of IPT or a modification of it (if required) for this and other personality disorders requires testing.

IPT FOR ACUTE DEPRESSION

The study of the treatment of acutely depressed, ambulatory men and women compared using IPT alone, amitriptyline alone, and the two in combination, against a nonscheduled treatment group for sixteen weeks (Weissman, 1979). IPT was administered weekly by experienced psychiatrists. A total of eighty-one depressed patients entered the randomized treatment study (DiMascio, 1979); (Weissman, 1979).

The control for IPT was nonscheduled treatment. In nonscheduled treatment, patients were assigned a psychiatrist and told to get in touch whenever they felt a need for treatment. No active treatment was scheduled but the patient could telephone. If the patient's needs were of sufficient intensity, a fifty-minute session (maximum, one a month) was scheduled. Patients requiring further treatment— who were still symptomatic after eight weeks, or whose clinical condition had worsened sufficiently to require other treatment—were considered failures of this treatment and were withdrawn from the study. Assessments of the patients' clinical conditions were made by a clinician who was blind to the treatment the patient was on and who did not participate in the clinical phase of the study. *IPT Compared to Nonscheduled Treatment for Acute Depression.*

Symptomatic failure over sixteen weeks was significantly less in IPT than in nonscheduled treatment. These results were upheld on assessments made by the independent clinical evaluator, the patient self-report, and the treating psychiatrist. The effects on the patient's social and interpersonal functioning took six to eight months to develop fully. At the one-year follow-up, patients who had received IPT, with or without tricyclics, were functioning at a less impaired level in social activities and with their spouses, children, and other relatives. *IPT Compared to Tricyclics.*

Overall, the rate of symptomatic improvement was similar to that of patients receiving IPT alone as compared to tricyclics alone, and both were better than nonscheduled treatment. However, the two regular treatments had a different effect on symptoms (DiMascio, 1979). IPT had its impact on improving mood, work performance and interest, suicidal ideation, and guilt. The effects became statistically apparent after four to eight weeks of treatment and were sustained

throughout the treatment. Amitriptyline had its impact mainly on vegetative signs and symptoms of depression—sleep and appetite disturbance and somatic complaints. The effect on sleep came early, within the first week of treatment.
IPT in Combination with Tricyclics.

Because of the differential effects of IPT and tricyclics on the type of symptoms and because patients have a range of symptoms, patients receiving combination treatment as compared to either treatment alone had greater overall improvement in symptoms, lower attrition, and lower chance of symptomatic failure (Weissman, 1979). Patients receiving combination treatment were less likely to refuse it initially and less likely to drop out before the end of the sixteen-week study treatment. Combination treatment was both more acceptable and better tolerated (Herceg-Baron, 1979). There were no negative interactions between drugs and psychotherapy. The effects were additive (Rounsaville, 1979).
Predictors of Response to Acute Treatment.

Patients who had an endogenous, nonsituational depression responded best to combined IPT and drugs and less well to IPT alone; those using IPT alone showed no differences in response from those in the nonscheduled treatment group. The response of patients who received drugs alone was more positive than that of patients with IPT alone and less positive than that of patients receiving the combination treatment. Patients with situational nonendogenous depressions did equally well on drugs alone, IPT alone, or the combination, and better than on nonscheduled treatment (Cohen et al., 1954); (Prusoff, 1980).

The patient's personality type, as measured by a variety of inventories or by the presence of a depressive personality diagnosis, did not affect response to any of the short-term treatments (Zuckerman, 1980). This finding suggests that the presence of a personality disorder in addition to major depression does not preclude the use of drugs or IPT for the acute episode.

FOLLOW-UP AFTER ACUTE TREATMENT

Patients were followed up one year after treatment had ended. Those who had received IPT either alone or in combination were functioning better in social activities, as parents, in their families, and overall (Weissman, 1981).

IPT AS MAINTENANCE TREATMENT

IPT as maintenance treatment was tested in an eight-month trial for 150 women recovering from an acute depressive episode. They were treated for six to eight weeks with amitriptyline. This study tested the efficacy of IPT (administered weekly by experienced psychiatric social workers) as compared with a low-contact control (brief monthly visits for assessments), with either amitriptyline, placebo, or no pill. Treatment was by random assignment (Klerman, 1974).

Maintenance IPT as compared with low-contact visits significantly enhanced social and interpersonal functioning for patients who did not relapse. The effects of IPT on social functioning took six to eight months to become statistically apparent (Weissman, 1974). Patients receiving IPT as compared to low contact were significantly less socially impaired, particularly in work, in their extended families, and in marriage. Overall improvement in social adjustment was significantly greater in IPT than in low contact.

Maintenance IPT as compared to amitriptyline was less efficacious in the prevention of symptomatic relapse. Patients on amitriptyline only as compared to IPT alone showed less evidence of depressive symptoms during maintenance treatment (Paykel, 1976).

Because of the differential impact of IPT and of tricyclics on relapse and on social functioning, overall the combination treatment was the most efficacious. Patients who received the combination drug and IPT had a lower risk of relapse and greater improvement in social functioning. Moreover, as was shown for acute treatment, the effects were additive. There were no negative interactions between drugs and psychotherapy.

All patients were followed up one and four years after the end of the eight-month maintenance treatment. At one year, thirty percent were completely without symptoms, 60 percent had had mild return of symptoms over the year, and 10 percent were chronically depressed (Weissman, Kasl, and Klerman, 1976); (Weissman and Klerman, 1977b). Although the presence of personality problems did not interfere with the short-term acute treatment, for the long-term outcome, patients who scored high on the neurotic personality scale and who did not receive maintenance treatment with either drugs or IPT were doing less well (Weissman, 1978). These findings suggest the value of maintenance treatment for patients with personality problems.

STUDIES IN PROGRESS

Four studies of the efficacy of IPT in ambulatory depressed patients are now in progress (Weissman, 1984):

1. A multisite NIMH sponsored collaborative study on the treatment of depression, testing the efficacy of IPT, cognitive therapy, imipramine and clinical management, placebo and clinical management for sixteen weeks with 240 ambulatory depressed patients at three sites (George Washington University, University of Pittsburgh, and University of Oklahoma) (NIMH, 1980).

2. A separate study at the University of Pittsburgh, testing the efficacy of maintenance IPT alone, IPT and placebo, IPT and imipramine, clinical

management and imipramine, clinical management and placebo, with 125 ambulatory patients with recurrent depression administered over a three-year period (Weissman, 1984).

3. A study at the University of Southern California, testing the efficacy of noritriptyline placebo versus IPT for 60–90 ambulatory depressed elderly patients over sixteen weeks.

4. A study at the University of Wisconsin, testing the efficacy of cognitive-behavioral (CB) group therapy with or without homework, IPT, or waiting list, for 140 depressed outpatients for ten weeks.

Because of the enduring nature of marital problems in depressed patients (Rounsaville, 1979); (Rounsaville, 1980) and the tendency for patients with marital problems to have enduring symptoms (Rounsaville, 1980), the Yale group is currently developing a manual for IPT in a conjoint marital context. After a training manual and a pilot test are developed, and therapists are trained, we will test the efficacy of individual vs. conjoint marital IPT for depressed patients with marital problems.

Psychotherapy outcome research is developing rapidly. In addition to the use of randomized treatment assignment and independent and blind clinical assessment of outcome, the work presented here has attempted to incorporate two important methodologic advances for psychotherapy clinical trials: operationalized and defined diagnostic criteria to allow for relatively homogenous patient groups, and operationalized and defined psychotherapeutic procedures to facilitate comparability of goals and focus between therapies and to allow for replication. This work has been evolving as we gain experience and new methodology becomes available. IPT has been refined further since the studies described here were completed and is now ready for replication studies outside the New Haven–Boston centers.

Substantively, we have demonstrated the efficacy of 1) maintenance IPT as compared to low contact in recovering depressives in enhancing social functioning; and 2) IPT as compared to nonscheduled treatment in acute depressives on symptom reduction and later on social functioning. The effects on social functioning take at least six to eight months to become apparent. These findings are consistent with the general concept of IPT.

Having compared IPT with other therapies for depression, we begin our study of IPT with an examination of the nature of depression itself.

PART I

THE INTERPERSONAL APPROACH TO DEPRESSION

". . . no, it's the small losses in life that strike at your
heart. Losing all of those things that other people value
as next to nothing."
—Henrik Ibsen
The Master Builder

Chapter 1

The Nature of Depressions—
Normal and Clinical

———

Observers of human endeavors are inclined to divide history into various stages. Thus historians refer to the Middle Ages, the Age of Enlightenment, the Edwardian Era. Recently, psychological terms have sometimes been used to describe historical periods. Probably the most successful instance of this was W. H. Auden's poem *The Age of Anxiety,* published in 1947, which seemed to capture the mood of widespread anxiety after World War II. Many writers, particularly Robert Jay Lifton (1976), have related this mood to awareness of the potential destruction of the whole human species with the advent of nuclear power.

In the 1960s, speculation began about whether depression and despair were becoming the dominant mood. By the 1980s, in contrast to the age of anxiety that followed World War II, we appear to be in the midst of an "age of melancholia." This age of melancholia appears in part to be associated with doomsday prophecies concerning nuclear warfare, overpopulation, and ecological destruction, and with the persistent economic difficulties in the United States and elsewhere that have followed the prosperity of the 1950s and 1960s.

Increasing public attention to depression and other affective emotional states during the 1970s and 1980s is reflected in numerous articles in newspapers and magazines and in television and radio broadcasts. There is greater public recognition of depression as a health problem, and media coverage of mental illness in general has reduced the stigma attached to depressive states. Political leaders, astronauts, figures in the arts and entertainment fields, and other celebrities now publicly acknowledge that they have suffered from depressions.

How good is the evidence indicating an actual increase in epidemiologic rates of depression? More scientific articles are being written about depression than before. More antianxiety and antidepressant drugs are being prescribed. An increase in the diagnosis of depression is evident in data from the United States, Great Britain, and Scandinavia. But the fact that more people are being diagnosed and treated for depression in general hospitals, community mental health centers, and clinic settings may be the consequence of more attention to the problem and of increased insurance coverage, rather then a true increase in incidence or prevalence. Moreover, it is still "nicer" to label someone depressed rather than schizophrenic or paranoid.

But there is certainly a worldwide rise in suicide attempts; indeed, the rate has increased almost tenfold among adolescents and young adults. Women have higher suicide attempt rates than men, with the highest rates occurring among women under thirty, and the most common technique is pill ingestion, a tribute to our new pharmacologic technologies (Weissman et al., 1973). Other findings, less well documented, also show that the median age of depressed patients is dropping.

The depressive experience is well described throughout the history of Western civilization. There are excellent descriptions in the Bible, particularly of Saul's depression, which David treated successfully. There are also clinical descriptions in Egyptian, Greek, and Roman medical literature from which the modern clinician has no difficulty in recognizing the symptoms of depression.

It is hard to know how much literary trends reflect epidemiological trends, but it is tempting to think that we are in an age of melancholia as a transition after an age of anxiety. Ours is a period in which rising expectations, generated after World War II, have come up against harsh realities of population explosion and doomsday prophecies, and one of the situations that psychologically predisposes individuals to depression is a gap between expectations and actuality. One feels despair not so much when a situation is actually bad as when one has given up hope.

The Range of Depressive States

The term depression has many meanings. For the neurophysiologist, depression refers to any decrease in the electrophysiological activity of an organ or system; as in "cortical depression." The pharmacologist uses the term to refer to drug actions that decrease the activity of an organ or system, so that the "central nervous system (CNS) depressants" include the barbiturates and the anesthetics, which are not clinically or pharmacologically related to "antidepressant" drugs. The psychologist designates as "depression" any decrease in normal performance, such as slowing of psychomotor activity or reduction of intellectual functioning. For clinical psychiatrists and other mental health professionals, however, depression covers a wide range of changes in affective state, ranging in severity from normal, everyday moods of sadness or despondency to psychotic episodes with risk of suicide.

As a mood or affect or emotional state, depression is part of normal human experience. Feelings of sadness and disappointment are within the vicissitudes of the normal human condition. The distinction between normal mood and abnormal depression is not always clear, although considerable research on diagnostic criteria is underway, and neither psychiatrists nor other clinicians agree on the precise line between normal and psychopathological affective phenomena. Diagnosis is especially difficult for the large number of patients with episodes of mood change in which a recent precipitating event appears significant, especially since clinicians tend to credit depressive reactions to such stressful events when they are apparent.

As a pathological symptom, depression often occurs in association with other psychiatric and medical illnesses, which makes precise diagnosis even harder. For example, in elderly people the differential diagnosis between early senile dementia and depression may be difficult. The term "secondary depression" has been proposed to encompass these symptomatic depression states (Robins and Guze, 1972). In clinical psychiatric practice, however, most depressive symptoms are "primary," that is, without apparent association with preexistent or concomitant illness.

Each year, between 4 and 8 percent of the population experiences a clinical depressive syndrome (Weissman and Boyd, 1983), a constellation of symptoms in which the mood disturbance is accompanied by sleep difficulty, change in appetite, retardation of thinking, and attitudes of hopelessness, helplessness, pessimism, and even suicidal tendencies. Moreover, since these symptoms often persist, the diagnostic criteria embodied in the third edition of the American Psychiatric Association's *Diagnostic and Statistical Manual,* known as DSM-III, require at least two weeks' duration of such symptoms, plus evidence that their intensity and pervasiveness have impaired the individual's usual social role performance and personal activities.

Depression as a Normal Mood

Although only a small minority of individuals experience depressive symptoms that meet the criteria of a clinical disorder, many more experience depressive moods: about 40 percent of the population report feelings of depression, disappointment, and unhappiness in a year (Bradburn, 1975). The evidence indicates that women are more prone than men to depression, not only in terms of prevalence but in terms of lifetime expectancy.

Although the capacity to become depressed is almost universal, and depression is thus a ubiquitous human experience, it is not a uniquely human condition. Many mammals, especially primates, also have this capacity. Naturalistic observations, particularly of dogs (Scott, 1970) and primates (Goodall and Hamburg, 1971), have demonstrated the occurrence of characteristic biobehavioral reactions to separation and loss, reactions with many similarities to human depression. These animal observations were anticipated in the writings of Darwin, who proposed that emotional expression, like anatomical structures, has had a biological evolution and has contributed to the survival of all mammalian species. This capacity, as Darwin was the first to point out, evolved as a response to the biological helplessness of the mammalian infant, which enters life incompletely developed and requiring a period of extrauterine nurturance and protection before becoming capable of independent biological survival.

Drawing upon these observations, Klerman (1974), (Harlow, Harlow, and Suomi, 1971), and others have concluded that the capacity to become depressed, developed through long periods of extrauterine dependence, has contributed to the development of social bonds and learned behavior among many mammalian and primate species and most particularly among humans. These social bonds and learning have greatly assisted the survival and expansion of the human species. Like all mammals, the human infant enters extrauterine life biologically helpless and dependent on adult figures for nutrition, warmth, protection, and survival. Adults may experience feelings of helplessness and dependence and may express the wish to be taken care of by some other person or parental surrogate, but the infant is in fact helpless even before conscious representations of wishes, perceptions, and memories is neurologically possible.

This biological fact of human extrauterine dependence provides the basis for the development of attachment bonds, especially between the infant and the mother figure, and for powerful reinforcement of social learning and group membership. Bowlby (1969) has expanded upon animal observations to emphasize the importance of attachment bonding in human experience. Development of these attachment bonds and the associated social learning involve complex brain structures that have been modified through the evolutionary process and are inherited as part of the human biological apparatus. In human infants, the depressive response (crying, facial change, postural change) is almost universally precipitated by separation from the mother figure. This has been documented not only in human infant studies but also in studies of animal separation, most importantly by Harlow (Harlow and Suomi, 1971), McKinney (Suomi and Harlow, 1973), and Kaufman and Rosenblum (1967).

Although the child grows and becomes biologically less helpless, humans retain the capacity to respond to certain stimuli with depression. In addition to real separations through death or physical distance, other forms of environmental change stimulate the depressive response. And the anticipation of separation from the parenting object also becomes a cause of depression, so that fear of abandonment is a prominent feature of the psychology of school-age children. Through social learning and the generalization of stimuli, other situations— disappointments, frustration of wishes, criticisms and reproaches, changes in interpersonal relations, and shifts in dominant-submissive relationships—may be precipitants for depressive symptoms.

Although humans share the capacity to become depressed with other mammals and primates, humans, because of language and cognitive abilities, can anticipate death, loss, and separation, not only for others but also for ourselves. This capacity for mental representation of attachments and their disruption lays the groundwork for the ultrapsychic dimensions of interpersonal relations.

The extent to which these normal reactions are related to the psychogenesis of clinical depressive syndromes has been a controversial area within psychiatry. There is disagreement about whether or not the clinical states represent a more intense and prolonged form of normal depressive emotion as seen in sadness or in periods of grief. Some investigators feel that the clinical states represent a qualitative discontinuity from normal states and reflect some impairment of the CNS mechanisms that mediate the normal mood states. Other investigators point to basic continuities and similarities. Moreover, there is disagreement as to whether psychosocial environmental changes are universal in all forms of clinical depression.

Distinguishing Normal Mood from Clinical Psychopathology

Clinical depression and related affective disorders involve an accentuation in the intensity or duration of otherwise normal emotions. Because almost all human beings experience unhappy, sad, depressed, and discouraged states, patients' distress readily gains the empathic understanding of clinicians and family members. This very familiarity sometimes renders clinical assessment and differential diagnosis difficult, however, because it obscures the boundary between normality and abnormality: family and friends tend to minimize the severity of the patient's difficulties because the manifestations seem to be normal responses to life situations.

In current clinical practice, the diagnosis of depression subsumes one or more syndromes in which there are abnormal persistent affective changes associated with feelings of worthlessness, guilt, helplessness, and hopelessness; anxiety, crying, suicidal tendencies, loss of interest in work and other activities, and impaired capacity to perform everyday social functions; hypochondriasis, accompanied by such physical alterations as anorexia, weight change, constipation, and psychomotor retardation, or by agitation, headache, and other bodily complaints. Even untrained observers can see severe depressive states as pathological because of their intensity, pervasiveness, persistence, and interference with normal social and physiological functioning. But all these symptoms seldom occur in any one patient. Rather, varying combinations are observed, and this has led to numerous attempts to identify the basic dimensions and develop diagnostic classifications that will reduce the heterogeneity. This nosological approach has in turn led to the development of new dichotomies, typologies, and symptom clusters.

In severe forms, most affective states are clearly seen as pathological by virtue of intensity, pervasiveness, persistence, and interference with usual social and physiological functioning. The difficult problems arise in the milder cases. A number of features distinguish clinically ill patients from those in a normal mood of depression. In addition to disturbances of mood, the psychopathological state involves some combination of these features:

1. impairments of body functioning, indicated by disturbances in sleep, appetite, sexual interest, and autonomic nervous system and gastrointestinal activity;
2. reduced desire and ability to perform the usual, expected social roles in the family, at work, in marriage, or in school;
3. suicidal thoughts or acts;
4. disturbances in reality testing, manifested in delusions, hallucinations, or confusion.

When suicidal thoughts and acts and impairment of reality testing occur, they usually indicate a need for psychiatric attention.

The individual symptoms are grouped in Table 1.1.

AFFECTIVE SYMPTOMS

In *depression*, the mood disturbance defines the syndrome. The patient complains of being "sad," "blue," "down," "bleak," "low in spirits," "discouraged,"

TABLE 1.1

Symptoms of Depression

Affective	Depression
	Anxiety
	Guilt
	Anger, Hostility, and Irritability
Behavioral Manifestations	Agitation
	Facial Expression
	Psychomotor Retardation
	Retardation of Speech and Thought
	Crying
Attitudes Toward Self and the Environment	Self-Reproach
	Low Self-Esteem
	Feelings of Helplessness, Pessimism, and Hopelessness
	Thoughts of Death/Suicide Attempts
Cognitive Impairment	Decreased Ability to Think or Concentrate
Physiological Changes and Bodily Complaints	Inability to Experience Pleasure
	Loss of Appetite
	Sleep Disturbance
	Loss of Energy
	Decrease in Sexual Interest
	Bodily Complaints

"disappointed," or "mournful." Sometimes the mood disturbance is experienced as an exaggeration or prolongation of normal sadness; at other times patients describe their depressed symptoms as qualitatively different from the normal mood. At intense levels, depression is experienced as painful, as mental anguish. The term "dysphoria" is often used for this distressing quality, but other emotions than depression—guilt, for example—can also be painful and distressing.

Approximately 60 to 70 percent of depressed patients report *anxiety*. It is difficult to assess these rates, since the term is often used in a casual sense to describe any unpleasant inner state, rather than in its precise sense—that is, a subjective state of inner distress with thoughts of dread, fear, foreboding, or anticipation of danger or harm, accompanied by autonomic nervous system dysfunctions such as sweating, palpitation, rapid pulse, or "butterflies in the stomach." Because of the frequent association of anxiety with depression, differential diagnosis may be difficult.

Freud identified *guilt* as the feature distinguishing melancholia, or morbid depression, from mourning. Guilt is a painful emotion in which one feels the gap between actual conduct and one's own moral or ethical standards. Some observers distinguish between guilt and shame, guilt being the awareness of not meeting one's own standards and shame involving failure to meet the standards of a significant other, the group, or the society. Guilt is internal; shame is interpersonal and cultural.

During clinical interviews, many depressed patients at first seem unable to express *anger, hostility,* or *irritability* even when provoked. Some psychodynamic formulations view this inhibition of hostility as turning anger against the self, and regard depression as the retroflection of aggression onto the self. Recent clinical experience and research indicate that the pattern of internalization is not universal. Many depressed patients manifest irritability, anger, and rage in family and marital relations, in child rearing, and with friends.

BEHAVIORAL MANIFESTATIONS

Agitation refers to increased psychomotor activity experienced by the patient as ego-alien and reported as restlessness or tension. The patient complains of being unable to relax, unable to sit still, "fidgety," or "jittery." In contrast to the overactivity of the elated patient, which involves socially purposeful acts (albeit often poorly timed, socially inappropriate, or grandiose), the activity of the agitated patient involves tension-releasing efforts such as pacing, wringing the hands, nail biting, finger tapping, or increased smoking. Some of these behaviors are within the range of the normal "tensions" of everyday life, and many, if not most, of the individuals labeled "tense" and "high-strung" are probably manifesting mild to moderate agitation. Although anxiety and agitation frequently occur together, distinguishing the two is clinically useful, particularly since moderate to severe agitation responds well to phenothiazines and other neuroleptic drugs but not to benzodiazepines.

Clinically it has been observed in animals and humans that one of the characteristic behavioral features of depression is change in *facial expression.* We almost instantly recognize depressive changes in our friends and loved ones by a narrowing of the gaze and the drooping of the sides of the mouth. These facial changes were first observed by Darwin (1872), and more recent work by Eckman (1973), using photographs has indicated that these facial changes associated with depression are in all societies. No direct measurements of the muscles involved were made until the 1970s, when Schwartz, et al. (1976) conducted a number of studies with electrophysiologic recording of various facial muscles. This study shows that in both normal and clinical depressions most of the facial change is due to the depressor muscle, which activates the sides of the mouth. In depressed patients, these muscle changes were long-standing and less responsive to environmental input. Moreover, in addition to the changes in the depressor muscle, there was also increased muscle tension in the masseter, the muscle at the temporal mandibular joint; such tension is usually associated with strain and hostility.

Psychomotor retardation often occurs in depressed patients. General activity levels are reduced, and the patient may spend hours slumped in a chair. The walk may be sluggish and the gait shuffling.

Retardation of speech and thought often occurs in parallel with psychomotor retardation. Many depressed patients have slowed speech, with long latency between questions and responses and with frequent pauses. These changes are often so characteristic that friends and loved ones can detect a mild depressive mood even in brief telephone exchanges; they are reacting to the quality of speech independent of its content and without nonverbal cues from facial expression or postural changes.

Crying is an almost universal expression of grief and of both normal and clinical depression. Some patients complain that they "cannot cry" and are "beyond tears." Others experience crying as relieving their depression and even as a sign of general improvement.

ATTITUDES TOWARD SELF AND THE ENVIRONMENT

In his classic paper "Mourning and Melancholia" (1917), Freud postulated that guilt and *self-reproach* are characteristic of melancholia (depression) but not of normal grief. Subsequent clinical research has revealed the inaccuracy of both parts of this formulation; many grieving persons feel ashamed and guilt-ridden, while many depressed people do not consciously experience, acknowledge, or report guilt. Guilt seems to be associated with Western societies, in which conflicts generated by religious beliefs are internalized as conscience or the Freudian superego. Cross-cultural studies indicate that guilt and feelings of worthlessness are far less common in African and Asian societies, where shame and complaints of bodily function and loss of energy are more prevalent (Marsella, 1979). In severe forms of depression, the patient's feelings of worthlessness may reach delusional proportions and be associated with condemning and critical auditory hallucinations. Whereas paranoid patients experience these ideas and voices as false accusations and see themselves as victims of persecution and malevolent intent, psychotic depressive patients feel that the criticisms are accurate and justified.

Low self-esteem and feelings of inadequacy and despondency are personality traits considered part of the psychodynamics of those predisposed to recurrent depression. Although there is controversy over the evidence supporting this view, clinicians and investigators generally agree that during an acute depressive state patients feel "inadequate," "incompetent," and "a failure" and believe that family, friends, and work associates regard them similarly. Beck (1969) emphasized this cognitive impairment among depressives, pointing out depressed patients' decreased ability to assess their own performance and others' views of them. Furthermore, these difficulties may persist even after remission of the acute depression. The self-esteem of patients who experience recurrent or chronic depression falls even lower as the illness progresses or recurs.

Feelings of helplessness, pessimism, and hopelessness are closely related to the depressed patient's difficulties in sustaining self-esteem. Patients complain that they feel helpless in the face of small tasks of dress, self-care, or grooming; parental, household, or occupational responsibilities are even more difficult to negotiate. Feelings of helplessness relate less to actual levels of performance than to failure to meet one's expectations or those of others. Cultural patterns, child-rearing practices, and family values condition many depressives to be perfectionist, achievement-oriented, and self-critical, and to have high ethical and moral standards. Internalization of such expectations renders these patients sensitive to the gap between wish and reality and therefore prone to consider themselves weak, inadequate, and helpless during depressive episodes. Handicapped by low self-esteem and feelings of helplessness, many depressives also report being pessimistic and hopeless. Fears and worries about health, finances, family affairs, and career concern many patients; they anticipate misfortune, experience gloom, and forecast doom. In severe forms, despair may be all-encompassing and may be associated with suicidal thoughts and acts.

Thoughts of death and suicide attempts are often part of clinical depression, and every therapist should be aware of the dangers. Death by suicide occurs at the rate of about 1 percent during the year of the acute episode and 15 percent over the lifetime of a patient with recurrent depressions (Klerman, 1982). By sympathetic but systematic interviewing, the clinician can elicit the patient's thoughts, impulses, and possible intentions. Many patients have suicidal thoughts, but only a few have suicidal intent. The period of risk extends from the acute episode into the weeks and months after symptomatic remission; the highest suicidal mortality occurs during the six-to-nine-month period after symptomatic improvement has occurred.

COGNITIVE IMPAIRMENT

During the clinical interview, the therapist may observe generally slowed movement, decreased facial expression, fixed gaze, and reduced eye scanning. All these physical manifestations are part of the psychomotor retardation that is characteristic of depression, and are usually correlated with the patient's subjective report of lethargy and decreased activity. Speech is slow and at times almost inaudible. Answers to questions are delayed and the lag between stimulus and response prolonged. The content of the response itself is often sparse; in severe forms, the patient's response may be only a few words or incomplete sentences. In the rare and serious syndrome of "depressive stupor," the patient may be completely inactive—mute, incontinent, and unable to eat. Fortunately, depressive stupor does not occur as frequently today as it did twenty or thirty years ago. There is a clinical problem of differentiating depressive stupor from catatonic schizophrenic states, particularly in young adults. Careful history taking is helpful, as is observation of changes in behavior and mental content, when the patient is interviewed while under the influence of sodium amytal given by injection.

Depressed patients often complain of difficulty in concentration, "slowed thinking," "mind a blank," "poor memory," and similar symptoms. Inhibition of thought and obsessional ruminations on self-doubts, worries over the future, self-reproach, and suicidal urges may cause patients to be preoccupied by inner thoughts and less attentive to environmental demands. On formal psychological tests, accuracy is usually retained but speed and performance are slowed. In severe forms, particularly among the elderly, differential diagnosis from early stages of dementia may be difficult.

PSYCHOLOGICAL CHANGES AND BODILY COMPLAINTS

An *inability to experience pleasure* is almost universal among depressed patients. Patients report that previous sources of gratification, such as food, sex, hobbies, sports, social events, or time spent with family, children, or friends, no longer provide pleasure. Patients with a severe form of this symptom are described as anhedonic.

About 70 to 80 percent of patients experience *loss of appetite* with accompanying weight loss. A minority, usually younger patients with milder forms of depression, experience a compensatory increase in food ingestion, often in the evening or at night.

The majority of depressed patients (80 to 90 percent) experience some form of insomnia. A small percentage, however, increase their sleep, often as a way of avoiding stressful situations. *Sleep disturbance* may involve difficulty falling asleep, with ruminations and reexamination of details of life circumstances; being awakened in the middle of the night by frightening dreams or uncomfortable body sensations; early morning awakening; or feelings of having slept poorly.

Loss of energy related to the inability to experience pleasure is shown in patients' reports of fatigue and lethargy. Sometimes diagnosed as neurasthenia or anergy, these symptoms are associated with reduced social, familial, occupational, and sexual activity, feelings of "being run down," "heaviness in arms and legs," and "energy being drained from my body." Patients often interpret these feeling states as indicative of nervous exhaustion, overwork, nervous breakdown, or vitamin or nutritional deficiency. When the symptoms are severe, the patient may believe, sometimes with delusional intensity, that they indicate some serious malady such as cancer or tuberculosis.

A *decrease in sexual interest* is common during depression and may go unrecognized if the therapist does not make detailed inquiries. In men, impotence is a frequent distressing symptom that may aggravate existing marital tensions and further diminish the patient's self-esteem.

Depressed patients frequently report multiple *bodily complaints* in which almost every organ system may be involved. These complaints include headache, neck ache, back pain, muscle cramps, nausea, vomiting, lump in the throat, sour taste in the mouth, dry mouth, constipation, heartburn, indigestion, flatulence, blurred vision, and pain on urination. General physicians, internists, and other medical specialists often prescribe extensive and at times expensive diagnostic workups for these patients.

The Depressive Syndrome

Just as no one patient will report all the symptoms listed in Table 1.2, there is no one depressive syndrome. The clinical state diagnosed by the criteria in DSM-III encompasses a wide range of depressive states.

TABLE 1.2
DSM-III Diagnostic Criteria—Major Depression

A.   Dysphoric mood or loss of interest or pleasure in all or almost all usual activities and pastimes. The dysphoric mood is characterized by symptoms such as the following: depressed, sad, blue, hopeless, low, down in the dumps, irritable. The mood disturbance must be prominent and relatively persistent, but not necessarily the most dominant symptom, and does not include momentary shifts from one dysphoric mood to another dysphoric mood, e.g., anxiety to depression to anger, such as are seen in states of acute psychotic turmoil. (For children under six, dysphoric mood may have to be inferred from a persistently sad facial expression.)

B.   At least four of the following symptoms have been present nearly every day for a period of at least two weeks (in children under six, at least three of the first four):

1.   poor appetite or significant weight loss (when not dieting) or increased appetite or significant weight gain (in children under six, consider failure to make expected weight gains);

2.   insomnia or hypersomnia;

3.   psychomotor agitation or retardation (but not merely subjective feelings of restlessness or being slowed down) (in children under six, hypoactivity);

4.   loss of interest or pleasure in usual activities, or decrease in sexual drive not limited to a period when delusional or hallucinating (in children under six, signs of apathy);

5.   loss of energy; fatigue;

6.   feelings of worthlessness, self-reproach, or excessive or inappropriate guilt (either may be delusional);

7.   complaints or evidence of diminished ability to think or concentrate, such as slowed thinking, or indecisiveness not associated with marked loosening of associations or incoherence;

8.   recurrent thoughts of death, suicidal ideation, wishes to be dead, or suicide attempt.

SOURCE: American Psychiatric Association Diagnostic and Statistical Manual of Mental Disorders, Third Edition, Washington, D. C., APA, 1980

SUBTYPES OF DEPRESSION

There has been considerable controversy in the clinical and research community over the best mode of subtyping depression. Some systems are based on presumed etiology, others rely primarily on symptom patterns and manifest behavior. Diagnosis and classification of the affective disorders are now being revised. The traditional psychotic-neurotic distinction and endogenous-reactive dichotomies have been critically reexamined and two new classifications are proposed: the primary-secondary distinction of Robins and Guze (1972) and Robins et al. (1972), and the unipolar-bipolar dichotomy first described by Leonard, Korff, and Schulz (1962) and subsequently developed by Perris (1966) in the United States and Angst (1966) in Switzerland. These new groupings have been advocated to resolve uncertainties derived from the concept of manic-depressive insanity first described by Kraepelin.

In modern scientific medicine, diagnostic assessment of individual patients and nosological classification of disease in patient groups would ideally be based on knowledge of etiology, pathophysiology, psychodynamics, and epidemiology. Unfortunately, knowledge in these areas for the affective disorders, though it is progressing rapidly, has not yet reached a level that provides comprehensiveness or certainty. Current diagnostic assessment of individual patients must be based predominantly on clinical and psychopathological information, supplemented by other sources. Nosological classifications are also based almost exclusively on clinical and psychopathological criteria.

Current research strategy is to define diagnostic groups as precisely as possible, using consistently applied criteria that are not confounded with etiological or therapeutic assumptions. It is hoped that the delineation of new groups according to these criteria will facilitate better communication among clinicians and produce categories capable of generating research that will, in turn, yield knowledge for sound etiological classification.

IMPLICATIONS FOR INTERPERSONAL PSYCHOTHERAPY

One of the major characteristics of IPT for depression is that it approaches depression as a clinical disorder. The justification for this is not only the widespread prevalence of depression but also the therapeutic importance of providing patients with a diagnostic label and legitimizing their assumption of the "sick role." Since this approach places IPT within the broad definition of the medical model, it is thus a different approach from that of many psychotherapists. In the psychotherapeutic community there has been an antidiagnostic bias and a tendency to depreciate symptoms. We feel that this approach is in error, both theoretically and therapeutically.

Theoretically, failure to attend to recent research advances in psychopathology can lead psychotherapists to miss important episodes of depression and to focus excessively upon conflicts, childhood antecedents, or enduring personality traits. Many psychotherapies fail to appreciate the vitally important role that manifest symptoms play in depressive episodes in the patient's life.

An essential part of our theory is a pluralistic point of view about the nature of depression. With regard to etiology, the pluralistic view maintains that no single cause in itself can explain depression. Genetics, early life experience, environmental stress, and personality combine in complex ways to produce the etiology and pathogenesis of depression. These factors will operate in different degrees for individual patients. Among groups of patients with various subtypes of depression, one or another factor may predominate, but it is unlikely that the "necessary and sufficient" etiological basis for the classificatory model that has prevailed in medicine is applicable to the depressions. Thus the pluralistic view also informs our attitude toward diagnosis and classification: depression is regarded as a syndrome, or rather, a group of syndromes.

Therapeutically, if the level of distress as manifested by symptoms and emotional states is sufficiently high, patients cannot attend to the learning necessary in psychotherapy and will be unable to make use of clarifications and insights relating their current situation to previous life experience, particularly to childhood developmental experiences. Accordingly, the interpersonal psychotherapy of depression rests on an understanding of depression as a normal mood, as a symptom seen in many medical and psychiatric conditions, and as a syndrome. The basic approach upon which IPT has been developed, both theoretically and therapeutically, begins with the conviction that the patient has a disorder, that this disorder is diagnosable, and that it is therapeutically to the patient's benefit to be labeled as such (rediagnosed), so that assumption of the "sick role" becomes legitimate. This view will be amplified in Chapter 5, "Dealing with the Depression and Diagnosing the Interpersonal Problem."

Chapter 2

The Interpersonal Approach

Armed with an understanding of the nature of depression, we may now explore the origins of the interpersonal approach we propose for its treatment. The interpersonal school of psychiatry and psychology is one of the several schools of thought in American mental health—in which, especially since World War II, theoretical and clinical schools have proliferated. Psychiatry, psychology, social work, and nursing have all experienced considerable ferment and competition among alternative schools. The extent of this diversity has been described by Armor and Klerman (1968), Havens (1973), and Lazare (1979).

Observers of the scene have catalogued the diverse schools in different ways. In their influential study of social class and mental illness in New Haven, Hollingshead and Redlich (1958) divided the practitioner community into two groups, "Analytic and Psychological" (A-P) and "Directive and Organic" (D-O). In the 1960s, using sociological survey methods in Chicago, Strauss et al. (1964) and Armor and Klerman (1968), using a nationwide sample of psychiatrists working in hospitals, identified three groupings, "biological" or "organic," "psychological" or "dynamic," and (the newest) "social psychiatric."

The 1960s and 1970s saw a proliferation of new theoretical and clinical viewpoints in American psychiatry. These included the community mental health center movement, as well as the emergence of behavioral techniques and many new forms of individual, group, and family psychotherapy.

Table 2.1 identifies the six schools that are most relevant to the present diagnosis and treatment of depression in the United States.

Observers of the American scene will note that a number of influential groups of practitioners are not represented on this list. For example, the existentialist school that Havens (1973) identified is omitted because, though it has strongly influenced philosophy, the arts, and the humanities, it has had less influence on clinical psychiatric practice and little impact on the theory, research, or treatment of depression. Theoreticians and practitioners in the community mental health center movement, which has caused major changes in the delivery of mental health services, tend to ignore issues of diagnosis in their writings and clinical practice and at times to criticize the "medical model." Many new schools of psychotherapy, including Gestalt Therapy, Humanistic Psychology, and Transactional Analysis, which have become especially popular among nonmedical practitioners, also reject the "medical model" and oppose diagnosis and classification. Although these facilities and practitioners deal with many depressed patients, their treatment is seldom discussed as a special issue.

TABLE 2.1
Practitioners and Writers

School	Major USA Writers	Remarks
Biological	Kety Winokur	Derived from nineteenth-century Continental schools of psychiatry.
Psychodynamic	Erikson Kohut	Strongly influenced by Freudian psychoanalysis, but modified by the American experience, particularly with ego psychology and self-psychology.
Social	Meyer Redlich	Leaning heavily on sociology, anthropology, and other social sciences.
Interpersonal	Sullivan Fromm-Reichmann Arieti	Applied to family therapy and psychotherapy with ambulatory patients but also with schizophrenia, depression, and other conditions.
Behavioral	Skinner Lewisohn	Mainly involving behavior treatment.
Cognitive	Beck	Mainly involving cognitive treatment.

Source: Klerman, G. L. 1983. The significance of DSM III in American psychiatry. In *International Perspectives on DSM III*, eds. R. L. Spitzer, J. B. Williams, and A. E. Skodol. American Psychiatric Press, Inc. Washington, D. C.. Used with permission.

Antecedents of the Interpersonal Approach

In the early to mid-nineteenth century, the concept of "moral treatment" was developed to refer to attempts to change the environment of the mental hospital to make it more conducive to recovery. "Moral," as used in the nineteenth century, was almost synonymous with what we would call psychological today. It did not mean judgments as to morality or ethical behavior. Toward the end of the nineteenth century the optimism of "moral treatment" gave way to pessimism, custodial practices and Social Darwinism. Social Darwinism was a widely held set of attitudes toward the end of the nineteenth century, which applied a caricature of Darwin's thinking about "survival of the fittest." It seemed to justify the hierarchy of social status in Victorian society by claiming that those who had been successful and risen to positions of power and status were endowed with qualities which enabled them to survive and thrive.

Most observers of the history of American psychiatry agree that mental health theory and treatment was at a low point when the nineteenth century ended. There was very little research and some of the practitioners attracted to psychiatry seemed inferior to those in other fields of medicine. The situation began to change in the first decades of the twentieth century, before World War I. It is probably no accident that this change in psychiatry coincided with the emergence of the Progressive movement in American political and cultural life. There seems to be a close historical correlation between periods of improved economic well-being, general intellectual and social ferment, and progressive political movements on the one hand, and cycles of reform in mental health practices and new ideas in psychiatric professional activities on the other. This pattern was clearly evident in the decade before World War I, when teaching and research activities developed in the new "psychopathic hospitals" in Boston, Massachusetts, Baltimore, Maryland, Ann Arbor, Michigan, and elsewhere. In this decade too, psychoanalysis had its early impact on American psychiatric and intellectual thinking; Freud and Jung were part of a group of psychoanalysts invited to Clark University in Worcester, Massachusetts, in 1908. They lectured there and in a number of other medical schools on the east coast.

The most influential leader in American psychiatry in that period, and for decades afterward, was Adolf Meyer of Johns Hopkins Medical School. Meyer had a profound influence on twentieth-century American psychiatry, creating the foundation for its unique development in this country (Klerman, 1979). This influence is paradoxical, since he was Swiss trained and German speaking and yet helped to bring neuropathology from Europe to America. He also helped introduce Kraepelin's ideas about dementia praecox into the United States. Yet Meyer turned away from his European origins and was strongly influenced by the emerging American philosophic school of pragmatism founded by William James since he was personally familiar with many of its leaders in the Chicago area.

Meyer was the first professor of psychiatry at Johns Hopkins University after it was reformed on the basis of recommendations in the Flexner Report, a study commissioned by the Carnegie Foundation in which Abraham Flexner undertook a study of medical education in the United States. With its emphasis on research, professional specialization, scholarship and full-time faculty, Hopkins became the model for American medical schools. The few other academic centers of psychiatry that emerged later were often led by students of Meyer, such as Campbell at Harvard and Diethelm at Cornell.

Meyer used the term psychobiology to describe his work and theories. Today, psychobiology refers to the influence of biological mechanisms upon behavior, but Meyer meant something much broader. Strongly influenced by Darwin, he viewed mental illness as an attempt by the individual to adapt to the changing environment. Because his concept of environment emphasized its psychosocial features, many of the distinctly American efforts in psychiatry, such as the modification of Freudian psychoanalysis, the development of the interpersonal school, and research in social epidemiology, were strongly influenced by Meyer directly or through his students, who dominated academic psychiatric centers until well after World War II.

Adolph Meyer's concept of psychobiology modified the Darwinian principle of biological adaptation to include the organism's adaptation to the social environment. According to David Rothman (1980), Meyer was very active in various social reform efforts of the Progressive era before World War II, but, in his psychiatric writings he was seldom specific about the particular features of the social environment that related to the emergence of mental illness. It was his students, however, especially Rennie (1956) and Leighton, et al. (1963), who created the field of social epidemiology in the United States after World War II.

From the 1950s on, five aspects of the social environment became the focus of interest for this group of theorists and investigators: civilization, urbanization, stress, social class, and mental hospital social structure.

CIVILIZATION

Among early speculations about the causes of mental illness are those of the Enlightenment, whose philosophers took the view that mental illness was the result of civilization. Rousseau's concept of the "noble savage" reflected an implicit epidemiologic hypothesis that mental illness did not occur when man remained in his natural—that is, uncivilized—state. This romantic view of non-Western societies, which Srole and Fischer (1980) have called the "paradise lost" doctrine of mental illness, rested on the presumption that people in preliterate societies do not have psychoses. It has been contradicted by cross-cultural research which shows that mental illnesses, including some forms of psychosis, occur widely throughout both literate and nonliterate societies (Murphy, 1976). In addition to cross-cultural methods, this doctrine of "paradise lost" has also been studied historically. Marshall and Goldhammer (1953) also tested this hypothesis using data on rates of mental hospitalizations in Massachusetts. Their research demonstrated that when the rates are corrected for the change in the total population over time, no trend toward increased hospitalization can be documented for psychoses in people below the age of fifty since the nineteenth century.

URBANIZATION

Closely related to the civilization thesis is the view that urban living has adverse mental health effects. This thesis is an expression of the implicit view that the city is "bad" and that illness will be more frequent in urban centers than in rural areas. Srole (1980) has recently tested this thesis in a follow-up to his study of people living in midtown Manhattan who were originally interviewed in 1954. After two decades of Manhattan living, those who were children in the 1950s showed better mental health compared to the earlier generation. This trend was mainly due to improvement in the mental health of the women. Srole suggests that this change results in a "new breed of women." Srole interprets this change as due to the improved status of women in the first half of the nineteenth century resulting from increased participation in the labor force, constitutional amendments giving women the right to vote, and increased longevity due to improvements in child-rearing practices and the conquest of infections associated with childbirth.

The work of Leighton (1963) and associates in Nova Scotia parallels Srole's Manhattan study. The Canadian research has been based on the thesis that rapid social change, particularly from a rural to an industrial social structure, results in the breakdown of social cohesion and increases social disorganization, which is reflected in increasing rates of mental illness. Their concept of social disintegration has many similarities to the ideas of the French sociologist Durkheim, especially his concept that increased anomie is related to increased incidence of suicide.

STRESS

During World War II, the U. S. Army conducted an extensive social science research program that included efforts to relate neurotic symptoms to combat stress (Stouffer, 1950). Since the soldiers had passed extensive Selective Service medical and psychiatric screenings, and since some nevertheless developed psychiatric symptoms during and after combat, the study concluded that the combat neuroses were precipitated by stress rather than due to predisposing factors or vulnerability. The thesis that mental illness is due to stress led to much further research on the relationship between psychosocial life events and mental disorders. For example, Holmes and Rahe (1967) did several studies on the role of various stress factors that increase the risk of becoming medically ill. Natural disasters such as hurricanes and floods, life events such as grief or loss of a job, and economic changes such as the closing of an industrial plant were shown to increase risk of medical and mental illness.

SOCIAL CLASS

The discovery that certain mental illnesses occur more frequently in lower social classes grew out of national concerns about poverty and other consequences of class structure. This influential line of research began with the Chicago school of sociology. Faris and Dunham (1939) used ecological methods to demonstrate differences in hospitalization associated with social class. Subsequently, Hollingshead and Redlich (1958) studied the prevalence of treated mental illness in New Haven, Connecticut. Although their work has been criticized for its failure to distinguish between incidence and prevalence and for restriction of the sample to treated cases, they nevertheless demonstrated a strong relationship between lower social class and increased incidence of mental illness, particularly schizophrenia. Moreover, they documented the powerful influence of social class on motivation to seek treatment and on access to treatment resources.

MENTAL HOSPITAL SOCIAL STRUCTURE

After World War II, psychiatrists and sociologists undertook a number of successful collaborations in researching the social, psychological, and institutional characteristics of mental hospitals. These studies demonstrated the powerful impact of hospital social structure on patients' clinical outcome. Excessive bureaucracy, hierarchical authority structure, the informal power exerted by nonprofessionals, and the pervasive role of ideology were rampant (Goffman, 1961). These findings revived interest in the "moral treatment" era of the nineteenth century because they brought up the question whether many of the poor clinical outcomes attributed to schizophrenia and other chronic psychoses were due to the illness itself or were results of the depersonalizing and dependency-producing features of the institution (Stanton and Schwartz, 1954). In England, the term "institutional neuroses" was proposed to draw attention to these effects. In the United States, Gruenberg (1966) identified the "social breakdown syndrome" as an adverse consequence of the social environment on the course of the illness, particularly the deterioration that can occur in schizophrenia.

Partly because of these studies, many attempts were made to reform mental hospitals. American hospitals adopted many of the techniques used in England, including "open door" policies, day treatment programs, and efforts at social and vocational rehabilitation. In the United States, this line of endeavor has become less prominent in recent decades because attention has shifted from the hospital to the community as the main focus of treatment. Early hopes that, like tuberculosis hospitals, many mental hospitals could be closed, have not been realized. Indeed, community placement and deinstitutionalization have often produced continuing chronicity and social disability among patients, which indicates that a considerable portion of chronic social disability is due to the illness rather than to adverse effects of institutional environments.

Social psychiatry efforts such as these have broadened the number of variables —the causal and risk factors—to be considered in understanding and treating mental illness. However, social epidemiology research has paid relatively less attention to specific mental disorders as dependent variables. If anything, some social epidemiologic studies tend to depreciate specific diagnoses and to rely upon single undimensional disability scales. This tendency has been reversed with the application of the APA's Research Diagnostic Criteria and other new diagnostic techniques. NIMH has set up an Epidemiologic Catchment Area program, which involves community surveys of large samples of patients in five sites in the United States using a structured interview, the Diagnostic Interview Schedule developed by L. Robins et al. (1981). The DIS allows for diagnostic assessment consistent with DSM-III categories. It is hoped that these efforts will bring about a rapprochement between the new emphasis on discrete diagnostic categories and the theoretical and methodological advances developed by social-psychiatric researchers.

The Interpersonal School

The interpersonal school has contributed a great deal to psychiatric theory and practice in the United States. Emerging in the Washington-Baltimore area during the 1930s and 1940s, it was initially based on the work of Harry Stack Sullivan (1956), but it soon came to include some of the theories of the neo-Freudians, Frieda Fromm-Reichmann, Erich Fromm, and Karen Horney.

It was probably no accident that this school developed where it did. One factor was Meyer's intellectual influence as he enlarged the scope of psychiatry's concern to include social and cultural forces. Another was the intellectual ambience in Washington during the New Deal era. Many economists, lawyers, social scientists, and government officials in Washington were sensitive to the psychological consequences of the economic depression and concerned with the quality of life in a modern industrial and urban society.

Although the earliest sources of an interpersonal approach are Meyer's ideas, Harry Stack Sullivan stands as the person who most clearly articulated the interpersonal paradigm. Sullivan was born in upstate New York and had psychoanalytic training in the New York area. He later became very individualistic in his approach and gradually developed his ideas after he moved to the Washington area. He lectured at Chestnut Lodge where a number of psychoanalytic emigrés, including Fromm-Reichmann, had migrated in the late 1930s. In his psychobiological approach, Meyer put great emphasis on the patient's current experience and social relations (Meyer, 1957), and he viewed the patient's response to environmental change and stress in adulthood as determined by early experiences—what he called "habits"—in the family and in various social groups.

Sullivan went further than Meyer, defining psychiatry as the field of interpersonal relations. He and his associates developed a comprehensive and consistent theory of the connections between psychiatric disorders and interpersonal relations for the developing child in the family and for the adult in the multiple transactions of life.

This approach has been applied mainly to therapeutics. Interpersonal modifications of intensive dynamic psychotherapy were proposed for schizophrenics (Fromm-Reichmann, 1960), for manic-depressive patients (Cohen et al., 1954), and for neurotics and children. The interpersonal school is responsible for the emergence of family therapy as a new form of psychotherapy.

Sullivan and his associates accepted most of the standard diagnostic categories. He discusses hysteria, obsessive-compulsive behavior, and manic-depressive illness in his writings. He retained Kraepelin's concept of dementia praecox to refer to a vaguely defined, genetically determined group with poor outcome, but he distinguished dementia praecox from what he called schizophrenia.

Although the interpersonal school has emphasized the role of family factors as possibly etiologic for psychoses, and has speculated upon intrafamiliar pathology, no consistent nosology or classification of family disorders has yet emerged. Efforts to relate family pathology to schizophrenia, including those of Lidz and Fleck (1965) at Yale, Bowen (1960) in Washington, D.C., and Wynne (1963) at Rochester, N.Y., have not been substantiated by research. Consequently, proponents of the interpersonal approach have attenuated their claims for its use in treating schizophrenia and now rely upon the observations of British investigators that "expressed" emotion and "communication deviance" facilitate or contribute to pathogenesis, probably by interacting with genetic or other biological factors, rather than being the necessary causative forces.

The theoretical foundation of the interpersonal approach has been best summarized by Sullivan, who taught that psychiatry involves the scientific study of people and the processes between people, rather than focusing exclusively on the mind, society, or the brain. Hence the unit of clinical study is the patient's interpersonal relations at any one particular time.

The emphasis on interpersonal and social factors in the understanding and treatment of depressive disorders has developed out of the work of the founders of the interpersonal approach. Its use in the treatment of depression, as distinguished from an exclusively intrapsychic or biological approach, begins with the work of Sullivan and Fromm-Reichmann in the 1930s and 1940s. The first major application of these ideas specifically to depression was made by Mabel Blake Cohen and her co-workers at the Washington School of Psychiatry, in a comprehensive clinical study of disrupted interpersonal relations in the childhood experiences of twelve manic-depressives (Cohen et al., 1954). The early family experiences of these manic-depressive patients were reflected in their adult personality structures, which were consistently associated with particular kinds of interpersonal problems, especially dependency. These interpersonal problems were also manifest in the way these patients functioned in psychotherapy.

THE IMPORTANCE OF SOCIAL ROLES

For the interpersonal approach, the unit of observation and therapeutic intervention is the primary social group, the immediate face-to-face involvement of the patient with one or more significant others.

The interpersonal approach is distinguished from social-psychiatric approaches by the different social unit it focuses upon. Social-psychiatric approaches focus upon large units of the society such as health care institutions; large-scale macrosocial processes such as urbanization; the influence of social class, racial membership, ethnic background; and historical, political, and economic forces. In contrast, but not necessarily in opposition, the interpersonal approach is most concerned with the individual's closest relationships, most notably family relationships—both in the family of origin and in the family of procreation; love relationships, both heterosexual and homosexual; friendship patterns, particularly in adolescence and young adulthood; work relations, and neighborhood or community relationships.

The roles of major interest to interpersonal psychotherapy occur within the nuclear family (as parent, child, sibling, spouse); the extended family; the friendship group; the work situation (as supervisor, supervisee, or peer); and the neighborhood or community.

During the period around World War I, this clinical focus on interpersonal relations borrowed heavily from the Chicago school of sociology and social psychology. Many of the early writings on social psychiatry and interpersonal approaches derive from the intellectual generation that included George Herbert Meade, Sapir, and other pioneer American social scientists. At that point in the history of American intellectual thinking the boundary between sociological psychology and philosophy was blurred, often nonexistent. Thus William James, the founder of American pragmatism, was also a major force in the founding of American psychology. The Chicago school emphasized the role of the self and argued from theoretical grounds that the self is not a disembodied psyche but arises out of the process of interaction between the child and significant others. More significantly, the adult self is sustained by the ongoing interactions between the individual and those around him.

These relationships between the individual and others, the self and others, have a structure, and this structure is provided by the position of the individual within the social system—most precisely by the specific roles the individual plays. Each person holds multiple hierarchical positions in the social system and plays specific roles appropriate to these positions.

The interpersonal approach views the relationship between social roles and psychopathology as occurring in two ways: disturbances in social roles can serve as antecedents for clinical psychopathology; and among its consequences mental illness can produce impairments of the individual's capacity to perform social roles. The classic psychopathologic approach, derived from the writings of Kraepelin and Continental European psychiatry, views impairment of social role performance as almost entirely the consequence of the patient's illness. This theory is generally applied to severe mental disturbances such as psychotic states of mania and schizophrenia, in which the progression of the illness is manifested by difficulties in communication, social withdrawal and isolation, inability to maintain occupational roles, and failure in sexual relations, intimacy, and the capacity to draw upon close relationships to sustain marriage.

The interpersonal approach, however, views disturbances in interpersonal relations as antecedents to mental illness. Drawing upon the general experience of psychoanalysis, it focuses on childhood experiences and family relationships as antecedents to specific mental illness. The hypothesis that has emerged is that disturbances in the child-rearing experience predispose certain children to the adult manifestations of schizophrenia and other illnesses.

CLINICAL APPLICATIONS

The interpersonal approach to mental health and mental illness is applied in both assessment and treatment.

In assessing patients, it is now recognized that a comprehensive appraisal requires more than the traditional review of symptoms and of prior hospitalizations and medical or psychotherapeutic treatment. It is also necessary to assess the patient's past and current interpersonal relations. This assessment involves the following components:

1. A complete inventory of current and past relationships with significant others, especially in the families of origin and of procreation but also at school and work, in love relationships and friendships, and in community activities.

2. The quality and patterning of the interactions, which extended over time become the history of the individual's interpersonal relations, similar to the history of symptoms, illness, and treatment that is an essential part of medical and psychiatric assessments. These patterns include issues of relationship to authority; dominance and submission; dependency and autonomy; intimacy; trust and confiding; demonstration of affection; sexual feelings and activities; residential and household arrangements; division of labor and tasks within families and at workplace; financial arrangements; shared recreational, religious, and community activities; and responses to separations and losses.

3. The cognitions the individual and the significant others develop, hold, and change about themselves, each other, their reciprocal roles, and the history of their relationship. Cognitions involve beliefs and attitudes about norms, expectations, and meaning ascribed to roles and role performance.

4. The associated emotions (also called moods, affects, feelings), including pleasure, joy, sadness, disappointment, anger, rage, hostility, trust, warmth, surprise, fear, guilt, envy, jealousy, shame.

The need for assessments other then symptomatic psychopathology and diagnosis of disorders has been increasingly acknowledged and is incorporated into the multiaxial system of DSM-III. In clinical practice, the main source of information about the individual patient's interpersonal relations comes from interviews with the patient and the significant other. Researchers are developing rating scales, inventories, and checklists to assess the complexities of past and current relationships and associated cognitions and emotions (Burdock, Sudilovsky, and Gershon, 1982). Although these measuring techniques will probably be helpful, clinical practice is likely to continue to rely primarily on interview and observation.

In treatment, the interpersonal approach has generated a good deal of experimentation and innovation. Many of the new psychotherapies introduced since World War II derive from this approach, especially group therapy and the numerous forms of marriage, couple, and family psychotherapies (Anchin and Kiesler, 1982).

In the United States the interpersonal approach has had great impact on the practice of psychotherapy, both by psychiatrists and by the increasing number of nonmedical psychotherapists trained in psychology, social work, nursing, marriage counseling, and religious counseling. The basic principles and concepts of the interpersonal approach have permeated the mental health professions in the United States and more recently in Western Europe and other urban industrial societies. Indeed, attention to interpersonal relations is one of the hallmarks of modernity. With its assignment of high value to individualism, personal satisfaction and happiness, economic and social well-being, rationality and justice, the modern world view creates expectations of individual choice and personal determination of goals, purpose, and meaning in life. In an individualistic society, the values emphasize the happiness, achievement and wishes of the individuals. Individuals often come to realize that they cannot achieve their wishes and goals without significant others. This is particularly the case where individual happiness requires close relations, as in marriage and in the family. But the focus is upon what the family, marriage, and small group can do for the happiness and satisfaction of the individual. In more family oriented societies, the unit of concern is the family or clan or ethnic group and the individual achieves his identity or happiness through the achievements and satisfaction of the larger group.

With increasing urbanization and industrialization, the traditional social supports that have characterized societies since the dawn of civilization in Egypt, the Middle East, India and China—religion, the church, the extended family and close neighbors—are less valued and less effective. We live in secular and mobile societies, and religion is less accepted as the source of truth, purpose, and consolation, and the church is less available as an agency of social support, charity and welfare, recreation and education; where the extended family and close communal ties of the immediate neighborhood are little more than nostalgic images to be revered at Thanksgiving and Christmas.

In the midst of these profound changes, individuals seek other means of meeting their needs for attachment, self-esteem, and purpose. There are limits to the extent to which modern society can proceed to reduce or even destroy the previous support systems. For whatever reasons, biological, psychological or social, individuals need attachments to provide for emotional sustenance, reinforce self-esteem and provide for sexual satisfaction and the development of families and children. Thus, although the traditional forms of family and neighborhood are less important, substitutes are being developed to provide the emotionally relevant equivalence in modern urban life. Psychological attention to interpersonal relations and the growth of professional psychotherapies offer secular, scientific, and rational responses to these needs.

Chapter 3

The Interpersonal Approach to Understanding Depression

In the preceding chapters we discussed the clinical features of depression and the interpersonal approach to understanding mental illness in general. Now we turn to the evidence relating interpersonal relations to depression.

While we believe that past and ongoing interpersonal relationships are related to depression, we cannot always establish the direction of causation. Henderson (1981) notes that persons with clinical depression may exaggerate and distort problems in their interpersonal relations because of their current affective state and cognitive dysfunction. The symptoms of the depression may be adversely affecting the patient's close interpersonal relations, and/or the patient's personality may make that person less competent to establish mutually satisfying interpersonal relationships and maintain attachments. Disrupted interpersonal relations often result in mood changes. And although disruptions of interpersonal relationships are not in themselves "necessary and sufficient" to produce clinical depressions, interpersonal difficulties are usually associated with clinical depression.

Thus we will first examine the relationship between changes in interpersonal relations and normal depressed mood, then explore the effect of disrupted interpersonal relationships on clinical depression, as correlates and as consequences.

Finally, we need to see how an individual's personality can be a predisposing vulnerability or factor in both problematic interpersonal relations and clinical depression.

Interpersonal Relations and Normal Mood

Sadness and an occasional depressed mood are a normal part of the human condition, and feelings of sadness are a nearly universal response to disruptions of interpersonal relations. The most useful discussions of the relationship between disrupted interpersonal relations and normal sadness are found in studies of attachment bonding and of bereavement.

ATTACHMENTS

Attachment theory, as developed by J. Bowlby (1969), proposes that humans have an innate tendency to seek attachments and that these attachments contribute to the survival of the species and to individual satisfaction. Attachments lead to reciprocal, personal, social bonds with significant others, and to experiences of increased warmth, nurturance, and protection and a decrease in levels of psychomotor activity such as attention, vigilance, and increased muscle tone.

Intense human emotions (love, hate, envy, rivalry, desire for nurturance) are associated with the formation, maintenance, disruption, and renewal of attachment bonds. Investigations by ethologists applied to mother-child relationships have demonstrated the importance of attachment and social bonds to human functioning. Humans of all ages are vulnerable to impaired interpersonal relations if strong attachment bonds do not develop early. Individuals are vulnerable to depression when attachment bonds are disrupted (Bowlby, 1969).

Bowlby argues that attachment bonds serve a survival function. The attachment of the helpless child to the mother insures proximity to the mother and thus aids the offspring's biological survival, especially by providing protection from predators. The continued presence of a secure attachment figure helps the child explore its physical environment, make peer contacts, and achieve group membership.

The way affectional bonds are made is determined and learned largely within the family, especially but not exclusively during childhood. The threat of loss of an important attachment figure creates anxiety and sadness, and frequent threats of such loss may predispose to later depression. Many psychiatric disorders are results of inability to make and keep affectional bonds. Bowlby concludes that human beings of all ages are happiest—most effective and competent—when they are confident that one or more trusted persons are available for help in time of trouble. For most adults in Western societies, the main attachments are with a few such persons, of whom the spouse is usually but not always the most prominent, followed by close relatives, offspring, and friends (Henderson, 1977). Bowlby's work has been extended by Rutter (1972), to show that the child's relationship with others besides the mother can also create attachment bonds, and that disruption and deprivation of these bonds can contribute to the onset of depression.

On the basis of such observations, Bowlby (1977) proposed a general approach to psychotherapy: Psychotherapy should help the patient examine current interpersonal relationships and understand how they have developed from experiences with attachment figures in childhood, adolescence, and adulthood. Parker (1978), among others, describes effective psychotherapy as similar to optimal parenting. Ideal psychotherapy should combine caring with nonpossessive warmth and should provide, as part of the interpersonal therapeutic relationship, a cognitive explanation of distortions of past relationships.

Thus the concept of attachment bonds provides a strong theoretical basis for understanding the interpersonal context of depression and for developing psychotherapeutic strategies to correct the distortions produced by faulty attachments in childhood. Moreover, attachment theory has stimulated a strong body of empirical research in the association between interpersonal relationships and depression.

BEREAVEMENT, GRIEF, AND MOURNING

The death of a loved one is an irreversible disruption of an attachment and almost universally produces sadness, grief, and mourning. The universality of this response has led many theorists to regard it as a normal variant of the clinically depressed state. Attention to the similarities and differences between grief and depression were first discussed by Freud and Abraham, who emphasized that mourning following the death of a loved one is not a pathological condition. Both saw mourning as similar to "melancholia" in the pattern of symptoms, with the exception that loss of self-esteem is absent in mourning but prominent in clinical depressions. As Freud (1917) put it, "In mourning it is the world which has become poor and empty; in melancholia it is the ego itself."

These observations have been partly confirmed by empirical studies of the bereaved (Lindemann, 1944). Both men and women respond to the death of a loved one with unhappiness and depressive symptoms (Weissman et al., 1979), but not all depressed patients have low self-esteem and feelings of worthlessness and guilt, and only a minority of mourners express guilt and fall in self-regard. Most grieving persons recover and only a few require treatment (Clayton, 1968). Grieving persons who are at risk for developing a depression are those who perceive themselves as having few emotional, physical, or financial supports available to them (Walker et al., 1977; Maddison and Walker, 1967; Maddison, 1968). Grief is a normal reaction to the disruption of a bond by death, but the presence of other attachments protects against a pathological outcome to grief (Parker, 1978).

Interpersonal Relations as Antecedant to Clinical Depression: The Role of Childhood Experience

While disruptions of attachment bonds produce feelings of sadness, they do not necessarily produce clinical depression.

CHILDHOOD EXPERIENCE AND ADULT DEPRESSION

Certain early childhood experiences are generally considered to predispose to development of psychopathology in adulthood. In particular, loss of a parent in childhood has been implicated in the development of adult depression. The parental bond can be disrupted through death, geographical separation, or divorce. Emotional separation of parent from child—lack of caring, emotional distance, overprotection, or child abuse—may also impair parent-child bonding.

The relationship between loss of a parent in childhood and subsequent adult depressive disorders has been studied extensively. When all research problems are taken into account, there is little evidence that it is the death of the parent itself that increases the child's vulnerability to later depression in adulthood (Tennant, Bebbington, and Hurry, 1980). The adverse effects can be explained by the quality of the parenting which replaces that of the dead parent or the qualities of the parenting before the loss. But the fact remains that death of a parent in childhood can increase likelihood of depression in the face of life stress in adulthood.

On the basis of these observations, recent research has been directed toward understanding the quality of parent/child relationships preceding loss by death or separation. First of all, it has become clear that the parenting role need not be provided by the biological parent (Birtchnell, 1980). Rutter found that children temporarily separated from parents because of family discord became better adjusted emotionally if they were later placed in a harmonious family setting. Parker (1979) found a close relationship between adult depression and poor parental care in childhood irrespective of whether the care was provided by the biological parent.

A disrupted, unloving relationship between a child and its parent or parent substitute can increase the child's vulnerability to depression as an adult. Parker found that adult depressed patients, compared with normal controls, reported more low maternal care and/or greater maternal overprotection. These associations were not influenced by the levels of symptoms and were confirmed by the mothers' independent reports of their interactions with their offspring. These patterns were not found in bipolar depressives. Bipolar disorder refers to individuals with multiple episodes of affective disorder, at least one of which must have been manic or hypomanic. They were previously called manic-depressives following Kraepelin. However, ambiguity arose because of a lack of criteria in Kraepelin's concept as to whether the term manic-depressive illness should be used for people with recurrent depressions or with perhaps only one depression. The term bipolar illness has gained wide acceptance since it was first proposed by Leonhard in 1959.

Three additional sources of evidence are relevant to understanding the impact of parenting on the later development of adult depression: (1) studies of children of depressed parents, which assess the effects of the parents' disorder on their offspring; (2) studies of the childhood histories of depressed adults; and, (3) studies of depression in children (Orvaschel, Weissman, and Kidd, 1980).

CHILDREN OF DEPRESSED PARENTS

A number of researchers have investigated the effects of depressed parents on their children. Children in families with one or two depressed parents are more likely to show psychopathology than the children of normal parents. Rolf and Garmezy (1974), for example, found more withdrawn, shy, and socially isolated behavior among the children of depressive mothers than for control children. Weintraub et al. (1975) noted higher levels of classroom disturbance, impatience, disrespectful or defiant behavior, inattentiveness and withdrawal, and lower levels of comprehension, creativity, and relatedness to the teacher for both the children of schizophrenic mothers and the children of depressed mothers than for their control counterparts. Gamer et al. (1977) found the children of psychiatrically ill parents to have disturbances in attention, particularly when confronting complex tasks. Welner et al. (1977) found that depressed mood, death wishes, fighting, psychosomatic concerns and anhedonia were significantly more common in the children with a depressed parent than in the controls. They also noted that 11 percent of the children of depressives had five or more depressive symptoms, with 7 percent meeting the criteria for probable or definite depression, as compared with none in the control group.

Weissman et al. (1972) investigated the parental role performance of a group of thirty-five depressed women and a matched group of twenty-seven normal women. During the acute depressed episode, they found the depressed women less involved with their children, had impaired communication, increased friction, lack of affection, and greater guilt and resentment. The depressed mothers were more overprotective, irritable, preoccupied, withdrawn, emotionally distant, and/or rejecting. Disturbed functioning in the children of these depressed mothers was noted in approximately 59 percent of the 109 children. This proportion was even larger (64 percent) when only those children at early adolescence or younger were considered. The children manifested hyperactivity, enuresis, depression, school problems, truancy, drug abuse, and delinquency.

It is now clear that children in families in which one or both parents are depressed are at greater risk for psychopathology in general, and for depression in particular. It is not clear how many of these effects are genetic and how many are due to social and environmental transmission; most likely there is usually a combination of both influences. Other factors, too, such as marital discord, low socioeconomic status, and peer relations, undoubtedly play a role.

THE CHILDHOOD OF ADULT DEPRESSIVES

Although adults' retrospective reports of their childhood are particularly prone to bias, they can be useful for generating hypotheses. Four studies have investigated adult depressive patients' descriptions of their early years. All four bear out findings that depression in parents is associated with similar emotional problems in their offspring. Adult depressives are more likely to have suffered in childhood from family discord, parental neglect, rejection, and abuse (Orvaschel, Weissman, and Kidd, 1980).

Depression Among Children. Childhood depression has been a controversial issue in child psychiatry. Recently, however, there has been a major shift in thinking about the diagnosis of depression in childhood (Malmquist, 1975). Current studies are beginning to overcome many of the difficulties surrounding the evaluation of childhood depression, such as the problem of distinguishing between symptom and syndrome and the need to separate symptom clusters according to developmental age (Malmquist, 1971). Depression is now recognized as a frequent symptom in adolescent clinic patients (Evans, 1975). In the Isle of Wight (Rutter et al., 1976), depression or suicide was not found to be frequent among the general preadolescent population, and only a small number of children overall were actually suffering from clinically significant depression. However, many of the adolescents in this British study reported feelings of inner distress, self-depreciation, and suicidal ideation (Rutter et al., 1976).

Connell (1972) proposed that depressed children be divided into two groups —those who had a precipitating event and those who manifested a long history of depression with no obvious precipitant. The latter group had a higher incidence of depressive illness in the family. In fact, among depressed children, a family history of psychiatric illness is commonly observed. Brumback et al. (1977) found a history of affective disorders in 89 percent of the depressed children's families and in over 60 percent of the mothers of the depressed children, as compared with 30 percent of the mothers in the nondepressed children. Poznanski and Zrull (1970) reported high rates of marital discord and parental depression in the families of depressed children and described many of the parents as rejecting and hostile, often suffering from personality problems. Puig-Antich et al. (1979) found serious family discord or mistreatment of children in 11 out of 132 cases and a family history of psychiatric disorder (depression, mania, alcoholism, or schizophrenia) in 61 percent of the relatives of the children.

It is now agreed that depressive illness occurs in preadolescent and adolescent children and that it can be reliably diagnosed on the basis of symptom criteria (Kovacs et al., 1977; Welner et al., 1977). The presence of a depressed parent and/or a positive family history of affective disorder strongly contributes to depression in childhood, particularly when the depression is chronic and does not appear to have a clear-cut psychosocial precipitant.

The families of depressed children are similar to those described by adult depressed patients recalling their childhood experiences. The depressed children's homes are characterized by family discord, parental rejection, and an increased frequency of parental psychopathology, although the psychopathology is not always depression.

Information obtained from the depressed patient, the children of depressives, depressed children, or the relative or patient report, and concerned with either current or past behavior, all carries certain consistencies. A disruptive, hostile, and generally negative environment is associated with depression in the parent, in the child, and in the child who becomes depressed as an adult.

Interpersonal Difficulties and Clinical Depression in Adulthood

As childhood interpersonal experiences can predispose to adult depression, so some aspects of interpersonal relations in adulthood can also be associated with onset and perpetuation of clinical depression.

SOCIAL STRESS AND LIFE EVENTS

Since Holmes et al. (1950) observed that the rate of upper respiratory illness increased with the number of stressful life events, research has frequently demonstrated the relationship between stress, especially over recent events, and the onset of many medical and psychiatric illnesses, particularly depression (Paykel et al., 1969; Rabkin and Struening, 1976; Schless and Mendels, 1977; Paykel, 1978; Uhlenhuth and Paykel, 1973).

The New Haven group's work is most relevant to depression (Paykel et al., 1969). In the six months following a stressful life event, they found a sixfold increase in the risk of developing a clinical depression. Marital discord was the most common event before the onset of depression. This research group also found that "exits" of persons from the individual's life during the preceding six months had occurred more frequently with depressed patients than with the control group.

Similar observations by Ilfeld (1977) were based on a survey of over 3,000 adults in Chicago. Depressive symptoms were closely related to the degree of stress, especially stresses in marriage and in parenting. In a further look at these Chicago adults, Pearlin and Lieberman (1977) found that persisting problems within an intact marriage were as likely to produce depressive symptoms and distress as the disruption of the marriage by divorce or separation.

In another study, Myers, Lindenthal, and Pepper (1975) interviewed a community sample in 1967 and again in 1976 and found a relationship between stressful life events and psychiatric symptomatology, often depression.

Bloom, Asher, and White (1978), in a critical analysis of several studies related to the consequences of marital disputes and divorce, linked these marital disruptions with a variety of emotional conditions, including depression.

SOCIAL SUPPORTS

Using Bowlby's concept of attachment, Henderson and associates in Australia have conducted a series of elegant studies that examine the importance of social supports in the production of psychopathology. Henderson's work began with a careful analysis of the concept of care-eliciting behavior, an essential part of attachment bonding. "Care-eliciting behavior" is described as "a pattern of activity on the part of one individual which evokes from another responses which give comfort" (Henderson, 1974, page 172). Comfort includes close body contact and verbal expressions of concern, esteem, or affection. These findings are based on animal observation by the ethologists Harlow (1971), Goodall (1971), and Scott (1970), on studies of human infant-parent interactions. Henderson notes that ethological studies of care-eliciting behavior have been limited to the young, and in agreement with Bowlby and Ainsworth, he proposes that attachment behavior, including care-eliciting behavior, remains part of the behavioral repertoire of humans throughout life. During childhood and adolescence, as the repertoire changes and enlarges, new relationships develop; these are usually quite strong with one or two people and less intense with a larger number. Adults, like infants and children, are distressed when separated from loved ones. When distressed, they seek the closeness of a few persons known or expected to be comforting. Such care-eliciting behavior has probably conferred considerable reproductive and evolutionary advantages; since it is one mechanism for male-female attraction and bonding, it provides a means of maintaining strong social bonds among members of the group.

Henderson further differentiates between normal and pathological care-eliciting behavior. Pathological care-eliciting behavior occurs when there is insufficient caring behavior from others, and this behavior includes such psychiatric syndromes as clinical depression. Most individuals require at least a minimum level of social interaction, and below this level the risk of psychiatric disorders increases (Henderson, 1977). Following Robert Weiss's (1975) ideas, Henderson notes that close personal relations—that is, social bonds—provide intimacy, social integration through shared concern, opportunity to receive nurturance, reassurance of worth, a sense of a reliable alliance, and guidance. He has also found that deficient social bonds in the adult environment are associated with neurotic symptoms. Patients with neurotic disorders, primarily depression, spent the same amount of time with their primary group as matched normal controls did, but proportionately more of the interactions were affectively unpleasant. Neurotic depressives had fewer good friends and fewer contacts outside the household; they had fewer attachment figures and felt that these attachment figures gave them insufficient support (Henderson et al., 1978).

Henderson (1979) confirmed the clinical association between weak social bonds and neurosis, mostly depression, in an epidemiologic study of a random sample of the general population in Canberra, Australia. The value of strong social bonds in protection against the development of neurotic symptoms was even stronger when the individual was faced with adversity (Henderson et al., 1978, 1980, 1980). Recognizing the considerable difficulty of teasing apart cause and effect, Henderson also conducted a longitudinal study in an attempt to determine the direction of causation (Henderson, 1980, 1981). He noted that the association between weak social bonds and neurosis could be due to "persons with a disturbance of mood reporting unfavorably on adequate relations or being uncongenial company driving away the support they need and seek. A third factor —personality—may lead to both the development of symptoms and to the inability to form mutually satisfying interpersonal relations" (Henderson et al., 1978). This study confirmed that lack of social bonds is a risk factor for the onset of neuroses, and that adequate social relationships, both closely affectional and more diffuse, can protect against neurosis. The crucial aspect of social bonds seems to be, not their availability, but how adequate they are perceived to be when one is under stress. Whether the deficiencies in social relationships were real or only self-perceived could not be tested in this study, but it supports the thesis that neurotic symptoms emerge when persons consider themselves deficient in care, concern, and interest from others; and that the symptoms themselves can appropriately be seen as care-eliciting behavior which can be adaptive (Henderson, 1981).

INTIMACY

Intimacy has been proposed as an important component of care-eliciting and supportive interpersonal relations. Research on this aspect of attachment bonding in relationship to the development of depression was reported by Brown, Harris, and Copeland (1977). In their survey of women living in the Camberwell section of London, they found that the presence of an intimate and confiding relationship with a man, usually the spouse, was a strong protection against the development of a depression in the face of life stress. Roy has replicated this finding in a study of eighty-four depressed women compared to a matched group without history of depression (Roy, 1978).

In similar research with medically ill patients, Miller and Ingham (1976) found that both men and women who reported the lack of an intimate confidant to general physicians had more severe psychological symptoms, usually depression.

MARITAL DISCORD

Marriage serves as society's response to the individual adult's need for human attachment (Hinchliffe, Hooper, and Roberts, 1978). Ideally, the social and legal contract provides a secure economic and social base for rearing children and creates an opportunity for each partner's needs for mutual care, concern, and affection to be expressed within the stability and security of a committed relationship. Therefore the actual or threatened disruption of the marital attachment through disputes, separation, or divorce is one of the most common and serious disruptions of attachment in adulthood and is often related to the occurrence of depression.

Although there is controversy about the sequence of marital problems and depression, some relationship has long been recognized and has become increasingly well documented. Marital difficulties, especially arguments, are the most frequently reported events in the lives of depressed women during the six months before they sought treatment (Paykel et al.). Weissman and Paykel found that marital relationships were the most impaired areas of functioning of acutely depressed women compared to their normal neighbors. The marriages of depressed women were characterized by disengagement, poor communication, friction, and sexual problems. These impairments were slow to resolve and persisted long after the women had symptomatically recovered from their depressions. These studies, as well as Brown's study of intimacy, highlight the importance of the marital relationship in the development and course of depression in women.

Following the evidence that persistent marital disputes are a common circumstance in the development of depressive symptoms for many women, Rounsaville et al. (1979–1980) studied the relationship between marital disputes and the clinical course of depression in women. Among a group of depressed women who received psychotherapy and/or antidepressant drugs for acute depression, they found that the majority of women coming for treatment had marital disputes. Depressed women with marital disputes differed from those without disputes in the process and outcome of psychotherapy, in that women with marital disputes showed less improvement in their symptoms and social functioning and had a greater tendency to relapse. However, within the marital dispute group, women who were able to effect an improvement in their marital relationships during treatment showed an improvement in depression and social adjustment equal to that of the patients who had no marital disputes at the onset of treatment, which demonstrates a correlation between improvement of marital disputes and im- provement of depression.

Follow-ups of these women one and four years after they completed their treatment provided further insight into the course of the marital disputes. The women who had disturbed marital relationships at the onset of treatment still had poor marital adjustment four years later. Even when there had been an improve- ment in the relationship during treatment, it was usually short-lived, unless the woman left a bad relationship and did not become involved in another bad relationship. The disputes usually persisted; the majority did not divorce despite continuing marital discord. The marital relationships of women who entered treatment with relatively good marriages and no marital disputes also tended to remain stable, and disputes tended not to develop in their marriages.

Sustaining marital disputes or repeatedly attaching to a partner who is unsuita- ble may reflect persistent personality difficulties. The majority of women who left their original partner and subsequently became involved with the same or a new man became further involved in marital strife. These women may be inadvert- ently seeking self-destructive attachments, suppressing their awareness of the partner's negative traits until it is too late, or their involvement in repeated disputes may be due to lack of an appropriate repertoire of social skills for close interpersonal relations.

The tendency of depressed women with marital disputes to continue living in discord over a period of years, often with the same partner, underscores the importance of dealing with marital problems in treatment of depressed patients.

Interpersonal Difficulties as a Consequence of Clinical Depression

In addition to the important role that difficulties in interpersonal relations play in the predisposition to depression that is derived from childhood experiences and in the onset and perpetuation of clinical depression in adolescence and adulthood, we must consider the impact of depression on the individual's interpersonal relations and the consequences of the depression for the patient's marriage, family, work, and community activities.

IMPACT ON COMMUNICATION AND INTERPERSONAL INTERACTIONS

Several studies that examine the impact on a nondepressed person of interaction with someone who is depressed can help us understand the processes by which interpersonal relationships become disrupted as a consequence of depression.

The usual response of others to normal sadness, disappointment, and depression, and to grief and mourning, is sympathy, support, encouragement, and offers of assistance. However, as time goes on, this positive response often gives way to frustration, friction, and withdrawal. Coyne (1976), studying the interaction between depressed patients and those around them, found that depressed people elicited unhelpful responses. When he asked college women to interact with both depressed and nondepressed women patients, and with nonpatients, they evaluated depressed patients more negatively than nondepressed. Furthermore, there was an increase in depression, anxiety, and hostility among the college women who talked with acutely depressed patients.

In similar work, Hammen and Peters (1978) had male and female college students rate other male and female students who played standardized depressed or nondepressed roles in telephone conversations. Depressed persons of the opposite sex were strongly rejected. Female raters made relatively little distinction between depressed males and females in role impairment. Male raters, however, considered the depressed females more impaired. And as in Coyne's study, the "normal" students were depressed after their interaction with the depressed ones.

The findings of these short-term studies are provocative. Depressed individuals are "depressing" to have around; they are evaluated negatively and often avoided. Not surprisingly, the effects of long-term interaction with depressed people can be even more adverse. Kreitman and associates (1971), Collins, et al. (1971), have investigated the effects on marital relationships of women living with a neurotic (mainly depressed) husband. Sixty male outpatients and their wives were interviewed and compared with sixty control couples (Kreitman et al., 1971). Wives of patients were five times as likely to be impaired as "control" wives in household roles, social activities, health, and child-rearing activities. Wives of patients were also twice as likely as control wives to have a psychiatric history. The longer the marriage, the more incapacitated the patients' wives became as compared to wives of controls. When the same authors interviewed couples about their activities, they found that patient pairs spent significantly more time together without others present than control couples did. Control wives spent significantly more time in separate social activities than patients' wives, and patients' wives scored lower on a scale of social integration.

The observation that spouses of depressed patients have higher than expected rates of mental illness and emotional problems could be due to assortative mating —the tendency of predisposed depressives to seek out and marry other future depressives even before the onset of clinical symptoms—or to pathogenic influence—that is, the adverse effects upon a clinically normal person of continued interaction with a depressed spouse. Kreitman et al. (1971) minimize the role of assortative mating. Since their studies show patient-spouse impairment increasing with the duration of the marriage, they argue for "pathogenic interaction," and conclude that disability increases as a result of the marital relationship, with the wives adjusting their social activity to the patterns of psychiatrically impaired husbands.

Similar findings about the detrimental impact of depressed patients' social communication patterns have been reported by Merikangas et al. (1979), who found in addition that a change in marital communication patterns predicted good treatment response. Patients who had responded to antidepressant drug treatment demonstrated improved communication with their spouses, including better dyadic conversation, less choppy speech patterns, and more interaction. The spouses of these patients interrupted the patients less during decision making and expressed less anxiety and depression themselves.

Hooper and Hinchliffe also observed the communication interactions of depressed patients and their spouses. In a detailed study, twenty depressed patients interacting with their spouses and with a stranger during the acute episode and at recovery were matched with a comparison group of surgical patient controls and their spouses. Using tape recordings, the researchers observed that discussions around everyday interpersonal and family situations and general philosophical issues which pose a problem may be dealt with in maladaptive ways (Hooper et al., 1977; Hinchliffe et al., 1975, 1977, 1978). The communication interactions of depressives were more negative, less responsive to the partners, more responsive to strangers, and more self-preoccupied. The high level of tension and hostility, a prominent feature in the marriages of depressed patients, arises from the patients' diminished social responsiveness. The diminished responsiveness in turn produces uncertainty and insecurity in the marital relationship and increases the patient's fear of possible loss of the loved person. This is followed by guilt and remorse, which in turn generates further anxiety and tension. Hostility leads to the spouse's withholding and remoteness and resultant angry demands by the patient for reassurance from the spouse.

MARITAL SEPARATION AND DIVORCE

Although marital disputes are most often viewed as a factor precipitating depression, Briscoe and Smith (1973) have examined the possibility that divorce is a consequence of depression. They interviewed 139 divorced individuals and assessed the presence of affective disorders before, during, and after the divorce. Thirty-two percent of the sample met the criteria of unipolar depression. In general, individuals who had been depressed before divorce were significantly more likely to be depressed afterward. Depressed divorced women were indistinguishable from nondepressed divorcées in all the characteristics studied, with the single exception that the former husband's relatives had more often disapproved of the marriage. On the other hand, depressed divorced men were older than their nondepressed counterparts at the time of their first date, were more likely to have engaged in sexual intercourse with their former wives before marriage, had married younger (under thirty), and had stayed married longer than the nondepressed men. Furthermore, depressed men were more likely to have seen a marital counselor and to have had sexual problems within the marriage.

Briscoe and Smith also found that the divorced women had more often been depressed during the marriage, whereas the men became depressed after the separation. Forty-five of the participants—more women than men—had depressive symptoms associated with precipitating events, such as the spouse's adultery or request for a divorce. Interestingly, the interviewers saw the depressive symptoms of seventeen of the forty-five as having contributed to the marital disruption rather than being the result of the divorce.

The depressed, divorced men and women had reacted differently to marital discord. The women seemed more likely to have become depressed during a troubled marriage, often as the result of specific stresses contributing to the friction. The divorced men, on the other hand, reported that precipitating interpersonal and sexual factors were not present, suggesting that the men saw their depression as contributing to marital friction and divorce rather than marital friction precipitating depression.

WORK, FAMILY, AND COMMUNITY ADJUSTMENTS

Weissman and Paykel (1974) studied forty depressed women and forty normal neighbors in an Italian working-class neighborhood to determine how the depression influences social, family, and community adjustment; whether the maladjustments associated with an acute episode persisted during treatment and after recovery; and to what degree the interpersonal difficulties reflected the illness and to what degree they represented preexisting personality patterns. The ethnic issues are probably important although we do not have direct data on this matter. The Italian working-class woman is brought up to conform to expectations around marriage and child-rearing. This is changing in Italian working-class and middle-class communities as the number of women entering the labor force has increased.

During the acute episode, the women suffering from depression were considerably more impaired in their daily lives and interpersonal relationships than their normal neighbors. The impairment was of moderate degree and was quantitatively rather than qualitatively different from the normal. The interpersonal difficulties fell short of the grossly disturbed patterns described in schizophrenic patients. Unlike schizophrenics, depressed women were not socially isolated; they were married, had children, and were living with their families. However, this was a sample of patients being treated and may not reflect the degree of impairment in depressed people who do not seek treatment.

The impairments of the acutely depressed woman reached into all her roles— wife, mother, worker, and community member. Role impairments were marked in work and in the intimate relationships of marriage and parenthood. They were less marked in relationships with friends, acquaintances, and the extended family. Consistent with the guilt and self-negation of depression, the patient's subjective distress about her performance was more marked than her objective signs of impairment. For example, dissatisfaction and distress reported at work were greater than the loss of attendance at work or decreased functioning there. Despite their discomfort, a considerable proportion of the depressed women remained at work during the acute episode. Interestingly, women who worked outside the home showed less impairment in their work than the housewives did in housekeeping and child rearing. Occupations outside the home seem to have a protective effect on depression. Women in the labor force report greater self-esteem and personal satisfaction which is contributed to not only by increased financial security but also by the sense of participating in the larger world, even if these jobs are not professional or leading to career advancement.

Social and leisure activities and relationships with the extended family showed similar role impairments. Although the depressed women were more impaired than their neighbors in both these role areas, the differences were not striking. Social relationships with the wide community were slightly impaired for both the patients and their neighbors; both groups showed rather limited participation, though the depressives were more withdrawn. This limited participation with the wider community could be interpreted as a cultural norm of Italian family life. In relationships with their extended families, neither patients nor normals showed serious maladjustment. The cultural patterns among housewives of Italian background, the majority of this sample, emphasize a close relationship with the extended family, and these relationships were maintained without unusual dependency or surface friction. However, when the relationships were disturbed by depression, and the depressed women withdrew somewhat and reduced communication, they felt resentment and guilt.

This relatively harmonious withdrawal from extended family interactions contrasts with the friction and tension that characterized the depressed women's interactions with their husbands and children. Marital relationships became the arena for friction, poor communication, and dependency, as well as diminished sexual satisfaction. Typically, the depressed woman feels a loss of affection toward her husband, mixed with guilt and resentment. Communication is poor and hostility overt. Although she is submissive and dependent, and overtly domineering behavior is absent, the depressed woman may exercise covert control through her symptoms and decrease in sexual activity. She continues to have sexual relations with her husband, although with reduced frequency; but she reports physical difficulties and is uninterested in sexual intimacy.

Depressed women express increased hostility in the family, and it is directed much more toward husband and children than work associates and friends. In good marriages the women withdraw from the spouse in an effort to protect him from the effects of depression, and the husbands in turn are more protective toward them. On the other hand, depressed patients with poor marriages blame the spouse for their depression, and the marital conflict is intimately involved with the patient's symptoms.

Relationships with children are also markedly impaired, according to Weissman and Paykel, although the manifestations vary with the stage of the family life cycle. Depressed mothers with infant children tend to be overconcerned, helpless, guilty, and sometimes overly hostile. With young school-age children, the mothers' attitude varies from irritability to lack of emotional involvement. There is often intense conflict with adolescent children. The adolescent learns to exploit the mother's helplessness rather than give her sympathy. Finally, the children's departure from home precipitates more feelings of loss and depression for the mother.

The role framework helps to illuminate the way depression works, but it does not by itself adequately describe the social dysfunctions of depression, since consistent patterns of malfunction are common across specific roles. These malfunctions involve six aspects: impaired work performance, interpersonal friction, emotional dependency, inhibited communication, withdrawal from family relations, and anxious rumination.

Recovery

As symptomatic recovery occurs, there is a tendency for social adjustment to improve, but the improvement is slower than that of symptoms. It is likely to be most rapid in the first two months and to continue more slowly for the next two months. Thereafter, the adjustment remains more or less static, or it may even worsen over the next year. Although the depressed person's improvement is considerable, it is not complete.

The Weissman and Paykel study showed that work performance improved rapidly as the patient improved. However, impairments in family relations were slower to improve, suggesting that enduring personality factors were operating independently of the depressive symptoms.

Symptomatic relapse is accompanied by a rapid worsening of social functioning. In particular, the patient's work performance worsens and her dependency and family attachment increase, which supports the idea that these dimensions are closely related to the symptomatic illness.

After eight months, patients in this study who were asymptomatic still had mild residual social impairments. Even after recovery, communication with close family and friends was inhibited. Instead, there was a pattern characterized by friction, resentment, and argumentative behavior. The trends which were evident after eight months of treatment were present at follow-up, twenty months after the acute episode. On the whole, the patients' social functioning had continued to improve. The general level of adjustment was fairly good, but not as good as that of the control group. Many patients sought further treatment, and for some of them the depressive symptoms recurred.

Many of the social disturbances of depression are a consequence of the illness; most impairments subside with recovery, but many return with symptomatic relapse.

Personality and Depression

The classic Greek medical writings of Hippocrates describe the role of temperament predisposing to melancholia. Through the centuries many clinicians have observed attributes of character and individual disposition that make some people vulnerable to depression. Twentieth-century views of the depression-prone personality derive mainly from the observations of clinicians working with clinically depressed patients. The psychoanalytic approach postulates that those who tend to be depressed are dependent on direct or indirect narcissistic inputs from others for their self-esteem. The cognitive approach holds that they have an enduring cognitive set of negative attitudes about themselves and are highly sensitive to situations that reinforce these negative attitudes. The learned helplessness theory proposes that people who can't alter or prevent negative situations become apathetic and reduce their goal-directed behavior. The behavioral approach would emphasize the deficient instrumental behaviors of depressives, such as social skills (the ability to behave in ways that elicit positive reinforcement from others); in this approach, low self-esteem is regarded as a consequence of the lack of positive social reinforcement.

The ideal design for testing these approaches would be to first study a group of people when they are without psychiatric disorders to assess their personality, then follow them to see which ones become depressed later on. This approach would come closer to disentangling personality traits from the symptoms of the disorder. Unfortunately, this research design is too expensive and time consuming to be practical. The alternative approach is to continue to study depressed persons after they have recovered. This method is not without its limitations, because personality assessments during and after the recovery period may still be contaminated by the consequences of having been ill or the presence of mild residual symptoms. Nonetheless, it is informative to review such studies.

Zuckerman et al. (1980) studied depressed outpatients who received psychotherapy, pharmacotherapy, or a combination of the two. Patients with premorbid low neuroticism and high extraversion, as measured by the Maudsley Personality Inventory (MPI-N), (1962) improved significantly in social and interpersonal adjustment compared to patients with premorbid high neuroticism and low extraversion. These findings, which were consistent regardless of which treatment was used, suggest that there is a subgroup of depressives with neurotic personality traits that predispose them to continued interpersonal difficulties. Similar results were found when these patients were followed up one year later (Weissman, Kasl, and Klerman, 1976 and four years later Weissman and Bothwell, 1977).

This approach to assessing the personality characteristics of depressed patients has been used systematically by Hirschfeld and Klerman (1979). Seventy-three depressed and twenty-four manic inpatients at four major university hospital centers were compared after their symptoms had abated. The depressed patients were significantly abnormal, with greater likelihood to break down under stress, less energy, more insecurity, interpersonal sensitivity, greater tendency to worry, less social adroitness, more neediness and more obsessionality. Manic patients were much more nearly normal according to the measures of personality included in the assessment battery.

The findings for the nonbipolar depressed patients were consistent with the excessive dependency described in psychoanalytic theory, the negative attitudes and learned helplessness emphasized by the cognitive theorists, and the deficient instrument behaviors of behavior theory. The depressed patient who emerges in this profile is introverted, lacking in self-confidence, unassertive, dependent, pessimistic, and self-perceived as inadequate.

Weissman and Paykel (1974), in their study of forty acutely depressed women, evaluated personality characteristics believed to be enduring, such as dependency, obsessionality, and difficulties in handling feelings. The fact that the residual impairments of these recovered depressed patients were considerably less than, and different in pattern from, those at the height of illness indicates that it is unwise to conclude much about lifelong social patterns from observation made during the acute depressed state. Theories that postulate dependency as a central and enduring feature predisposing to depression (Abraham, 1978; Rado, 1968) were not fully supported. Although dependency was characteristic of the depressed state, it was reduced to near-normal levels on recovery. In their work performance, the depressed women could not be regarded as obsessional. Although work performance improved strikingly as the depression remitted, it tended to remain poorer than that of the control group.

Hostility increased during the acute episode, but there was only a small decrease after recovery, so that the recovered depressed women still displayed more hostility than their neighbors. Clearly, formulations which relate depression to an internalization of hostility and an inability to externalize must be revised. Of course, the classical psychoanalytic formulations suggest something more complex than simply, "depression equals anger turned inward": they do not posit a direct inhibition of external hostility but an increase of hostility directed inward on an introjected object.

The Weissman and Paykel finding that recovered patients showed residual impairments in many facets of their lives is borne out by English writers. They have proposed a tendency to neuroticism in depressives (Foulds, 1965). Two areas of neurotic maladjustment most characteristic of the recovered depressive in the Weissman study were interpersonal friction and inhibited communication. These impairments are both problems of communication: the inability to communicate freely, directly, and appropriately with the family and friends, often combined with pathological communication of hostility and resentment. These maladaptive patterns seem most likely to be manifested in intimate relationships such as marriage. Persistent inability to communicate directly may in turn contribute to hostility and friction, ultimately even creating the marital stress that often precedes the depressive episode.

In most of this study, interpersonal adjustment is necessarily dealt with as if it were an attribute of the depressed person alone. This of course is not so; interpersonal relations involve an individual's interaction with the social environment, and the nature of that environment may make a substantial contribution to the development of depression. Some impairments may reflect recent situational crises or long-standing stressful situations that have contributed to the development of the depression.

PART II

CONDUCTING INTERPERSONAL THERAPY OF DEPRESSION

> . . . the last three years have been like one endless work-day without rest for me. Now it's over . . . My poor mother doesn't need me . . . nor the boys either.
>
> How free you must feel.
>
> No . . . only unspeakably empty. Nothing to live for now. . . .
>
> —Henrik Ibsen
> *A Doll's House*

Chapter 4

Goals and Tasks of IPT

There are many ways of conceptualizing any psychotherapy. We have conceptualized IPT at three levels: strategies for specific tasks, techniques, and therapeutic stance. IPT is similar to many other therapies at the level of techniques and stance, but it is distinct at the level of strategies.

The strategies of IPT occur in three phases of treatment. During the first phase, the depression is diagnosed within a medical model and explained to the patient. The major problem associated with the onset of the depression is identified and an explicit treatment contract to work on this problem area is made with the patient. When this phase is completed the intermediate phase begins. It is here that work on the major, current, interpersonal problem areas is accomplished. The termination phase is not unique to IPT, in that feelings about termination are discussed, progress is reviewed, and the remaining work is outlined. As in other brief treatments the arrangements for termination are explicit and are adhered to.

To understand the IPT structure, including techniques and stance, the following outline will be useful. This outline is the basis for the detailed discussions and case illustrations in Chapters 5 through 12.

I. The Initial Sessions
   A. Dealing with the Depression
      1. Review depressive symptoms.
      2. Give the syndrome a name.
      3. Explain depression and the treatment.
      4. Give the patient the "sick role."
      5. Evaluate the need for medication.

B. Relate Depression to Interpersonal Context
  1. Review current and past interpersonal relationships as they relate to current depressive symptoms. Determine with the patient the
    a. nature of interaction with significant persons;
    b. expectations of patient and significant persons from each other and whether these were fulfilled;
    c. satisfying and unsatisfying aspects of the relationships;
    d. changes the patient wants in the relationships.
C. Identification of Major Problem Areas
  1. Determine the problem area related to current depression and set the treatment goals.
  2. Determine which relationship or aspect of a relationship is related to the depression and what might change in it.
D. Explain the IPT Concepts and Contract
  1. Outline your understanding of the problem.
  2. Agree on treatment goals (which problem area will be the focus).
  3. Describe procedures of IPT: "here and now" focus, need for patient to discuss important concerns; review of current interpersonal relations; discussion of practical aspects of treatment—length, frequency, times, fees, policy for missed appointments.

II. Intermediate Sessions—The Problem Areas
  A. Grief
    Goals
    1. Facilitate the mourning process.
    2. Help the patient reestablish interest and relationships to substitute for what has been lost.
    Strategies
    1. Review depressive symptoms.
    2. Relate symptom onset to death of significant other.
    3. Reconstruct the patient's relationship with the deceased.
    4. Describe the sequence and consequences of events just prior to, during, and after the death.
    5. Explore associated feelings (negative as well as positive).
    6. Consider possible ways of becoming involved with others.
  B. Interpersonal Disputes
    Goals
    1. Identify dispute.
    2. Choose plan of action.
    3. Modify expectations or faulty communication to bring about a satisfactory resolution.

Strategies
1. Review depressive symptoms.
2. Relate symptoms' onset to overt or covert dispute with significant other with whom patient is currently involved.
3. Determine stage of dispute:
   a. renegotiation (calm down participants to facilitate resolution);
   b. impasse (increase disharmony in order to reopen negotiation);
   c. dissolution (assist mourning).
4. Understand how nonreciprocal role expectations relate to dispute:
   a. What are the issues in the dispute?
   b. What are differences in expectations and values?
   c. What are the options?
   d. What is the likelihood of finding alternatives?
   e. What resources are available to bring about change in the relationship?
5. Are there parallels in other relationships?
   a. What is the patient gaining?
   b. What unspoken assumptions lie behind the patient's behavior?
6. How is the dispute perpetuated?

C. Role Transitions

Goals
1. Mourning and acceptance of the loss of the old role.
2. Help the patient to regard the new role as more positive.
3. Restore self-esteem by developing a sense of mastery regarding demands of new roles.

Strategies
1. Review depressive symptoms.
2. Relate depressive symptoms to difficulty in coping with some recent life change.
3. Review positive and negative aspects of old and new roles.
4. Explore feelings about what is lost.
5. Explore feelings about the change itself.
6. Explore opportunities in new role.
7. Realistically evaluate what is lost.
8. Encourage appropriate release of affect.
9. Encourage development of social support system and of new skills called for in new role.

D.   Interpersonal Deficits
Goals
1.   Reduce the patient's social isolation.
2.   Encourage formation of new relationships.
Strategies
1.   Review depressive symptoms.
2.   Relate depressive symptoms to problems of social isolation or unfulfillment.
3.   Review past significant relationships including their negative and positive aspects.
4.   Explore repetitive patterns in relationships.
5.   Discuss patient's positive and negative feelings about therapist and seek parallels in other relationships.

III. Termination
1.   Explicit discussion of termination.
2.   Acknowledgment that termination is a time of grieving.
3.   Moves toward patient recognition of independent competence.

IV. Specific Techniques
1.   Exploratory.
2.   Encouragement of Affect.
3.   Clarification.
4.   Communication Analysis.
5.   Use of Therapeutic Relationship.
6.   Behavior Change Techniques.
7.   Adjunctive Techniques.

V. Therapist Role
1.   Patient advocate, not neutral.
2.   Active, not passive.
3.   Therapeutic relationship is not interpreted as transference.
4.   Therapeutic relationship is not a friendship.

Chapter 5

Dealing with the Depression and Diagnosing the Interpersonal Problems

---

IPT has two focuses: to reduce depressive symptoms and to deal with the social and interpersonal problems associated with the onset of the symptoms. The initial sessions are devoted to establishing the treatment contract, dealing with the depressive symptoms, and identifying the problem areas. During the initial sessions, both the depression and the interpersonal problems are diagnosed and assessed. In these sessions, the therapist should accomplish six tasks:

1. begin dealing with the depression;
2. complete an interpersonal inventory and relate the depression to the interpersonal context;
3. identify the principal problem areas;
4. explain the rationale and intent of interpersonal therapy;
5. set a treatment contract with the patient; and
6. explain the patient's expected role in the treatment.

The Initial Sessions: Dealing with the Depression

The first session begins with the patient's description of what has caused the need for treatment, the recent history of the depressive condition, a review of the depressive symptoms, and an evaluation of the need for medication. A physical examination with a comprehensive medical workup should be required for all patients. If there has been no examination within the past six months the patient should be asked to have one; people over forty should have had one even more recently.

The history of the depressive state should include a review of past episodes and of particular interpersonal precipitants and/or consequences of the depressions and the ways in which previous depressive episodes were resolved. The patient's level and constellation of depressive symptomatology is assessed in light of a possible need for concurrent pharmacotherapy. Suicidal intent must be carefully assessed.

Educating the patient about the depressive condition, including reassurance and guidance in managing symptoms, should be part of the first two sessions. This is important in establishing the patient's commitment to the treatment and in creating a sense that the problems are being "worked on" right away.

REVIEW OF SYMPTOMS

A detailed review of the patient's symptoms—of their presence, duration, and severity—should be undertaken in the initial session. This review of symptoms has three purposes: 1) It allows the psychotherapist to confirm the diagnoses. 2) It reassures the patient that the problems fit into a pattern that is anticipated by the psychotherapist and is understood as a clinical syndrome. Thus the patient understands that inexplicable, aberrant symptoms and behaviors are part of a pattern, time-limited, and, though uncomfortable, treatable. 3) It centers the symptoms in a specific time frame and in the interpersonal context that will be the focus of the psychotherapy.

As part of this review, a detailed account of the patient's suicidal feelings, thoughts, and behaviors, past and present, should be obtained (see Part III, Chapter 14, for a discussion of the special problems of dealing with suicidal patients). Guidelines for this review are the Research Diagnostic Criteria and the DSM III criteria for depression listed in Chapter 1. The Hamilton Rating Scale for Depression (see Appendix) can also be a useful guide to the systematic review of symptoms.

The review of symptoms should cover inquiries into the following areas:

Depressed Mood

The mood is assessed through replies to such questions as: How have you been feeling over the past week, including today? Can you describe what your mood has been? Have you felt blue, down in the dumps, depressed? How would you describe it? How bad has it been?

Have you wanted to cry? Does crying help? Have you felt that you would like to cry but that you were beyond tears?

Have you felt hopeless, unable to control what happens to you, at the mercy of others, or unable to do anything for yourself?

How have you felt about the future? Can you see yourself getting better?

Feelings of Guilt

Have you blamed yourself for things you have done? Have you been down on yourself? Do you think you are a bad person?

Have you let your friends and family down? Do you feel guilty about it?

Have you felt that you are to blame for your illness? In what way? A lot? Do you think about sin?

Suicide

Do you think much about death? Have you felt that life is not worth living? Have you wished you were dead?

Have you had any thoughts of taking your life? Have you made any plans to do so? Have you started to do things to work out that plan?

Have you actually made an attempt on your life?

Insomnia

Early

When you go to bed do you fall asleep easily? Have you been taking sleeping pills?

Do you have difficulty getting off to sleep every night? How long does it take you to fall asleep? What goes through your mind as you lie there?

Middle

When you fall asleep, do you sleep well? Are you restless or do you keep waking? Do you get out of bed?

Late

Do you wake early in the morning? Stay awake or fall asleep again? Is this earlier than you would normally get up?

Work and Activities

What have you been doing in work, housework, hobbies, interests, and social life? Is this any different from what you used to do?

Retardation

Assess retardation solely on the basis of observation in the interview, not on subjective complaints of slowing down. Note slowness of thought and speech, impaired ability to concentrate, decreased motor activity, or apathy and stupor.

Agitation

Rate agitation on the basis of behavior during the interview also. Agitation is defined as restlessness associated with anxiety. It should be differentiated from anxiety, since it refers to observable phenomena of motor restlessness that are experienced as distressing.

Psychic Anxiety

Have you been feeling nervous, anxious, or frightened? Have you felt tense or found it hard to relax? Have you been worrying about little things?

Have you had a feeling of dread, as though something terrible were about to happen?

Have you tended to become fearful in special situations—being alone at home, going out alone, being in crowds, traveling? Do heights or elevators bother you?

Somatic Anxiety

Have you suffered from any of the following: trembling, shakiness, excessive sweating, feelings of suffocation or choking, attacks of shortness of breath, dizziness, faintness, headaches, pain in the back of the neck, butterflies or tightness in the stomach?

How often? How badly?

This group of problems encompasses a number of somatic complaints common in anxious patients, including gastrointestinal problems such as flatulence and indigestion; cardiovascular problems such as palpitations; headaches; respiratory complaints; and genitourinary complaints.

Gastrointestinal Symptoms

How has your appetite been? Have you had a heavy feeling in your stomach?

What is your pattern of bowel movements? Is this different now from your usual pattern?

General Somatic Symptoms

Do you tire easily? Do you feel tired all the time? Is it an effort to do anything? Do you spend a lot of time in bed? Asleep?

Do you have any aches and pains? Feelings of heaviness?

This group includes heaviness in limbs, back, or head; diffuse headache; loss of energy and fatiguability—subjective feelings. Consider changes in intensity and frequency. In depression these are characteristically vague and ill defined, and it is extremely difficult to get a satisfactory description of them from the patient.

Sexual Symptoms

I want to ask you a few questions about your sex life. Have you lost interest in the opposite sex/your spouse/your partner recently? Have you had less sexual drive than usual? Difficulty in becoming aroused? Sexual relations less often? Difficulty in obtaining an erection (men) or reaching a climax?

Attitudes Toward Bodily Complaints

This category refers to the patient's concern with bodily complaints, whether or not they have a realistic basis. The hypochondriacal patient is concerned with and keeps coming back to bodily symptoms rather than psychic complaints.

Loss of Weight

Have you lost weight since the trouble started? How much?

Assess the patient's maximum weight loss since the start of the illness.

Insight: Awareness of Condition

What would you say is the nature of your trouble? Do you regard yourself as being emotionally or psychologically ill?

What caused this?

Insight refers to the patient's being aware of a psychological disturbance and that it has a depressive component. Degree of self-awareness, as well as understanding of psychodynamics and psychological causation, must always be considered in relation to the patient's thinking and background knowledge. It is important to distinguish between a patient who has no insight and one who is reluctant to admit having "mental problems."

Everybody has a set of ideas and beliefs about illness, bodily or mental, and most people have their own classification and diagnostic systems. The patient's ideas should be elicited without disagreement or challenge. Some patients will see their experience in religious terms: "God is punishing me for being so selfish." Others will blame someone—a mother for not being "loving enough" or a spouse for being cruel and insensitive.

Diurnal Variation

At what time of day do you feel best? Morning? Afternoon? Evening? At what time of day do you feel worst?

These queries are designed to discover consistent fluctuations of mood and other symptomatology in the first and second half of the day. As a rule, a patient will feel better during one or the other. Occasionally a patient feels better in the afternoon and worse both morning and evening.

Depersonalization

Have you had the feeling at all that everything is unreal, that you are unreal, or that the world is distant, remote, strange, or changed? I don't mean just the feeling that you could not really imagine this illness would happen to you.

Paranoid Symptoms

Are you suspicious of other people? Do you think people are talking about you or laughing behind your back?

If a patient answers yes, probe for elaborations. Look for ideas of persecution that do not have a depressive element, that is, are not associated with guilt and a feeling that the persecution is deserved. If paranoid ideas do have such an element, this may be part of guilt or other depressive delusions.

Obsessional and Compulsive Symptoms

Do you find you have to keep checking or repeating things you have already done? Do you have to do things in a special way, a special order, or a certain number of times?

Do you find that unpleasant, frightening, or ridiculous thoughts or words come into your head and won't go away, even when you try to get rid of them?

Are you afraid you might commit some terrible act without wanting to?

GIVING THE SYMPTOMS A NAME

After the review of symptoms, if the patient does indeed have a depressive disorder (see DSM-III criteria, Chapter 1) then it is important to say so explicitly —to tell the patient that these multiple symptoms have a single clear name. The patient should be told that the syndrome of depression has been diagnosed, and that the sleep and appetite problems, the headaches, the hopeless outlook, the lack of interest, the fatigue, are all part of the depression. If the results of the physical examination show no specific somatic causes for these symptoms, the therapist can confidently reassure the patient that they are due to depression. Patients need to know that they do not have a serious organic illness, they are not "going crazy," the sleep problems or difficulty in concentration are not due to senility.

The diagnosis should be conveyed to the patient in some such words as these:

> Your symptoms [state them specifically: headaches, sleep problems, fatigue, etc.] don't seem to have a physical basis. The lack of a physical basis doesn't mean that the symptoms are not real and that you are not feeling well [your headache, fatigue, etc., are real]. The symptoms you describe are all part of being depressed. Your appetite and sleep are disturbed. You've lost interest in your usual activities. You're more irritated with your children and not getting along with your spouse. You can't imagine taking the job you were interested in before. You don't have energy and zest. This is all part of the clinical picture of depression. Your thoughts about death, your tiredness and feeling of futility, the question about where your life is going, your lack of energy, are part of the constellation of depression. The symptoms you describe are common ones for depressed persons. You are in the throes of a depression.

EXPLAINING DEPRESSION AND ITS TREATMENT

After the specific diagnosis the patient should be given some general information about depression and told what to expect:

> Depression is a common disorder. It affects about 3 to 4 percent of the adult population at any one time. Even though you are suffering now, depressions do respond to treatment. The outlook for your recovery is excellent. A variety of treatments is available, and you do not need to feel hopeless if the first approach doesn't work. Most people with depressions recover promptly with treatment and the prognosis is quite good. You will feel better and will return to your normal functioning when the symptoms disappear. Psychotherapy is one of the standard treatments of depression. It has been shown

to be effective in a number of research trials. Psychotherapy should help you understand the problems that led to the depression.

GIVING THE PATIENT THE "SICK ROLE"

The symptom review, the diagnosis, and the description of what the patient may expect, including the type and course of treatment, all serve deliberately to give the patient the "sick role." This role allows patients to receive in a compensatory but time-limited way the care that has not been adequately received—or felt as received—from others.

The idea of the sick role was first presented by Talcott Parsons (1951). Parsons, a Professor of Sociology at Harvard Medical School and one of the founders of the field of medical sociology, noted that illness is not merely a "condition" but also a social role. The essential criteria of a social role concern the attitude both of the incumbent and of others with whom he interacts, in relation to a set of social norms defining appropriate behavior for persons in that role.

Parsons described four functions of the sick role.

1. The sick person is considered exempt from certain normal social obligations. This exemption must be socially defined and validated.
2. The person is exempt from certain types of responsibilities.
3. The person is considered in a state that is socially defined as undesirable, to be gotten out of as expeditiously as possible.
4. The person is considered "in need of help" and taking the role of patient, which carries obligations of its own, especially affirming that one is ill and cooperating with the helper in the process of getting well.

In the context of the sick role concept, the review of symptoms allows the psychotherapist to discern whether the patient is entitled to the sick role. If the answer is yes, then this information is conveyed explicitly to the patient and, at times, to the family; this legitimizes the sick role and defines the patient as in need of help. It also temporarily exempts the patient from certain social obligations and from responsibility for the state of depression.

Describing the recovery process is essential, because it limits the sick role and informs the patient of the obligation to cooperate in getting well and relinquishing the sick role as soon as possible. A key element of this role is helping the patient to relinquish it and recover (Suchman, 1965a; Suchman, 1965b) and the recovery phase should begin almost as soon as the patient is engaged in treatment.

The psychotherapist might give the patient the sick role by saying something like:

It's O.K. if you don't feel like entertaining and being sociable now, while you're feeling so badly. Why don't you explain directly to your husband that for the next month, during this phase of active treatment for your depression, you would rather not invite guests and would like a chance to consider social obligations with him before he commits both of you to any? You are going to be actively engaged in treatment with me now, and over the next month we will be working hard toward recovery. The expectation is that you will be able to assume your normal life gradually and at the end of two months should be quite active. As time goes on and we begin to understand and cope with the problems around your becoming depressed, we have every reason to hope that you will feel even better than before.

The central concept that should be shared with depressed patients is that depression is a disorder in which they are not fully in control but from which, with treatment, they will recover without serious residual damage. Patients often take a moral view of their illness: that depression is failure, a sign of weakness, a just punishment for past misconduct, or even a deliberate act. They should be reassured that this negative view is part of the depressive affect.

EVALUATING THE NEED FOR MEDICATION

The need for psychopharmacologic treatment, typically a tricyclic antidepressant, will depend on the severity of symptoms, the patient's preference and previous experience, and medical contraindications. (Pharmacotherapeutic treatment is discussed in detail in Chapter 13.) In general, patients with severe sleep and appetite disturbances, agitation, or lack of reactivity are good candidates for tricyclic antidepressants in addition to psychotherapy, in the absence of medical contraindications. Patients whose depression has endogenous features (see Table 5.1) may not respond as rapidly to psychotherapy alone as to psychotherapy and tricyclic antidepressant combined (Prusoff et al., 1980).

The presence of life stress as a precipitating factor in the depression does not preclude the effective use of medication in addition to psychotherapy. In fact, the majority of patients, even those with endogenous features or melancholia, identify a stress associated with the onset of depression. Nor does an acute depression superimposed on chronic depression or depressive personality preclude the use of tricyclic antidepressants in addition to psychotherapy (Rounsaville et al., 1981). The key clinical features to identify in evaluating the need for medication are the severity of the symptoms and the presence of specific ones: agitation, retardation, and loss of interest or reactivity. The criteria described in Table 5.1 are from the Research Diagnostic Criteria (RDC) (Spitzer, 1976) for major depressive disorder —endogenous subtype. These criteria are similar but not identical to the DSM-III criteria for major depressive disorder with melancholia. In clinical practice, the two criteria sets identify almost identical groups of patients. They have been shown to be useful in making decisions about the use of medication.

TABLE 5.1
Criteria for Endogenous Depression

Endogenous major depression as defined by Research Diagnostic Criteria is:
From Groups A and B a total of at least four symptoms for probable, six for definite, with at least one symptom from Group A.

Group A

1. Distinct quality to depressed moods, i.e., depressed mood is perceived as distinctly different from the kind of feeling the patient would have or has had following the death of a loved one;
2. Lack of reactivity to environmental changes (once depressed the patient does not feel better, even temporarily, when something good happens);
3. Mood is regularly worse in the morning;
4. Pervasive loss of interest or pleasure.

Group B

1. Feelings of self-doubt or reproach or excessive or inappropriate guilt;
2. Early morning awakening or middle of night insomnia;
3. Psychomotor retardation or agitation (more than a mere subjective feeling of being slowed down or restless);
4. Poor appetite;
5. Weight loss (two pounds a week over several weeks or twenty pounds in a year when not dieting);
6. Loss of interest or pleasure (may not be pervasive) in usual activities or decreased sexual drive.
    These criteria are similar but not identical to the DSM-III melancholia.

SOURCE: Spitzer, R. L., Endicott, J. and Robins, E. 1978 Research Diagnostic Criteria (RDC)

Relating Depression to the Interpersonal Context in the Initial Sessions

THE INTERPERSONAL INVENTORY

Once the review of the depression has been completed, the therapist should direct the patient's attention to the onset of symptoms and to the reason for seeking treatment: What has been going on in the patient's social and interpersonal life that is associated with the onset of symptoms? The review of key persons and issues often follows easily. If not, it is useful to begin an inventory of current and past relationships, to get a full picture of what the important current social interactions are in the patient's life.

The systematic review of current and past interpersonal relationships involves an exploration of the patient's important relationships with others, beginning with the present. This may all be done during the sessions or the psychotherapist may ask the patient to write an autobiographical statement containing interpersonal information.

In this inventory, the following should be gathered about each person who is important in the patient's life.

1.   interactions with the patient, including frequency of contact, activities shared, and so on;

2. the expectations of each party in the relationship, including some assessment of whether these expectations were or are fulfilled;
3. a review of the satisfactory and unsatisfactory aspects of the relationship, with specific, detailed examples of both kinds of interactions;
4. the ways the patient would like to change the relationship, whether through changing his or her own behavior or bringing about changes in the other person.

Although the inventory is concentrated in the first two sessions, it may be added to less systematically as treatment progresses.

IDENTIFICATION OF MAJOR PROBLEM AREAS

As the psychotherapist guides the patient through the review, the primary interest is in determining which interpersonal issues are most central to the patient's current depression and which aspects of the patient's difficulties are open to change. The therapist should obtain enough information to define the *primary problem area.* Discussion of the problem area proceeds naturally in tandem with dealing with the depression itself, and it also helps move the patient away from sole concern with the present overwhelming symptoms. Since the discussion of the depression focuses on a discrete onset period, this is usually the best transition to a discussion of the interpersonal problems associated with the onset.

With the phrase "Let's try to review what has been going on in your life," the psychotherapist begins asking the patient about recent changes in life circumstances, mood, and social functioning:

> What else had been happening in your life about the time you started feeling bad? At your work? At home? With your family? Your friends? Any changes? How have you been feeling lately? Have you been worrying a lot? Have you had less contact with people lately? Have you lost interest in or are you getting less pleasure from things you used to enjoy—your job, friends, family, food, sex, hobbies, eating, watching t.v?

Determine how life circumstances relate to the onset of symptoms.

> When did you start feeling depressed? What was going on in your life? When you learned of your husband's affair, was this around the time you started to get sad?

It is important to define the problem areas because they can help the psychotherapist formulate a treatment strategy with the patient. Since IPT is short-term, it is usually concentrated on one or two of the four problem areas that depressed patients commonly encounter. (These areas are defined and discussed

in detail in Chapters 6 through 9.) This classification of problem areas conceptu-
alizes interpersonal problems according to a system that focuses on potential areas
of change in treatment. The classifications are not exhaustive and they do not
represent in-depth formulations, nor do they attempt to explain the dynamics of
the depressive disorder. Instead, this classification system is intended to help the
therapist outline realistic goals and follow appropriate treatment strategies.

The problem areas are:

1. grief;
2. interpersonal disputes with spouse, lover, children, other family members,
    friends, co-workers.
3. role transitions—a new job, leaving one's family, going away to school,
    relocation in a new home or area, divorce, economic or other family
    changes; and
4. interpersonal deficits—loneliness and social isolation.

These areas are not necessarily mutually exclusive. Patients may come for
treatment with a combination of problems in several areas, or there may be no
clear-cut, significant difficulties in any one area. For each person the psychotherapist assesses individual needs and what the patient considers the factors that
have contributed to the depression. For patients with wide-ranging problems, the
therapist may be guided in the choice of focus by the precipitating events of the
current depressive episode.

Occasionally the patient and the psychotherapist disagree about the appropriate focus. Patients are sometimes unwilling or unable to recognize the degree to
which a particular problem is distressing them. For example, patients with marital
role disputes may be reluctant to complain of problems because they feel threatened by the possibility of endangering the marital relationship. Patients with
pathological grief reactions may be unaware consciously of the source of annual
episodes of depression. When the therapist and the patient do not agree about
the desirable focus of treatment, the therapist can take one of three tacks: (1)
delay setting treatment goals until the patient realizes the importance of the
issue; (2) set very general goals in the hope of being able to focus more specifically
as therapy progresses; or (3) accept the patient's priorities in the hope that after
those issues are looked into, the focus can shift to more central matters. The third
tack worked well for a woman patient who came in with the complaint "My
children are driving me crazy." Several sessions later, however, she brought up
her more pressing distress at her husband's extramarital affair.

The specific stress area is usually determined by focusing on one or two areas
which seem most troubling: threat of loss of job, problems with children, marital
friction, relocation. The purpose is to identify and clarify the most recent stresses

the patient is trying to cope with, and to determine the problem areas that will be the focus of the remaining sessions.

It is important to listen—to let patients describe the problems in their own terms and unburden themselves. But patients should not be allowed to dominate the interaction with irrelevant preoccupations. A systematic outline in which all salient historical points are listed can be useful in finding the best focus for a brief treatment. These points do not have to be applied in mechanical order, but all the areas should be adequately covered. They should include the history of present symptoms; the history of current life circumstances; the history of current close interpersonal relationships; and the history of recent changes in all three.

The psychotherapy task is to help patients identify the key persons with whom they are having difficulties; what the difficulties are; and whether there are ways the patient can make the relationships more satisfactory. The problems should be stated explicitly to the patient in formulations that show their derivation from what the patient has been describing. It should also be made explicit that the purpose of the next visits is to help with the problems.

The therapist might say,

> It seems from what you have been telling me that you have been [state the current problem or problems clearly—having trouble in your marriage, arguing with your spouse, afraid of losing your job, uncomfortable in your new apartment, lonely in the city, missing your old friends, etc.]. These problems can certainly be related to your depression. I'd like to meet with you over the next few weeks, as we have been doing, for about an hour each time, to see if we can figure out how you can better cope with the situation.

Patient reactions to this type of exploration of the interpersonal nature of depression can be of at least three types:

1. Patients may insist that they have an undetected physical illness.
2. They may remain focused on the symptoms of the depression—the sleep disturbance, the fatigue—and deny that these have any connection to life stress.
3. They may acknowledge to varying degrees some current life stress.

The first response is the least frequent and the most difficult to deal with. Obviously the third response is the easiest to handle. In any case, a patient who responds in either the first or the second way—that is, with denial—should not be pushed or lectured. If the attitude persists, it may be necessary to postpone further sessions and offer the opportunity for a further physical examination, or perhaps a second opinion from another physician. At this point the therapist should go gently—reassuring the patient, not getting into an argument, not trying to change the patient's mind. It is more useful to follow the patient's lead, never denying the reality of the symptoms and the real discomfort they cause. When patients continue to deny current problems, always leave the door open for the next visit; tell them you'd like to help explore again what is going on in their life and see how they are getting on:

> I can understand that these [state patient's symptoms—headaches, sleep problems, etc.] are uncomfortable. I'd like to try to understand over the next few weeks what may be causing them. Let's see how you are doing next week.

In some cases it may be appropriate to negotiate with patients about their perceptions:

> We both agree that you have problems with [state symptoms—sleep, energy], but we have different ideas about what is producing them. Together let's see how things go for you and what we can find out over the next few weeks.

If after several sessions patient and therapist remain unable to agree on problem areas and/or treatment goals, IPT treatment may not be possible. The lack of an agreed-upon therapy contract may lead the patient to express his dissatisfaction through silence, missed appointments, or termination. (The handling of such special problems is discussed in Chapter 14.)

IPT CONCEPTS AND THE TREATMENT CONTRACT

Even when taking the symptom history described above, it is important that the therapist ask questions in a way that conveys the message that depression is not a disease mysteriously visited upon the patient but is related to interpersonal functioning.

Many depressed patients are aware that problems with others play an important part in their condition, but they often see their problems as entirely individual, related only to their personal failures or inadequacies. They may have social relationships that are overtly untroubled or they may be so socially isolated that they cannot see that interpersonal deficits increase their vulnerability to depression. These patients may need some such explanation as this:

> We live in a world in which other people play a large part, even if we tend to think that we face life alone. Although the causes of depression are unknown, it is frequently associated with problems with personal relationships, including dealings with your spouse, children, family, or colleagues. Problems in relating to others or loss of loved ones may bring on depression in some people, while for others the symptoms of depression prevent them

from dealing with other people as successfully as they usually do. In this treatment we will try to discover what you want and need from others and help you learn how to get it.

After this general explanation, the psychotherapist should give the patient an outline of the psychotherapist's initial understanding of the problems the patient is currently having in social relationships. To demonstrate the vital nature of interpersonal issues, patients may be asked what changes would make them feel better. The reply will usually involve improved interpersonal relationships, even if it does not do so obviously. Wanting more money, for example, can be seen as a step toward developing more satisfying relationships with others: more money is expected to bring more respect from others, less bickering, and so on.

The psychotherapist should then give the patient an explanation of the techniques of IPT. The "here-and-now" emphasis on current social functioning should be made clear:

We'll be discussing your life as it is right now.

The patient should know that the general strategy of treatment is to review in detail current relationships (and relevant past ones) with the purpose of clarifying the problem areas and working toward resolution of them.

We'll be reviewing your relationships with important people in your life.

The patient's part in the process will be to decide, with the psychotherapist, on the focus of treatment and to bring in new material that pertains to the work at hand. Patients should know that they are largely responsible for choosing topics to discuss. Whenever necessary, however, the therapist will refocus the discussion on the problem area after that has been agreed on.

I'll expect you to be willing to discuss these relationships and your feelings honestly with me. If I feel the direction of the session is not going to be useful, I'll let you know.

SETTING THE TREATMENT CONTRACT

The setting of two to three treatment goals takes place. Although improvement of interpersonal relationships is the goal of IPT, symptom reduction (eating better, sleeping better) is also an important component, and as people work on their problems in therapy, they usually experience a relief of symptoms. Goals set should be attainable within the course of treatment, so that the emphasis is on progress toward solving a problem rather than lifetime solutions.

To further explain treatment goals, it is sometimes helpful to ask the patient to rate goals in the manner of the Goal Attainment Scale Kiresuk (1976) describes. For each problem area the patient is asked to define what would be the best possible outcome, the most expectable outcome, and the worst possible outcome. Being clear about hoped-for outcomes at the start may help patients see small increments of progress in the therapy.

Since treatment goals are set jointly by psychotherapist and patient, the therapist can use this process to provide evaluative feedback to the patient. This may include assessments of the psychotherapist's general understanding of the patient's particular interpersonal problem area and of the severity of the patient's difficulties. Many patients, experiencing psychiatric symptoms for the first time, may have an unrealistic sense of the severity of their problems.

For example,

> a twenty-seven-year-old man came for treatment with a depression of moderate severity following his third loss of a job in the past several years. Reacting to his depressive symptoms, he was frightened that he was "going downhill" permanently. In the course of the initial interview, it became clear that the loss of the most recent job had been in part precipitated by the patient; as with previous jobs, when he began to get involved in the work, he also began to feel that co-workers and employers were "taking advantage" of him. He reacted to this with withdrawal, work slowdown, and absenteeism, behavior that always led to his quitting or being fired.
>
> In setting up the treatment contract, the psychotherapist explained to him that he was suffering from a depressive condition of moderate severity, that there was a good prognosis for improvement, and that it did not portend more severe impairment or hospitalization. The therapist went on to say that there seemed to be some regularity in the patient's problems at work, since the feeling of being exploited developed in each situation, and that one goal of treatment might be to figure out how this came about and help the patient find more satisfactory work in the future.

At this point, the practical aspects of treatment (length of sessions, frequency, appointment times, fee, missed sessions policy, and so on) should be agreed upon, and by the end of the first session an explicit treatment contract should be stated. The contract should emphasize:

1. The social interpersonal context of the intervention:
We will try to understand what current stresses and relationships in your life may be contributing to depression.

2. The short-term duration (twelve to sixteen additional sessions, once a week, for about one hour):

I'd like to meet with you once a week for twelve to sixteen more times for about an hour each time, to try to understand with you the stresses in your life and how they relate to your depression.

3. The problem area:
From what you tell me, your depression began with recent transitions from college to graduate school. I'd like to discuss with you the critical areas you seem to describe as related to your depression. One is the kind of transition you've had to make from being a college student to being a graduate student, and where this leads in terms of career directions as you would like to think about them. The second issue centers on how you develop and maintain intimacy with someone, whether a man or a woman. When we say intimacy, we mean a close and confiding relationship with someone you trust and feel understands you. The third problem seems to be how you fit into a larger social scheme of things, how you can have some sort of sense of being part of things rather than being isolated, looking on from the outside rather than integrally involved and buddies with everybody. Do these sound like the issues we should discuss?

TEACHING PATIENTS THEIR ROLE IN IPT

In the first several sessions, while taking the history and helping the patient to delineate treatment goals, the psychotherapist is comparatively more directive and active than will usually be necessary in later sessions (although psychotherapy is an exploratory process which does not always proceed logically or smoothly). It is important to convey to patients that they will be responsible for choosing the topics in the remaining sessions and that the psychotherapist will be less active. To prepare patients for their role in the exploration that therapy involves, a statement such as the following may be given:

> Now that we have some sense of where we are going, I think I should tell you how we will proceed. Your task will be to talk about the things that concern you, particularly the things that affect you emotionally. We have already identified specific areas where there is room for change, and we have agreed upon certain specific goals. Naturally, we will be discussing material relevant to these issues. However, as we work together, other important issues may emerge—and you should feel free to raise them. I will be interested not only in what happened but, even more important, in your *feelings* about these events. It will be your responsibility to select the topics which are most important to you. After all, it is you who are most in touch with the way you are feeling and the relationships that seem to present problems

for you. There is no "right" or "wrong" thing to talk about, as long as it concerns you—is something that you have strong feelings about. This includes feelings about me, our relationship, or the therapy.

Sometimes ideas or feelings will come to mind—ideas that don't make much sense to you or seem embarrassing. These are important to bring in and discuss. It is important that you talk about feelings that arise during the session or when you think about it later.

Patient and psychotherapist have specific roles in IPT. As a preliminary to the therapy, and as a prototype for other relations, the reciprocal role expectations should be explicitly stated. This is a negotiation of the treatment contract, and the experience of negotiation can provide an example for the patient of dealing with interpersonal relations in the "here and now."

Beginning the Intermediate Sessions

The intermediate sessions begin after the treatment contract is set and the problem areas to be worked on are defined. The psychotherapist's strategy during these sessions is based on the assessment of the problem areas.

The intermediate sessions focus on one or possibly two problem areas in each session. The therapist has three interrelated tasks:

1. helping the patient discuss topics pertinent to the problem area;
2. attending to the patient's affective state and to the therapeutic relationship, to maximize the patient's intimate self-disclosure; and
3. preventing the patient from sabotaging the treatment.

TOPICAL FOCUS

The patient is encouraged to take the initiative in choosing topics for discussion, and each session begins with the psychotherapist receptively waiting for the patient to begin or asking some general question such as "Where should we start today?" In keeping with the goal of exploring new material, this allows the patient to change the focus of treatment, when appropriate, and to bring up previously unrecognized or suppressed problems.

If a patient is bringing in material that is relevant to treatment goals, the psychotherapist need not be as active in focusing the session, but if a patient seems to be discussing irrelevant material, or avoiding a subject of presumed concern, the therapist should give the patient time, to see whether the material is truly irrelevant before trying to shift the focus to material more closely related to the goals of treatment. Relevance does not necessarily emerge at once. For example,

> a forty-three-year-old man with marital problems began one of his sessions with a lengthy discussion of his disgust with the slovenly, undisciplined ways of the residents of a poor neighborhood he drove through on his way to the session. This led, however, to a productive exploration of similar disgust with his wife's slovenly ways, and those of his mother earlier.

A patient's initial statements about the nature of the problem are often revised in the course of treatment. Either because of distrust of the psychotherapist or genuine misunderstanding of the problem, the patient may at first present relatively minor issues as the important areas while deemphasizing major concerns. Alternatively, the psychotherapist may suspect that a problem area deemphasized by the patient is the most important one. In such cases it may be difficult to settle upon a treatment contract after only a few sessions. Possibly the focus of treatment may change in intermediate sessions as issues are put into perspective. In general, though, the content of IPT sessions will follow directly from the interpersonal inventory and goal setting of initial sessions. With each problem area the sequence of movement in therapy is, *first,* general exploration of the problem, *second,* focusing on patient's expectations and perceptions, *third,* analysis of possible alternative ways to handle the problem area, and, *finally,* attempts at new behavior.

In exploratory phases of treatment, the patient is asked to review systematically the relationship with the person or persons with whom problems have arisen. In giving this history, including some explanation of mutual expectations and detailed descriptions of important interactions, the patient frequently reveals problem areas, such as poor communication or unrealistic expectations, that warrant more focused attention. Sometimes interpersonal difficulties do not result from maladaptive behavior by those involved but simply contradictory demands or expectations of each other. In such cases this situation should be made clear.

Upon discovering conflicting expectations, the patient is usually faced with a choice of either changing in some way or going on as at present while learning to accept limitations. At this point the psychotherapist's role is to guide the patient in a thorough exploration of which options are open. If the patient chooses to attempt new behavior, the psychotherapist can then act as a collaborator in helping the patient assess his progress and develop new strategies of handling problems.

Chapters 6 through 9 focus on the second task of IPT, which deals with a social or interpersonal problem related to the onset of the depression.

Chapter 6

Grief

———

Grief associated with the death of a loved one can be normal or abnormal. IPT deals with depression associated with abnormal grief reactions that result from failure to go through the various phases of the normal mourning process.

Normal Grief

The experience of normal grief after a beloved person dies has much in common with depression, but the conditions are not equivalent. In normal bereavement a person experiences symptoms such as sadness, disturbed sleep, agitation, and decreased ability to carry out day-to-day tasks. These symptoms tend to resolve themselves without treatment in two to four months, as the bereaved person goes through a process of gradual weaning from remembered experiences with the loved one (Lindemann, 1944; Siggins, 1966). People who are experiencing normal grief do not generally seek psychiatric treatment.

Abnormal Grief

The principal assumption behind the therapist's strategy for dealing with abnormal grief is that inadequate normal grieving can lead to depression, either immediately following the loss or at some later time when the patient is somehow reminded of the loss.

Abnormal grief processes of two general kinds are commonly noted in depressed persons: delayed grief and distorted grief.

In *delayed grief reaction*, grief is postponed and experienced long after the loss. When this grieving occurs, it may not be recognized as a reaction to the original loss, but the symptoms are those of normal grieving. A delayed or unresolved grief reaction may be precipitated by a more recent, less important loss. In other cases delayed reactions may be precipitated when the patient achieves the age of death of the unmourned loved one. Questioning the grieving person about earlier losses will show that this person is actually mourning the prior loss.

A *distorted grief reaction* may occur immediately following the loss or years afterward. There may be no sadness or dysphoric mood but instead nonaffective symptoms may be present. These manifestations may involve different medical specialists before a psychotherapist is called to the task of deciphering the nature of such reactions.

DIAGNOSIS OF ABNORMAL GRIEF REACTIONS

It is often clear that the patient's depression began with a significant loss, but in other cases there may be only an indirect relationship between the current depression and a previous loss. In reviewing the patient's interpersonal relationships it is highly important to obtain a history of significant relationships with those who are now dead or otherwise absent. This should include the circumstances of the death and the patient's behavioral and emotional reaction to it. Evidence that may suggest a pathological mourning process are found in Table 6.1.

To diagnose abnormal grief the psychotherapist might say,

> I notice that you didn't mention your mother when discussing your parents. Has anyone you've been close to died recently? Could you tell me about the death? When? Where? What circumstances? How did you feel when you learned of the death? How were you the next few weeks? Did you carry on as usual?

GOALS AND STRATEGIES OF TREATMENT

The two goals of the treatment for depression that center on grief are (1) to facilitate the delayed mourning process, and (2) to help the patient reestablish

TABLE 6.1
Evidence of Abnormal Grief

Task	Therapists' Questions
1. Multiple losses	What else was going on in your life around the time of the death? Has anyone else died or left? What has reminded you of it since? Has anyone died in similar fashion or when your circumstances were similar?
2. Inadequate grief in the bereavement period	In the months following the death, how did you feel? Did you have trouble sleeping? Could you carry on as usual? Were you beyond tears?
3. Avoidance behavior about the death	Did you avoid going to the funeral? Visiting the grave?
4. Symptoms around a significant date	When did the person die? What was the date? Did you start having problems around the same time?
5. Fear of the illness that caused the death	What did the person die of? What were the symptoms? Are you afraid of having the same illness?
6. History of preserving the environment as it was when the loved one died	What did you do with the possessions? The room? Were they left the same as when the person died?
7. Absence of family or other social supports during the bereavement period	Who could you count on when the person died? Who helped you? Who did you turn to? Who could you confide in?

interests and relationships that can substitute for what has been lost. The therapist's major tasks are to help patients assess the significance of the loss realistically and emancipate themselves from a crippling attachment to the dead person, thus becoming free to cultivate new interests and form satisfying new relationships. The therapist adopts and utilizes strategies and techniques that help the patient bring into focus memories of the lost person and emotions related to the patient's experiences with the lost person.

Elicitation of Feelings and Nonjudgmental Exploration.

Abnormal grief reactions are often associated with lack of a supportive social network to help the bereaved person in the normal process of mourning. Consequently the major psychotherapeutic strategy is to encourage the patient: (1) to think about the loss; (2) to discuss the sequence and consequences of events prior, during, and after the death; and (3) to explore associated feelings. Thus the psychotherapist substitutes for the missing social network.

Tell me about ———. What was [the person] like? What did you do together? How did [the person] die? When did you learn about the illness? Describe it. How did you learn about the death? How did you feel about all this?

Reassurance.

Patients often express fear of bringing up something that has been "buried." They may be afraid of "cracking up," of not being able to stop crying, or of otherwise losing control. In such instances the psychotherapist may let the patient know that the fears expressed are not uncommon and that mourning in psychotherapy rarely leads to decompensation. Recent research has indicated a number of common themes in the mental life of persons experiencing stress, particularly the stress of bereavement.

Horowitz (1976) has identified typical themes in the dysphoric thoughts of those who have experienced a stressful event such as a painful loss: (1) fear of repetition of the event even in thought; (2) shame at helplessness in being unable to postpone or prevent the event; (3) rage at the person who is the source of the event (in the case of death, the dead person); (4) guilt or shame over aggressive impulses or destructive fantasies; (5) survivor guilt: the loved one has died and oneself has not, and the person who survives is relieved to remain alive; (6) fear of identification or merging with the victim; and (7) sadness in relationship to the loss. It is helpful for the therapist to be alert to the expression of these themes and to help the patient articulate them. In fact, it is frequently reassuring if the therapist can "anticipate" the patient's complaints by inquiring about thoughts and feelings along these lines.

It is quite normal to feel upset and confused when you talk about the loss. You will feel better again.

Reconstruction of the Relationship.

Patients with abnormal grief reactions are frequently fixated on the death itself, thus avoiding the complexities of their relationship with the deceased. The therapist should lead a thorough factual and affective exploration of the patient's relationship to the dead person both when the person was alive and in the present context. The patient may not wish to acknowledge angry or hostile feelings toward the deceased, which may be due to feeling abandoned by the loved one. When the mourning process is blocked by strongly negative feelings toward the dead person, the therapist should encourage the patient to express these feelings, but the encouragement should not be via confrontation, which could provoke a shift of hostility from the deceased to the psychotherapist. If negative feelings emerge too rapidly, the patient may decide not to continue psychotherapy because of the guilt that is likely to accompany them. However, if the psychotherapist reassures the patient that the negative feelings will be followed by positive and comforting feelings, as well as a positive attitude toward the deceased, the patient will be much better prepared to explore his/her ambivalence.

> Tell me, how was your life with ———? How has it changed since ——— died? Every relationship has its ups and downs—that's normal. What were yours?

Development of Awareness.

The steps described above will help the patient formulate a new and healthier way to understand memories of the person who has died. For instance, a patient may no longer consider a parent a villain but instead realize that the mother or father was a sick person, and thus be able to accept both the parent's behavior and his or her own reaction to it. To help achieve this new understanding, the therapist may try to elicit both affective and factual responses that will lead to more knowledge of the elements that contribute to the difficulty of mourning. A patient who feels a need to maintain a pathologically strong bond to the deceased can be comforted by answering such questions as:

> What were the things you liked about ———? What were those you didn't like?

Behavioral Change.

As patients lose their investment in maintaining continued; abnormal grieving, they may be more open to developing new relationships to fill the "empty space" left by the lost loved one. At this point the therapist may be very active in leading the patient to consider various alternative ways (dating, church, organizations, work) to become more involved with others again.

> What is your life like now? How have you tried to make up for the loss? Who are your friends? What activities might be enjoyable?

Abnormal Grief—The Case of Mary T.

Mary T., a married woman in her late fifties, was admitted to a local general hospital because of paralysis of her right leg from the hip down. Until the symptoms started to appear two months earlier, this woman had been very active in her community, dedicated to her church, and happily married. Until about a year before her admission, she and her husband had lived on the upper floor of a two-family house, with her mother living on the first floor. This patient defied the efforts of internists, neurologists, neurosurgeons, and orthopedic surgeons. Sophisticated laboratory procedures repeatedly confirmed a healthy person who should be up and walking.

The patient was clinically depressed. She spoke slowly, reported difficulty sleeping and early morning awakenings with ruminations about past failings. She looked sad and she had lost ten pounds over the past six weeks. She had no previous history of depression. Careful evaluation revealed that about three months before admission Mrs. T.'s doctor, who had cared for her since she was a young girl, had died of a painful and unpleasant disease. She did not know precisely what the illness was but said his death had greatly affected her. She mentioned only in passing that her mother had died about a year earlier, and said that death had not caused her much difficulty.

In the third session more information about the mother developed. The patient's mother had lived downstairs in the same house for the past few years. The patient had to wait on her mother, coming down several times a day, because the mother's right leg was paralyzed and she could not move. When Mrs. T.'s mother died, it must have been a great relief, and it caused only a very mild grief reaction. About a year later, however, there was a reaction of intense guilt. The patient started to carry her mother's cane and progressively stopped walking downstairs and outside. It appears that the paralysis was the patient's way of coming to grips with the guilt caused by her feelings about her mother's death, and her grief at her doctor's death compounded the problem. The patient entered the hospital on the first anniversary of her mother's death.

The therapeutic stance with the patient was supportive and nondirective. Reconstruction of the patient's relationship with both deceased persons was the first step in the therapy. She was encouraged to describe in detail the circumstances around the death of her mother, including the physical care she had provided during the last few years, the details of their daily activities, and her reactions both during these years and at the time of the death. She was also encouraged to describe the circumstances and her reactions when she learned of her physician's illness and death, since she particularly turned to him for comfort.

No joint interpretation of the possible meaning of the paralysis could be attempted. In fact, when the therapist in one session referred to the relationship between her mother's paralysis and her use of the mother's cane, the patient nearly terminated treatment.

INITIAL PHASE (SESSIONS 2–3)

In the first session, the patient described her guilt about not providing sufficient care for her mother. She felt that had she made her mother adhere to the special diet prescribed and massaged her good leg, her mother might be alive today. She also regretted her lack of compassion toward her family physician, who himself was ill though she hadn't known it, and whom she called repeatedly for help and advice about the mother.

By the second session, the patient had gradually begun to walk with the cane, and by the third week she could walk without it. She was discharged from the hospital but continued the weekly psychotherapy. Her sleep and appetite disturbance improved, although she was still slowed down.

MIDDLE PHASE (SESSIONS 4–9)

During the middle phase of treatment, more of Mrs. T.'s anger at both her mother and her doctor became overt. The patient described her mother's unreasonable screaming at her to come downstairs and care for her, so that for the six months before her death the patient was virtually never out of the mother's apartment. Mrs. T. resented not being able to visit her grandchildren and having to give up church activities and all social life with her husband. Though he didn't complain overtly, her husband became more withdrawn and less emotionally available to her.

Further discussion revealed long-term bitterness between the patient and her mother, who had forced her to leave college and go to work because "college is wasted on a girl." In contrast, her brother had attended law school. She felt angry that she had to carry all the family burdens and he could visit once a week, bring flowers or candy, and be viewed as the "good son," while she who was giving virtually all the physical care could never please her mother.

During the terminal phase of the mother's illness, when Mrs. T. went to see her doctor because she felt so drained and fatigued, she was told he couldn't see patients and was referred elsewhere. She felt abandoned and rejected by the doctor, whom she had used as a confidant since she was a girl.

TERMINATION PHASE (SESSIONS 10–12)

As therapy ended the patient was asymptomatic and was not using the cane. She had resumed her church activities and was planning to move downstairs and rent the less convenient upstairs apartment. She and her brother had had a good talk about the circumstances of her leaving college and she had been able to tell him her feelings about it. She described her satisfaction with her own children and grandchildren and the full life she and her husband had together.

Mrs. T. expressed some reluctance at termination, but she had found a new family doctor who would probably act as confidant in periods of stress. She left without ever having discussed the possible psychogenic origins of her paralysis, but she was completely without depressive symptoms at termination.

In some ways this case is not typical for IPT since the therapeutic contract was not explicit. Nevertheless, the reexamination of the relationship and the opportunity to express the appropriate feelings directed toward the dead mother contributed to a more successful resolution of the grief.

Chapter 7

Interpersonal Role Disputes

An interpersonal dispute is a situation in which the patient and at least one significant other person have nonreciprocal expectations about their relationship. An example of nonreciprocal role expectations is the wife who expects the spouse to take care of her financially but has to have an outside job to help meet their bills, whereas the spouse expects his wife to share financial responsibility. Another is a mother who expects her teenage daughter to confide in her fully the details of her friendships as the mother did with her own mother, while the teenage girl feels that to grow up she must figure some things out on her own.

The IPT therapist focuses on interpersonal disputes if they seem important in the genesis and perpetuation of the depression. This usually occurs when the disputes are stalled or repetitious, with little hope for improvement. In such circumstances depressed patients lose self-esteem because they feel they can no longer control the disputes and there is a threatened loss of what the relationship provides, or because they feel incompetent to manage their own lives. Typical features that perpetuate role disputes are the patient's demoralized sense that nothing can be done, poor habits of communication, or truly irreconcilable differences.

Diagnosis of Interpersonal Disputes

For the therapist to choose role disputes as the focus of IPT, the patient must give evidence of current overt or covert conflicts with a significant other. Such disputes are usually revealed in the patient's initial complaints or in the course of the interpersonal inventory. In some IPT research, role disputes with the spouse have been the most common problem area. In practice, however, recognition of important interpersonal disputes in the lives of depressed patients may be difficult (Paykel, 1982).

Typically, depressed patients are preoccupied with their hopeless feelings and consider themselves solely responsible for their condition. When there is no clear precipitant to a depressive episode, and when the patient does not identify problems in current interpersonal relationships, it is important while performing the interpersonal inventory (as described in Chapter 5), to listen as much for what is omitted as for what is said. Insufficient or overidealized descriptions of current or recent relationships that seem to be important may be clues to difficulties that the patient is unwilling to recognize or explore. The patient should be carefully questioned about how relationships have changed prior to or after the onset of depressive symptoms. An understanding of how interpersonal problems may have precipitated the depression or how they are involved in preventing recovery may suggest a strategy for therapy.

Goals and Strategies of Treatment

The general goals for treatment of interpersonal role disputes are to help the patient first identify the dispute, then make choices about a plan of action, and finally modify maladaptive communication patterns or reassess expectations, or both, for a satisfactory resolution of the interpersonal disputes. Improvements may take the form of a change in the expectations and behavior of the patient and/or the other person; changed and more accepting patient attitudes, with or without attempts to satisfy needs outside the relationship; or satisfactory dissolution of the relationship. The IPT therapist has no particular commitment to guide the patient to any particular resolution of difficulties and makes no attempt to preserve unworkable relationships.

In developing a treatment plan, the therapist first determines the stage of the role dispute:

1. *Renegotiation* implies that the patient and the significant other are openly aware of differences and are actively trying, even if unsuccessfully, to bring about changes.
2. *Impasse* implies that discussion between the patient and the significant other has stopped and that the smoldering, low-level resentment typical of "cold marriages" exists.
3. *Dissolution* implies that the relationship is irretrievably disrupted.

The therapist's tasks and expectations at these three stages differ. For example, intervening in an impasse situation may bring on increasing apparent disharmony as negotiations are reopened, while the task of treating a dispute at the stage of unsatisfactory renegotiation may be to calm down the participants to facilitate conflict resolution. The treatment of disputes at the stage of dissolution has much in common with the treatment of grief described in Chapter 6, in that the therapist tries to help the patient put the relationship in perspective and become free to form new attachments.

The IPT therapist's general treatment strategy with interpersonal disputes is to help the patient understand how nonreciprocal role expectations relate to the dispute and begin steps that will bring about resolution of disputes and role negotiations. This movement from exploration to action may take place over the entire course of therapy, with early sessions devoted to exploration and communication analysis, and later sessions to decision analysis. In dealing with particular, circumscribed problems, however, exploration and decision making may occur in a single session.

In exploring role disputes the therapist seeks information on different levels. At a practical level, these questions are answered: What are the ostensible issues in the dispute? What are the differences in expectations and values between the patient and the significant other? What are the patient's wishes in the relationship? What are the patient's options? What resources does the patient have to bring about change in the relationship?

To understand the importance of the particular dispute under discussion the therapist looks for parallels in previous relationships. The parallels may be obvious —for example, when a patient has repeatedly gotten involved with alcoholic men. Others are more subtle, as when patients keep manipulating others into rejecting them. Useful questions are:

Has this happened to you before? Do you have other similar relationships? The relationship you describe sounds like the one you had with ———.

When parallels are discovered, the key questions to explore are: What does the patient gain by the behavior? What are the central unspoken assumptions that lie behind it? Why does the patient get into similar unpleasant situations?

Special attention to the interpersonal strategies of the disputants frequently reveals problems in communication patterns. For instance, repetitious, painful disputes are frequently perpetuated when the participants are afraid of confrontation and expression of negative feelings and try to ignore solvable problems by simply waiting for things to "blow over." It may be useful to ask the patient:

Have you told ——— how you feel directly? What do you think would happen if you did? Could you try?

The aim here is to help patients recognize their complex, mixed feelings of anger, fear and sadness, and devise strategies for managing them, such as avoiding situations in which they arise, expressing wishes directly, and reducing impulsive behavior based on irrational suspicions.

When a patient has developed a sufficiently clear understanding of role disputes, including the part he or she plays in them, therapist and patient can proceed to a thorough consideration of the consequences of a number of alternatives before taking action.

A role dispute can be renegotiated successfully if the patient becomes able to express needs and wishes directly to the other person and together they are able to work out a resolution that takes the needs of both into account. There will be some understanding of each other's needs and some compromise on both sides.

An Interpersonal Role Dispute—The Case of Alice E.

Alice E. was twenty-eight years old and had been married for ten years when she began treatment. She worked with her husband in his business. Her chief complaints were a lack of interest in everything around her, increasing irritability, and marital problems. Her symptoms included sad mood, difficulty falling asleep, loss of appetite and interest, and a profound sense of her inadequacy as a woman. Her relationship with her husband had deteriorated markedly over the previous four or five months. She believed he took her for granted and was interested in her only insofar as she fulfilled his needs as a sex partner and as an employee. The patient vacillated between self-blame and feelings of helplessness, on the one hand, and angry accusations about her husband's inattentiveness and lack of concern for her wishes, on the other. As she talked of first one area and then the other, she tended to lose track of what she was saying. She related her depression to her husband's all-consuming interest in his business and what she perceived as the resulting change in their relationship.

Although she dated the onset of her difficulties as four or five months before seeking treatment, she was unable to identify any specific event. Instead, she spoke about her growing dissatisfaction with what she perceived as her husband's selfish and controlling attitude, and his lack of consideration for her feelings.

As Mrs. E. reviewed the history of their marriage, she expressed nostalgia for the "good old days" when they were poor but happy. She reported feeling increasingly left out since he purchased the business five years ago. Exploration of her interpersonal relationships revealed a paucity of social supports as well as lifelong feelings of loneliness associated with her inability to establish and/or maintain intimate relationships. She had been one of nine children from a somewhat fragmented family. Although they all lived in the same city, she had only minimal contact with them now. She had felt fairly close to her mother, but this relationship was somewhat strained by the patient's belief that her mother had never approved of her husband.

After gathering information about the current depression, the events surrounding the onset, and her perception of its effect on her relationship with her husband, the therapist tried to explore what Mrs. E. hoped to get out of therapy—how she expected therapy to be helpful to her. She indicated that she wanted: 1) "someone to talk to" because she felt unable to discuss these issues with her husband; 2) to learn how to stand up to her husband; and 3) to get her husband to respect her, to relate to her as a wife and not as an irresponsible child or employee.

At the end of the first session the therapist was still uncertain how to conceptualize the patient in terms of IPT problem areas. Although the social history made it clear that the patient had interpersonal role deficits, she had come for treatment with the specific problem of an interpersonal role dispute with her husband, and as the session developed, marital disputes in an impasse phase became the central focus.

INITIAL PHASE (SESSIONS 2–4)

In the early sessions Mrs. E. focused on her ambivalence vis-à-vis her marriage and her dependence on her husband. She continued to express disappointment with what it meant to be a "married woman," and she described the gradual process by which she had become more and more dependent upon and controlled by her husband. She related to him as if he were a disapproving father; she was afraid of offending him yet angry that she seemed unable to please him. She had a severely restricted view of the options available to her, thinking she must either deny her own wishes to please her husband or get out of the marriage. The interpersonal inventory revealed a pattern of withdrawal, denial, and/or indirect communication of her wishes. She seemed to expect others to "know" what she needed and felt rejected if her needs were not magically anticipated and met.

Much of the work in these sessions focused on sorting out with Mrs. E. her expectations in the marriage and how she thought things would have to change if she were to be more comfortable. Since she was committed to the marriage, goals were set in terms of working on improving communications with her husband and in developing some independent interests so she would be less dependent on him to fulfill all her needs.

The patient's communication problems with her husband were discussed first. She described a fight they had had the previous night. She acknowledged that her customary way of avoiding confrontation on the real issues was related to the couple's increasing estrangement. She said she could express her real wants only when she was angry, but the depth of her rage frightened her and made her feel guilty—and so she would withdraw into silence but continue to seethe. During these sessions she started to talk, albeit indirectly, about her suspicions that her husband was "fooling around" with a young woman who worked in the store with them. As if she couldn't trust her own judgment, she remarked, "Everybody says it's so but I just can't see it . . . I don't know." Later she said that her husband had had a series of girl friends over the past few years, but she felt certain he wouldn't leave her. The fourth session ended with her assertion that she was going to try to begin to talk to him about what she expected of him without waiting until she blew up, but, typically, she put a damper on it by saying, "But you'll see . . . it won't work."

INTERMEDIATE PHASE (SESSIONS 5–8)

Mrs. E. began the fifth session by bringing a letter her husband had written to her the previous night. Many individuals communicate by letter since they find face-to-face discussion of difficult issues made easier if they first communicate in writing. In the letter he talked about his love for her, his sadness about their deteriorating marriage, and his frustration about his seeming inability to "turn things around." She expressed doubts about her husband's sincerity: "I just can't get myself to believe it—it seems he just wants to get me where he wants me, and then it just starts all over again." When the therapist suggested that it might be helpful to have him join them for one session, she became quite restless and said, "I don't want to talk about him any more. I just want to talk about my problems." Later she agreed to ask him but felt that he wouldn't come.

When Mr. and Mrs. E. came for the conjoint session, the communication problems reported in previous sessions were played out in this hour. Alice remained silent for most of the hour, allowing her husband to do most of the talking. When she reluctantly began to talk about her complaints, she finally confronted her husband, Mark, about his involvement with the saleswoman, which he promptly denied. By the end of the hour they had begun to talk to each other more directly, rather than entirely through the therapist.

After the conjoint session there was a marked change in Alice's appearance. Up to now she had looked rather shabby and sullen—usually dressed in black. She started wearing bright colors and her overall attitude had a bright, confident, "up" quality. She and Mark had gone out to dinner a couple of times, and had visited relatives whom they hadn't seen for a long time. Although she acknowledged feeling some satisfaction with this broadening of their activities, she nevertheless continued to express doubt about Mark's motives. She described several occasions on which she felt rebuffed when she had begun to express her wishes to him. What was most impressive, however, was her determination to "let him know what's on my mind whether he wants to hear it or not." She also spoke about her fear that people (especially her family) might think that she had gotten "uppity" since she and her husband had become financially secure. She described her humble background and her own discomfort with Mark's new, "classy" ways. Whereas Mark enjoyed his success and the community respect it brought him, Alice felt somewhat embarrassed by it because it seemed to represent yet another barrier separating her from her family and former friends. She was cut off from her roots, so to speak, yet ill at ease with her new status in the community.

During these middle sessions much of the time was devoted to exploring the couple's efforts to reestablish some contact with each other and with their families. Toward the end of the eighth session, Alice acknowledged her anxiety about termination. The following week Mark telephoned to cancel his wife's appointment because "Alice is sick and she didn't want to call you herself."

TERMINATION PHASE (SESSIONS 9–12)

At the next scheduled session, Alice once again started to talk about difficulties with her husband over his business. Both the content and the quality of her comments were reminiscent of the first sessions. The relatively introspective stance of the previous sessions had all but disappeared. Midway into the hour, however, Alice became quiet and somewhat thoughtful. She finally said, "I'm scared to show Mark my love, that's all it is." As the therapist began to discuss these feelings, she commented, almost casually, that her husband had been talking about getting a divorce. Despite her insistence that she really didn't take it seriously, it seemed to have a disorganizing effect on her functioning. Toward the end of the hour, she again raised the issue of termination and voiced her concern about not yet feeling strong enough to go it on her own.

In the following sessions the therapist continued to explore with Alice her feelings about termination, but Alice had a tendency to avoid the issue or deny having any special feelings about it. The couple had been arguing more frequently. Part of the conflict seemed to focus on Mark's desire for a child and Alice's extreme ambivalence about being further tied down. She was also afraid Mark might leave her if she had a baby, and this was not completely irrational, since both Mark's and Alice's fathers had abandoned their families. Another part of her resistance to becoming pregnant was her feeling that this would represent just one more way she would be "giving in" to her husband. Despite the increase in arguments between them, she reported feeling less depressed than she had the previous week; "letting it out is better than keeping the stuff inside," she said. At the final session, Alice was somewhat agitated and attempts to explore her feelings about the termination were met with denial and thinly disguised anger.

Three days after this stormy termination session, however, Alice telephoned to "apologize" and to say she was in fact feeling better after all. She refused referral for further treatment: "I think I'd like to try it on my own."

An Interpersonal Role Dispute—The Case of Sal D.

Sal D., a thirty-one-year-old married man, was unemployed at the time of the first interview but within a week found a job as a t.v. repairman's assistant. Mr. D.'s chief complaint was a history of decreased energy and motivation over the past several months. He reported having difficulty finishing projects on his house because he quickly became physically exhausted. He also slept less and had little interest in sex. "My feelings have left me," he said.

INITIAL PHASE (SESSIONS 1–4)

Sal D. was the oldest male in a traditional Italian family. His mother was the emotional caretaker for the family and his father was a stern, "cold" man whom Sal could never get along with. He was critical, unavailable and "browbeating." The son described himself as an underachiever in school: he was not interested in schoolwork. He dropped out of high school in the eleventh grade and joined the Marines as a challenge to his father's assertion that he'd never make it. After his hitch was up he became a construction worker under the direction of his father, who was a foreman. Their work relationship was often stressed by disagreements.

Five years ago Sal had had a fall that injured his knee and leg; he could no longer do construction work, which he had found productive and lucrative. He then became more dependent on his wife, who quit her job to care for him while he was in a wheelchair. Sal said that if he had not had the fall, or if he had been able to go back to his old job after it, he would be a foreman by now. As a result of this physical handicap, he changed jobs and became a t.v. repairman, receiving vocational training through workman's compensation.

He tended to minimize the effect of his injury on his self-esteem, and talked mainly about his marital difficulties. He often came to his appointments looking tired and disheveled, and did not spontaneously volunteer information. As a result, the therapist maintained an active profile by asking specific questions and taking a careful interpersonal inventory. The central theme that emerged was his feeling of inadequacy and powerlessness in relation to life in general, but more specifically in relation to his father and his wife.

By the end of the initial sessions it had become clear that Sal's depressive symptomatology was associated with marital disputes with his wife. These seemed largely related to his difficulty in expressing his wishes to his wife and their increasing estrangement. Treatment centered on his understanding the impediments prohibiting him from constructively communicating with his wife.

INTERMEDIATE PHASE (SESSIONS 5–8)

When Sal D. began to explore his relationship with his wife in more detail, in Session 5, he started crying as he described his unhappiness in his marriage and his difficulty articulating his feelings because he felt "numb." He said that he had been "holding on" to many of his feelings, which was causing a break in the relationship with his wife.

In the next session he again addressed family issues, and for the first time he began to see some similarities between himself and his father. He said he thought he was treating his wife in many of the same distancing ways that his father treated him.

Session 7 proved to be a turning point. He was more self-revealing, and he described the ways he and his wife had been very "emotional" and close with each other during the past week. They had talked more openly and had finally been able to make a joint decision to accept a lump sum of money from an insurance company for the leg disability rather than accept compensation in the form of disability payments. This decision, which would relieve the couple of a great deal of their financial burden, had been worrying them for more than a year.

In Session 8, Sal D. said he felt improvement in his overall attitude. He stated that as he tried to change, to share thoughts and feelings with his wife, she began to meet him halfway, which favorably surprised him. He and the therapist discussed possible ways in which he could further involve his wife in how he was feeling.

TERMINATION PHASE (SESSIONS 9–12)

During this phase Sal D. was laid off. He explored some of the circumstances leading up to the layoff and the feelings of hurt and anger surrounding the event. He was puzzled that he did not go out and look for work immediately, but thought this was due in part to receiving the insurance settlement and in part to a need to assess his job situation and plan more carefully. He had made use of the layoff to seek his wife's opinion. He thought that in the past he would have picked a fight with his wife, indirectly thrusting his job worries onto her. He planned to start looking for work the following week, after he had a chance to consider his options.

In Session 10, Sal said that before he began treatment he had withdrawn too much from his wife, and he was now risking more openness with her. He had been surprised to find that she had not responded negatively or "violently" when he expressed his feelings. He went on to say that he could not continue to prejudge his wife's responses, but he still felt he could not share too many intimate feelings with her for fear she would get upset. In discussing termination, he said that initially his major concern about involving himself in treatment was his fear of disclosing feelings that he did not want to reveal. He was afraid the therapist would "jump into my head" and force feelings out. Rather, he had been pleasantly surprised to experience therapy as enabling him to explore and find out about himself.

In Session 11, the patient initiated the session by stating that he had a great deal to say. He was happily thinking about going into work as a subcontractor in which he would be his own boss. He felt more confident and less lethargic at home, able to accomplish home chores more willingly; as a result, he experienced less pressure from his wife. He had been communicating more directly with her, saying so when he wanted to help her and not pushing her away without explanation. He acknowledged that the financial problems and the enforced idleness after his injury had been extremely demoralizing. And his feeling like a failure while he was working as a repairman had also contributed to the depression, because he was not producing up to his potential. In talking about terminating, Sal said he was still baffled that he hadn't been able to share as much with his wife as he had with the therapist.

In the last session Sal D. expressed positive feelings toward the therapy and said he had experienced a sense of "reawakening" within himself. He felt relaxed in the treatment and wanted to create the same openness with his wife that he felt with the therapist.

An Interpersonal Role Dispute—The Case of Iris M.

Iris M., a twenty-seven-year-old married woman, came for treatment because of depression that had been troubling her for nearly three years, since the birth of her second child. She related her depression to long-standing dissatisfaction with her marriage and said that her pregnancy with the second child was in part an attempt to keep herself involved in the marriage, since her older child was four at the time and needed less intensive caretaking. But the birth of the second child only made her feel more burdened and more trapped in an unsatisfying marriage.

INITIAL PHASE (SESSIONS 1–4)

Mrs. M.'s depression had been at a mild/moderate level for most of the first two years; then, about a year ago, she had felt very desperate and had considered suicide. However, she was able to fight off these feelings and, shortly thereafter, became involved in an extramarital affair with a man who lived in her neighborhood. As this relationship developed, the patient at first felt some hope. However, this was short-lived, because she and her lover's wife soon became good friends. Her husband became friendly with the lover and the two couples spent a great deal of time together.

Mrs. M. was sure that neither her own husband nor the lover's wife was aware of the affair, but her depression had worsened significantly over the past year as she became obsessed with the relationship. She was flooded with a wide range of feelings—guilt at betraying both her husband and her best friend, jealousy of the lover's relationship with his wife, disappointment in her own marriage, and disappointment with her relationship with the lover. At the beginning of treatment she felt unable to tolerate the continuation of this arrangement but also unable to bring about any change.

Mrs. M.'s symptoms of depression included sad mood, worry and guilt, low self-esteem, pessimism, moderate anxiety with fears of being left alone, difficulty falling asleep, low levels of energy during the day (with frequent nap taking), impaired ability to perform household tasks, difficulty concentrating, loss of interest and pleasure in nearly all activities, poor appetite, and weight loss. She neglected many of her household duties but reported that her husband had been willing to do many of them for her as it became obvious to him in recent months that she was depressed. She had recently quit a part-time sales job because she could not concentrate or make herself get to work. Her initial statement of what she hoped to get out of treatment was simply to feel better so that she could "stop hurting my husband and do my share in my marriage again."

In planning a strategy for continued evaluation and initial phases of treatment the therapist saw two main tasks: a) helping the patient manage the current depression; and b) helping her renegotiate the current marital situation. To manage the depression the therapist planned to review with the patient the details of her day and the circumstances surrounding her mood changes in the course of the day. Through this kind of evaluation the therapist hoped to find ways to help the patient mitigate the depressive symptoms and impairment of functioning. To understand the marital dispute, which was at an impasse, the therapist found it helpful to start conceptualizing the patient's case by considering possible options for change. These included continuing in the marriage and trying to understand and alter the factors contributing to Mrs. M.'s dissatisfaction with it. The kinds of change that might help would include: attempting to change the relationship with her husband and/or helping her find sources of satisfaction outside the marriage that produced less inner conflict than the extramarital affair. To evaluate the viability of such options the therapist would need to assess in detail the history of the patient's relationship with her husband, the types of behavior and attitudes of both partners that might be contributing to the dissatisfaction, and the likelihood that either partner could change these things. As to satisfactions outside marriage, the therapist would evaluate the patient's current social network and the options for changing and expanding it. Given the patient's high level of conflict over the extramarital affair, it seemed unlikely that the marriage could become stronger as long as the affair was going on.

Separation or divorce, with or without continuing the affair, was another option. To help the patient assess its viability the therapist would need to evaluate what the affair was providing and what the patient's intentions were about it. It would also be essential to help her evaluate what she thought it would be like to leave her husband: how the children would be cared for, how relationships with her family and her husband's family would change, and so on.

The patient had married immediately after graduating from high school and said she'd had doubts about the marriage from the start because she had gotten involved with her husband immediately after being rejected by a much idealized former boyfriend. She felt less passion for her husband but considered him safe and supportive. However, on her wedding day she was obsessed with thoughts of the former boy friend and had a premonition that she would never truly love her husband. This seemed to have become a self-fulfilling prophecy.

The patient blamed most of the marital problems on her husband's failure to show his love for her openly. She recounted several attempts to get him involved in projects around the house only to have to do them herself. He seemed more interested in a social life with male friends than with his family. A year after she married the patient had become pregnant and from then on tried to devote herself to being a housewife and mother.

Although Mrs. M. described her husband as being uninterested in her, he seemed to have been rather solicitous and helpful as she became more depressed. He had done household chores, taken a more active role with the children, showed what appeared to be genuine sympathy, and encouraged her to seek treatment. Although she was able to recognize that this behavior was indicative of her husband's caring about her, that view of his intentions was hard to accept because it only increased her guilt about the love affair. Another aspect of the patient's contribution to the problems in the marriage was her way of handling anger and disappointment with her husband by emotional distancing and pouting, without ever really telling him what she was displeased about. She reported that, despite her dissatisfaction with the marriage, she and her husband rarely argued or raised their voices about disagreements. She usually simply acquiesced.

Review of the patient's childhood revealed that she had married primarily to get out of her parental home. The patient was the middle of three children in a household in which both parents were alcoholics who had frequent violent fights.

Over the course of the next three sessions it became clear that although the patient was obsessed with her current love affair, she did not take the lover himself seriously. She described him as being irresponsible and in many ways less attractive than her husband. She talked excitedly about the secret meetings but was disappointed by the superficial nature of the relationship, which revolved around brief sexual encounters in which she was frequently unaroused. She was tormented by jealousy of the lover's wife and suspected that she was being used merely as a diversion. Despite her preoccupation with the relationship, she saw no future in it. Even if she were interested in leaving her husband, she said, she would not want to marry a man like her lover, and besides, he was not interested in leaving his wife. Nevertheless, the patient felt unable to break off the relationship, just as she felt hopeless about finding more satisfaction in her relationship with her husband.

Since the patient was less depressed in the third session, she discussed the material in a bland, affectless way, which was in great contrast to her professed guilt and the conflicted feelings she reported. In addition, the discussion of the relationship with the lover had a playful, exhibitionistic quality about it. Attempts to confront the patient about such issues as her expectations about that relationship and about her not trying to get her husband to change were ignored or avoided. At the end of the early sessions the therapist tried to discuss treatment goals. The patient relatively quickly named two: a) feeling less depressed; and b) feeling more love for her husband. Questioned about what loving her husband would involve, she expressed pessimism but also said that she had not given the marriage a chance.

Iris M.'s depression seemed to be related to her marital unhappiness, which she and her husband had been unable to acknowledge and work on. Although the husband was aware that the patient was depressed and felt that there were limitations in the relationship, the patient had never clearly expressed her dissatisfaction nor tried to get him to change to make their relationship more satisfactory. The marriage was free of overt conflict but it was lifeless and at an impasse. With the goal of helping the patient get beyond this state of affairs, the therapist focused primarily on the patient's attitudes and behaviors that kept the marital relationship stalemated.

Her most obvious contribution to the marital dispute was her failure to define and communicate her wishes. The central theme of her dissatisfaction was the feeling that her husband did not show interest in or love for her, that he left her out of his life and did not want to share activities. However, she made little attempt to get him involved with her, since she felt he should know what she wanted without being told. The therapist intended to help the patient think clearly about specific things she wanted from her husband and was not getting, and from there, to help her develop more direct and satisfactory ways to communicate these things to him. To some extent the emphasis on communication would be educational, concentrating on ways the patient was missing opportunities to make herself understood. The therapist also intended to deal with the possibility that Mrs. M.'s communication problems were related to fears of causing violent arguments like those of her parents.

At a second level, the therapy was intended to help the patient understand her pessimism about being able to have a happy marriage. This fundamental insecurity in close relationships was demonstrated in her relationship with the idealized high school boy friend who deserted her and in her preoccupation with trying to assure herself that the exciting new lover truly cared for her. Although she also felt her husband did not love her enough, she was able to tolerate this because she had devalued him to a point where she could nearly convince herself that he didn't matter. The therapist planned to deal with these basic fears of intimacy by contrasting the husband's demonstrations of real concern and caring with the patient's statements that he was not involved, and by contrasting her husband's capacity to care for her with her parents' inability to do so.

A third tactic would involve helping the patient recognize the destructive nature of the extramarital relationship. As the patient had already acknowledged, the relationship provided little satisfaction and had no future. It was in fact an energy-draining distraction that prevented her from investing herself in the task of trying to make her marriage work.

A fourth way of improving the relationship would be to help identify other and better sources of satisfaction outside the marriage. Involvement with a social network outside the nuclear family might well help Iris M. gain perspective on her marriage. In addition, involvement outside the home would help her develop independence and a sense of competence; she could express aspects of her personality that could not be expressed within the marriage.

INTERMEDIATE PHASE (SESSIONS 5–10)

During the middle phase of treatment the therapist tried to elicit descriptions of interactions with the husband, to determine exactly what had been said and felt.

The overall process of working with Mrs. M. was characterized by great variability, because her moods and involvements fluctuated. Although she tended to be avoidant and unfocused in all sessions, in about half of them she was able to get involved in useful discussions of her marital problems. In the others she complained about various sources of dissatisfaction without being able to evaluate her role in the problems. Despite these variations, she made progress in several areas during this part of the treatment. First she reported numerous small instances in which she had tried to be more direct with her husband about ways she felt he slighted her. She was surprised at his positive response to her demands and felt that the relationship was improving. She began to draw away from the lover, seeing him far less frequently and being less obsessed with thinking about him.

Iris M.'s movement during this phase of treatment resulted in part from the therapist's strategy of focusing discussion on issues between Mrs. M. and her husband in general and on their communication in particular. When the patient tried to shift to other issues, such as problems with the lover or women friends, the therapist either failed to ask questions about these areas or confronted the patient directly about avoiding what both agreed to be her central problem. Maintaining this focus resulted in some movement toward improved communication in the marriage. Interestingly, the patient also made changes in areas that were not the major focus, such as going back to work and reducing the time spent with the lover. She also reported starting to feel more loving toward her husband.

TERMINATION PHASE (SESSIONS 11–12)

Although the end of treatment had been mentioned explicitly in several earlier sessions, the nature of the interactions changed qualitatively during the final two sessions. The focus was more on where the patient wanted to go from here. She restated her need to be more assertive and direct in her communications with her husband, and she ended the extramarital affair, although she continued to feel some anxiety about having done this. Her depression had lifted and she did not feel that additional treatment was needed at this time.

Chapter 8

Role Transitions

Depression associated with role transitions occurs when a person has difficulty coping with life changes that require role change. Almost everyone has multiple roles in the social system, and these roles become indelibly interwoven with the sense of self. The roles themselves, as well as the status attached to them, have an important influence on the individual's social behavior and patterns of interpersonal relationships. Impairment in social functioning frequently occurs in response to demands for rapid adaptation to new, strange roles, especially changes that are experienced by the individual as loss. Not all individuals undergoing role transitions experience the change as a loss. Those who are clinically depressed are more likely to experience role changes as loss. The loss may be immediately apparent, as in the case of divorce, or it may be more subtle, like the loss of freedom following the birth of a child. Retirement or some other change of social or professional role, especially one that brings diminished social status, is often another kind of subtle loss. Moving, changing jobs, leaving home, economic change, and changes in family roles due to illness, new responsibilities, or retirement are other examples of role transition.

The most frequently encountered role transitions occur with progression to another part of the human life cycle. Since these changes are expected as part of the time table of biological growth and development or are dictated by social and cultural patterns, they are considered normative transitions. The transition to adolescence, childbirth, the end of childbearing potential, the decline of physical capacity with aging are biologically normative. Social transitions, which are heavily determined by social class and historical era, include entering college or leaving home for the first time, marriage, job promotion, and retirement.

People who feel they are failing in a new role, or who are not satisfied with the role or its status, may become depressed. These difficulties are often related to ideas about the new role that the patient is only partly aware of and that may be discovered through a systematic attempt in therapy to find out what the change means to the particular person. Men who, paradoxically, become depressed after a sought-after promotion are commonly troubled by conflicts about responsibility and independence; they were actually more comfortable in the old subordinate role, in a less demanding job with more direction from others.

Depression frequently results when a person recognizes the need to make a normative role transition but has difficulty with the necessary changes required, or when a person correctly recognizes failure in a particular role but is unable to change the behavior or to change roles. In depressions associated with role transitions, the patient feels helpless to cope with the change in role. The transition may be experienced as threatening to one's self-esteem and sense of identity, or as a challenge one is unable to meet.

In general, difficulties in coping with role transitions are associated with the following issues:

1. loss of familiar social supports and attachments;
2. management of accompanying emotions, such as anger or fear;
3. demands for a new repertoire of social skills; and
4. diminished self-esteem.

Attention to stages of development in adult life has increased in recent years. Levinson (1978), Lidz (1976), Erikson (1968), Keniston (1968), among others, have explored the types of problems and key tasks associated with stages of adult development. Depression that is related to role transitions often involves developmental role transitions also. For example, depression in late adolescence or early adulthood (late teens and early twenties) typically involves difficulties in achieving a satisfactory sense of role identity or in forming intimate relationships outside the family. Patients with these problems may remain overattached to their parental families. Other role transition problems that are typical of young adult life include adapting to occupational or marital roles and to the role of parent.

In the middle adult years, depression may be related to failure to find satisfaction or success in one's chosen career, marriage difficulties, or a decrease in the parental role. In old age, depression may be related to a loss of role and status through retirement, decline in health, loss of social supports through illness, or the death of relatives and friends.

Diagnosis of Role Transition Problems

To diagnose role transition as a problem area for IPT, there should be evidence that the patient's depression and related clinical problems have followed life changes related to role transitions. In most instances this relationship will be apparent to patients and their significant others, and the patient will readily identify the transition: for example, leaving school, seeking a first job, impending marriage, recent divorce, or retirement.

In exploring role transitions such inquiries as these have proven helpful:

> Could you tell me about the change [retirement, leaving home, the divorce, etc.]? How did your life change? What important people were left behind? Who took their place? How did you feel in the new role [as retiree, divorcée, student]?

Planning Treatment for Role Transition

Although the issues may vary according to the life phase the patient is in, certain elements common to all role transitions can help define the tasks and goals of IPT treatment for depression connected with these transitions. Problems in managing role transitions center on four tasks: (1) giving up the old role; (2) expressing guilt, anger, loss; (3) acquiring new skills; and (4) developing new attachments and support groups.

Table 8.1 outlines these tasks and offers suggestions for questions the therapist can ask to check the patient's progress with them.

EVALUATION OF OLD ROLE

The first task has similarities to the facilitation of grief described in Chapter 6. The psychotherapist helps the patient put the lost role in perspective by evaluating the activities and attachments that were given up. In general, patients who are having difficulty managing role transitions tend to idealize the benefits offered by the old role while minimizing the negative aspects of it. In reviewing the aspects of the role that is lost, it is useful to help the patient acknowledge the difficulties of the old role, while also trying to discover its positive aspects. For example, one patient had a great deal of difficulty managing her separation from her husband because to her being married, regardless of the circumstances, was socially expected of women. She had suppressed the extent to which her

TABLE 8.1
Checking the Patient's Progress

Task	Therapists' Questions
1. Facilitate evaluation of role that has been lost.	Tell me about the old [whatever has been left or lost or changed—the old house, the former job, living with parents, the former spouse, etc.]. What were the good things? The bad? What did you like? Not like?
2. Encourage expression of emotions.	How did it feel to give up or leave ———? Tell me the details of your leaving. How did you feel in the new situation? What was it like at first?
3. Develop social skills suitable for the new role.	What is required of you? How hard is this? How does it make you feel? What is going well? Badly?
4. Establish new interpersonal relations, attachments and social supports.	Whom do you know? Who can help you? Are there persons you want to get to know?

marriage had been a failure and a destructive element in her life because the role of divorcée was unacceptable.

ENCOURAGING EXPRESSION OF AFFECT

Even when a change is desired and sought, giving up the old role may be experienced as a loss, so that a mourning process occurs. In an old and familiar role the patient may have experienced the satisfaction of mastering the requisite social skills needed to perform in it and derived great pleasures from rewards that were unique to that phase of life. In addition, management of the old role may have involved development of a satisfying system of social supports that has been vital to maintenance of self-esteem.

To facilitate the transition it is useful to elicit the feelings about the change, including grief, guilt—perhaps at not having entirely lived up to self-expectations —anger, and disappointment.

DEVELOPING NEW SOCIAL SKILLS

Most important transitions involve acquisition of new skills. The IPT psychotherapist is not a vocational counselor whose task is to determine the patient's aptitude for taking on different kinds of jobs. The therapist instead helps the patient assess the meaning of the role expectations and tries to discover the beliefs and emotions that are hindering the patient from making full use of potential coping skills. The new role may require new skills, both to respond to new role demands and to form new relationships and attachments.

The therapist may help the patient go through a realistic assessment of assets and skills for managing the transition, while carefully looking out for areas in which the patient may be over- or underestimating them. Such skills might include finding an apartment on one's own, learning to get around in a new community, finding a new job, learning to entertain. Frequently, difficulty in managing new demands is related to performance anxiety. To help with this, the therapist may engage the patient in a kind of rehearsal of difficult situations, asking the patient to imagine, for example, the worst thing that could happen.

Another important type of difficulty involves incorrect or stereotyped assumptions about the new role. These attitudes are often formed through observation of and identification with key individuals in the past who provided undesirable models. To counter these attitudes, the therapist can frequently help the patient recognize examples of specific cases that contradict the stereotype. For example, one sixty-two-year-old woman had a great deal of difficulty getting involved with a senior citizens' group because this meant that she was "old." However, an evaluation of what she meant by "old"—which included isolation, lack of activities, and lack of interests—actually described her own socially isolated situation. In contrast, even the little contact she had with the senior citizens' group showed her that they were less "old," and more lively and involved, than she was.

ESTABLISHING SOCIAL SUPPORTS

Taking on a new role often means developing a new system of social supports, forming new types of relationships as well as familiar kinds of relationships with new people. In addition, the types of rewards offered by the new social role may be unfamiliar and less avidly desired than those offered by the old one. This sort of change may occur when a woman returns to the work force after her children no longer need her as a full time caregiver. Although she may have had previous work experience, the demands of the job may have changed markedly since then, or they may seem more difficult to manage after a lapse of some years. Often too, the kind of job that is wanted or available is entirely different from the earlier one. Many women feel apprehensive about entering what is still often perceived as the "man's world" of the workplace, and though they have less time to enjoy old friendships, they may hesitate to form comparable relationships with work associates.

To help patients develop the needed social supports, the therapist might review the opportunities available for getting involved with others. Depressed patients are likely to have overlooked opportunities for forming supportive relationships and to have become socially isolated.

Role Transitions—The Case of Ellen F.

Ellen F. is a twenty-seven-year-old mother of a six-year-old son, who works part time as a sales clerk. She came for treatment three weeks after a suicide attempt with a combination of nonprescription medications. The precipitant of this had been the end of an extramarital affair. She had been chronically dissatisfied with her marriage of ten years to an alcoholic husband who provided her with steady financial support but little affection. Moreover, when the husband was drinking, which occurred several times weekly, he was verbally abusive and sometimes physically assaultive. The patient's extramarital affair "made me realize what I had been missing." The affair had lasted only a few months and the lover had returned to another woman. Feeling abandoned and hopeless, Mrs. F. made her impulsive suicide attempt immediately after getting the news. She was treated in an emergency room and sent home, where she developed severe depressive symptoms. When these persisted for three weeks, she sought professional help. This was her first depressive episode.

INITIAL PHASE (SESSIONS 1–3)

Mrs. F. saw her depression as clearly related to her difficulty in ending the marriage and disrupting the attachment. She had left her husband several years before, but his treatment of her improved while they were apart and she returned after two months. However, old patterns had quickly been resumed and Mrs. F. had felt trapped again. She said that she hoped treatment would "help me to leave him." She felt she deserved better treatment than she received from her husband but was unsure that she could actually make the break. She was feeling apathetic, anhedonic, and pessimistic that any positive changes could take place.

Mrs. F. and a sister five years younger were raised by a domineering, passive-aggressive mother, her father having left the family for another woman when the patient was six years old. Her mother did not become involved with other men, and the patient recalled feeling that the family seemed to her to be unattractive, outcast women who could not gain the attention of a supportive man. This view of herself and her family was in contrast to her personal attractiveness and social abilities. In fact, she herself was a popular student, as well as a good one, throughout her high school years. Her mother's relationship with her was excessively close—overwhelming—and her marriage at the age of seventeen was seen as a means of leaving mother and home. However, this did not completely interrupt her mother's intrusiveness into her affairs. She still had qualms about contradicting her mother and felt that this was also something that she would like to work on in treatment.

By the second session, the patient had asked her husband to leave the house and he had willingly agreed, expressing his own discontentment with the marriage. The patient felt elated and reported an improvement in the depressive symptoms. She also described being surprisingly free of conflict about breaking up with her husband, in spite of her years of being unsure about doing it. She also described becoming more forthright and direct with her mother in discussions about such matters as when she would take a vacation. These two sessions were largely taken up with reviewing her relationships with her husband and mother. From this discussion it emerged that she avoided taking responsibility for her decisions and got others, such as her mother or her husband, to make decisions for her. She distrusted her own judgment and was hesitant about thinking things through. Related to her discomfort with taking responsibility for herself was her conviction that losing her man (or getting him to leave) would mean being unattractive, unwomanly, and devalued, as she felt her mother and she were after the father left. Her pattern of relations with a man was to get involved and stay with the man at all costs, overlooking all faults. She also, however, expressed fears of being alone, having never lived on her own as the head of a household.

From the information gathered in the first three sessions, it was decided that the focus of therapy would be helping Mrs. F. manage the role transitions involved in separating from her husband. It was anticipated that this would involve the following steps: a) helping her identify new sources of emotional support to replace her husband and her husband's family, b) exploration and correction of fears of being alone and her tendency to distrust her own judgments, c) helping her develop a new repertoire of social skills, such as the discipline of her child, and d) helping her recognize the distinction between her own value and having a man, any man. It was decided to treat her case as one of role transitions rather than role disputes because of Mrs. F.'s conviction that the differences between her and her husband were irreconcilable, and her professed certainty that she wanted to end the marriage.

INTERMEDIATE PHASE (SESSIONS 4–10)

The patient continued to feel good about the separation from her husband. In search of alternative sources of support, she had first turned to her extended family, including her in-laws and her mother, who had all urged her to reconcile with her husband, describing, for instance, how "pathetic" he seemed to be without her. She realized that seeking help from these people had contributed to her previous reunion with her husband, and she began to reestablish old relationships with women friends. Before the fifth session, the husband had come to ask her to take him back and she had refused. She noted that he was drinking at the time of the request. The psychotherapist then explored the possibility of a reconciliation asking the circumstances under which she would find reconciliation acceptable. Mrs. F. felt that there were no circumstances under which she would be willing to reestablish the marriage.

Four weeks after the separation, she began to date again. She found this a positive experience, though she felt strange, after ten years, at having to consider what she wanted and expected from the men she went out with. Just at this time she began to have trouble with her son, who was beginning to act up at school and at home. She realized that she had tended to leave the disciplinary role to her husband and that she had been uncomfortable about discussing the separation with the child. Several sessions were spent discussing in detail how she related to her son, how to talk with him about the separation, and alternative approaches to discipline. The son's behavior improved at home and at school, and she began to feel closer to him.

From Session 5 on, the patient's symptoms improved. She still had good and bad days, but the anhedonic, lethargic, hopeless feelings had passed.

The patient continued to date and became interested in one man. In treatment she examined her initial attraction to her husband. He was "safe" because he had become dependent on her and because he was so "pathetic" without her. She realized that she was attracted to men who were quickly and unconditionally interested in her because she felt so fearful of being rejected by men. As a result she was not discriminating about the men she became involved with. She also began to discuss with the psychotherapist early signs she might use to help her detect similar nonproductive patterns in her future relationships with men.

TERMINATION PHASE (SESSIONS 11–13)

As the end of treatment approached, Mrs. M. reported feelings of emptiness and boredom, and a sense that her life was going nowhere. She did not relate this to the end of treatment but spoke principally of her reemerging sense of worthlessness in living without a man, even if this was recognized as not necessarily a permanent situation. More material about her adolescent feelings of self-condemnation and worthlessness without a father were discussed, and the patient began to talk about such dismaying things as growing old and ugly. The therapist related these feelings to the termination and the patient's fears of being on her own, and tried to contrast her fears with her actual level of competence and indicators of her attractiveness. At this time the husband made another attempt to induce the patient to take him back. Although tempted, she again reminded herself of the old patterns and decided that even though she felt lonely and unhappy now, she would be condemning herself to a more enduring unhappiness if she resumed the marriage. In the final session she reviewed the changes in attitudes and behaviors that she had made during the treatment, including her improved relationship with her child, her growing circle of friends, both male and female, her dating, her greater ability to communicate her needs and disagreements to others, and her improved sense of independence and competence. On the basis of this she concluded that she did not want to resume her old life, even if she had to put up with a certain amount of loneliness.

The patient's immediate depressive episode was precipitated by an extramarital affair that brought into focus the things that were missing in her marriage. Although she had long recognized her dissatisfaction with her husband, she had been able to ignore it until she experienced what an alternative relationship would be like. She came to treatment wanting to get out of her destructive marriage but not feeling able to make the change on her own. The therapist helped the patient evaluate the new demands, available social supports, and rewards associated with becoming a more independent single parent. The demands of separation from her husband included: (a) tolerating loneliness; (b) maintaining her self-esteem without being identified with a man; (c) managing her child; and (d) making new friends and dating. In each case the therapist helped her examine the fears associated with the demands and determine that she in fact had the resources to meet them. In the situation of disciplining her son, the therapist not only evaluated Mrs. F.'s attitudes about being a single parent but was active in teaching the patient ways to think about and talk with him, information that she had not obtained elsewhere. As to social supports, the therapist helped the patient identify new ones that were less conflicted than her relationships with her mother and in-laws. To help the patient enter the new role the therapist helped her clarify her feelings about the role she wanted to leave—being married to her husband and highly involved with her mother. From this process the patient decided that she lost far more than she gained in these relationships, and this view helped provide incentive for accepting the strain of making the transition she wanted. And in considering the rewards of the new role, the therapist helped the patient recognize the relief and pride she felt in relying on herself.

Chapter 9

Interpersonal Deficits

Interpersonal deficits are chosen as the focus of treatment when a patient presents with a history of social impoverishment that involves inadequate or unsustaining interpersonal relationships. Patients with such deficits may never have established lasting or intimate relationships as adults. In general, patients with a history of extreme social isolation tend to be more severely disturbed than those with other presenting problems.

Diagnosis of Interpersonal Deficits

Optimal social functioning includes close relationships with intimates or family members, less intense but satisfying relationships with friends and acquaintances, and adequate performance and relationships in some sort of work role. For patients with interpersonal deficits it may be useful to focus on those who are socially isolated. The socially isolated group may lack relationships with either intimates or friends, or may not have a work role. They may have long-standing or temporary deficiencies in social skills.

Goals and Strategies of Treatment

The goal of treatment of interpersonal deficits is to reduce the patient's social isolation. Because there are no current meaningful relationships, the focus of treatment is on past relationships, the relationship with the therapist, and beginning to form new relationships.

The three tasks involved in handling a problem of interpersonal deficits are:

1. review of past significant relationships, including negative and positive aspects;
2. exploration of repetitive or parallel problems in these relationships; and
3. discussion of the patient's negative and positive feelings about the therapist and parallels in other relationships.

The review of past significant relationships, particularly childhood relationships with family members, assumes a greater importance with these patients. As each one is reviewed, it is important to determine both the best and the worst part of the relationship. Discussion of past relationships at their best may provide a model for helping the patient to develop satisfying new relationships. The therapist might ask:

Tell me about your current friends. Your close family. How often do you see them? What do you enjoy with them? What problems do you have with them?

Continue reviewing relationships from most current to less recent:

How can you find friends and activities now that you used to enjoy in the past?

A positive relationship in the past was used to help Joe B., a highly withdrawn twenty-eight-year-old man, find more satisfying current relationships. Although he had broken off contact with his parents in his late teens, Joe B. remembered with satisfaction the task-oriented work he and his father had done together. Since he was unable to enjoy the company of others in unstructured situations, he reduced his isolation by taking a volunteer job at a local hospital.

Detailed evaluation of failed relationships or of past interpersonal difficulties may alert the therapist about predictable problem areas in new relationships. The therapist should look for regularities in the kinds of situations that lead to difficulty for the patient and help the patient identify these situations, with the hope of avoiding them in the future or of working on gradual resolution of the difficulties. For example:

A thirty-year-old woman had closed herself off from social contacts with others and had lost a job largely because of extreme anxiety at interacting socially with more than two or three people at a time. She developed psychophysiological symptoms in group situations and absented herself in an embarrassing manner on many occasions. She felt excluded, disliked, and anxious, and these feelings were related to her earlier family situation. When she was able to identify her problem, she found more acceptable employment in a small business in which she had frequent interactions with only one boss. She also reduced her isolation somewhat by entertaining friends at home one at a time.

Attention to the patient-therapist relationship is more important for socially isolated patients than for those with other types of problems. This relationship provides the therapist with the most direct data about the patient's style of relating to others. In addition, solving problems that arise in this relationship may provide a model for the patient to follow in developing intimacy in other relationships. Open discussion of the patient's distorted or unrealistic negative feelings about the therapist or the therapy is especially important. Typically, patients in this group prefer severing relationships to openly confronting others and resolving issues. For example:

A twenty-four-year-old man was particularly silent at the beginning of the seventh session and began to discuss quitting. He stated that he did not think that he could be helped. When the therapist asked whether he had been upset about something the therapist had done or not done, he replied that the therapist was just rejecting him as others had done. When he was asked to explain what he meant, it turned out that he had completely misheard an encouraging statement the therapist had made. The patient was relieved at having discovered his mistake and also at having expressed his complaint. This interchange provided the basis for more extended discussion of the patient's generally inhibited communication with others.

For patients with interpersonal impoverishment, dealing with negative feelings toward the therapist not only provides a model of interpersonal learning but also acts as a safety valve to prevent the patient from terminating treatment prematurely because of some imagined slight.

In helping the patient apply the learning that takes place in treatment to outside situations, the therapist may make extensive use of communication analysis and role playing. When the patient has tried, successfully or unsuccessfully, to increase his interactions with others, a detailed review of these attempts may reveal easily correctable deficits in the patient's communication skills. In helping the patient overcome his hesitation in approaching others, the therapist may invite the patient to role-play difficult situations:

Let's pretend you are going into a room full of strangers at a party. What could you do to meet people?

It should be emphasized that brief treatment of interpersonal deficits is especially difficult, and goal setting should therefore be limited to "starting" to work on these issues, not necessarily resolving them.

Interpersonal Deficits—The Case of Bob R.

Bob R. was twenty-two years old, single, and was working as a cook while going to a local college part time. He lived with his mother. Mr. R. came for treatment at his employer's suggestion. He complained of depressed mood and irritability for the past one or two months. His symptoms included anorexia (with a ten-pound weight loss over the previous month), sleep disturbance, crying spells, decreased interest in his normal activities, lack of energy, anhedonia, and irritability. He denied suicidal ideation. Two weeks before the evaluation he had had an argument with his mother and struck her. He denied ever having hit her before. He had had no previous psychiatric contact.

Mr. R. dated the onset of symptoms to approximately a month before the breakup of a three-year relationship with a woman, J. He said that J. had decided to end the relationship because of his "moodiness" and emotional unavailability. He had not seen or talked with J. since the breakup.

Mr. R. was born out of wedlock to a nineteen-year-old woman in rural Alabama. During the pregnancy the patient's father was said to have run off with another woman, settled in a nearby town, and had other children. Mr. R. was raised solely by his mother and had no further contact with his father. When he was thirteen, he and his mother moved to New England. The patient experienced this as a very difficult transition: he felt out of place, embarrassed about his southern accent and his ineptitude at sports. He had few friends and led a rather lonely existence. Over the next few years he did poorly at school and argued constantly with his mother about his behavior. Soon after entering high school, he met J., who would subsequently become his girl friend. J. was a successful student who attended a special community high school geared toward encouraging academic achievement for students of ability but prior poor performance. She persuaded B. to transfer to this alternative school, and he soon took much greater interest in his studies, developed himself as an athlete, and stopped his self-destructive behavior. He became interested in a career in teaching, and after graduation he enrolled in college and began working part time to pay for his education.

Two years before he began treatment, the patient's mother, who had been working as a key punch operator, was hospitalized because of complications resulting from diabetes mellitus and subsequently became depressed. Because she had no health insurance, there were substantial medical bills to pay. Shortly before his mother's hospitalization, Mr. R. had made plans to move out on his own, partly because J. wanted him to have his own apartment so the couple could have some privacy. Concern about his mother's psychological state as well as her debts made him decide to continue living with her and to cut back on his studies and work full time. At the time of the evaluation the patient's mother had still not returned to work.

INITIAL PHASE (SESSIONS 1–4)

During the initial evaluation the patient was wearing wrinkled, loose-fitting clothes. He sat slumped in his chair and spoke so softly that it was often difficult to hear him. He was severely depressed. After the appropriate medical workup, he was given a course of tricyclic antidepressants, beginning with imipramine 100 mg., which was gradually increased over the first week to 200 mg. at bedtime, and then held at that dose. In addition, it was agreed that the patient would meet with his therapist twice a week until there was a significant improvement in his symptoms, at which time the meetings would be held once a week. During each of these early sessions, time was spent reviewing the patient's symptoms and discussing questions relating to the medication regimen. Beginning with the second session, the patient gradually appeared less depressed, talked more, and began taking more care with his appearance. The therapist was highly active in helping the patient manage day-to-day problems at work which had arisen because of his severe depression.

The therapist also began exploring the patient's relationship with his girl friend, J., his lack of social skills, and the events leading to the breakup. The relationship with J. had been vital to him because she was his model for adapting to life in the Northeast and helped coach him in ways of relating to other people. However, the relationship was much like that with an older sister. The patient was frightened of the intimacy and attachment J. wanted and tended to withdraw when her demands increased. He couldn't sustain the attachment. He felt inferior to his girl friend and unworthy of her interest. He felt guilty, too, since he perceived that his involvement with J. meant being disloyal to his mother. In fact, the immediate precipitant of the breakup had been his refusal to move into an apartment with her.

Review of the patient's relationship with his mother showed how his perception of the mother's expectations was affected by his being a male only child of a woman who married neither his father nor anyone else. His mother treated him as very special but also as someone she could rely on to replace the need for a man in her life. His mother had told him that when he was born she had been urged to give him up for adoption but had chosen to keep him despite the humiliation and inconvenience this had caused. Although the patient's mother made him feel that he was essential to maintenance of her well-being because she needed his love and care, she also made him feel that he represented the residue of the totally irresponsible father who had left her pregnant with him. The bad father was frequently brought up as an example of what the boy might become. Hence Mr. R. saw his desire for relationships with other women and his plans to leave home as indications that, like his father, he was a worthless man who wronged his mother.

Discussion of current relationships revealed that B. felt close to no one but his mother at the time he began treatment. Relationships with men were avoided because he felt clumsy, inarticulate, and inadequate in comparison with them. Moreover, although he felt unmasculine and overidentified with strong women such as his mother and J., he also felt contempt for many male friends because of their irresponsibility about drugs and women. His only relationship with a woman that had been more than casual was with J. Although he felt able to meet women, he lacked the ability to sustain relationships. The patient's relationships at school and at work were relatively superficial. He worked hard to escape notice for either very good or very poor performance.

Because of the paucity of current interpersonal relationships and the patient's lack of social skills, the problem area was defined as interpersonal deficits and the strategy was as follows:

1. to focus on past significant relationships, to clarify perceptions of his mother's expectations of him, to identify positive experiences that could be models for new attachments, and to help him reexamine his view of his father, with a more realistic and balanced picture emerging—by reviewing these relationships, the therapist hoped to help the patient clarify how he used them as models in a way that prevented him from forming meaningful adult attachments; and

2. to focus on the patient-therapist relationship as a direct source of information about Mr. R.'s style of relating to others, in order to modify current interpersonal problems.

The immediate focus was on the patient's current living situation and his relationships with his mother, girl friend, and peers.

INTERMEDIATE PHASE (SESSIONS 5–8)

By the end of the fifth session, the patient was virtually asymptomatic on imipramine 200 mg. His mood was brighter; his appearance had changed rather dramatically as he paid more attention to his clothes and grooming; and he felt an increased interest in activities.

The fifth session occurred after a one-week break due to the therapist's planned vacation (which had been discussed with the patient at the beginning of treatment). Mr. R. reported that he had gone out to a few sporting events by himself, and was spending time painting and writing, two activities he had avoided for the past few months. To the therapist's question about whether he was considering beginning to date again, he responded that he was frightened of involvement with a woman because he became emotionally attached quickly and then, as he put it, "get *de*-tached quickly." He did not comment directly about the therapist's absence the previous week. Because he appeared to be doing well, the therapist recommended meeting once a week for the remainder of the treatment, and Mr. R. agreed.

On the day of Session 6, a co-worker of his called to say that he was out of town and would not be able to keep his appointment but would be there the following week. However, he did not appear for—nor call to cancel—his next scheduled appointment. When the therapist reached him at work the next day, he said he had forgotten about the appointment but would come for his next appointment the following week at the regular time.

Thinking about the two successive missed appointments and reviewing Session 5, the therapist decided that Mr. R. was probably quite angry about the therapist's vacation, and perhaps about the change from twice-a-week to once-a-week meetings.

B. arrived the next week at the regular time. He explained that he had missed his session two weeks before because he had gone to another city to visit his two stepsisters, his father's other children. He had not mentioned the sisters before. Now he said that he had talked to them about his father and they had confirmed his view that the father was indeed an irresponsible man. Mr. R. went on to say that he had missed the next session because he had met a woman he liked and had been with her on the afternoon his appointment was scheduled. He had realized he was missing the appointment but thought it more important for him to remain with the woman.

The therapist raised the question that the patient had never commented on his feelings about the therapist's vacation. After maintaining that he had not minded it, he acknowledged that he had really been furious with the therapist for leaving "just when we were getting started" and had even considered stopping treatment at that point. The therapist pointed out that Mr. R. had in fact taken a vacation (to see his sisters) just as the therapist had, and he allowed that there might be a connection between the two events. The therapist then raised the question of why he had not said anything about his feelings earlier. This led to a productive discussion of his difficulty expressing angry feelings, and specifically his fear that if he were to express those feelings, things would inevitably get out of control and he would either be thrown out or have to leave in order to "save face." He was able to acknowledge his attachment to the therapy, and said he was surprised and grateful that the therapist didn't have a negative reaction to his anger. During this period Mr. R. also brought up recent efforts to make friends at work, describing his discomfort at approaching one of the co-workers. Role playing was undertaken in which the patient practiced what he might say.

TERMINATION PHASE (SESSIONS 9–11)

In the next session, Mr. R. discussed his feelings about a man his mother had begun dating. He felt the man was irresponsible, as his father had been, and thought his mother was using poor judgment in spending time with him. The patient was considering talking either with her or with the man about his disapproval of the relationship. The therapist questioned the appropriateness of getting involved in his mother's social life, but the patient asserted that it was appropriate for him to "look out for" his mother. This led to a further discussion of his feelings of indebtedness to his mother because of her decision not to give him up as a child, and of his fear that he, like his father, had an irresponsible streak. He talked about how difficult it had been for his mother during his early adolescence, and his wish to "make it up to her." In response to this, the therapist suggested that the patient's mother's dating might be an indication that she too was getting ready for a separation, and explained that although B. need not give up helping his mother, being more concerned with his own needs and relationships was appropriate at his age. He was encouraged to discuss directly with his mother what her wishes and expectations about separation were.

In the following session he expressed more strongly than before his wish to be out on his own and his feeling that not having moved out sooner had contributed to the breakup with J. He talked of his wish to "see the world" while still young. He also discussed his wish to learn more about his father and described a poignant scene: when he was sixteen he had visited his southern relatives and an aunt had spent a few hours telling him about his father's early life. Although he wanted to talk with his mother about his father, he had felt from a very early age that this would make his mother too uncomfortable, and had never done so. Mention of his father had been limited to brief angry episodes. Now he said he intended to talk with his mother about his father but was not ready to do it quite yet. The therapist helped him practice what he might say to his mother and he speculated on what he might expect to hear. The patient discussed his feeling that even to understand the negative side of his father would be preferable to the emptiness he felt when he thought about him.

At the beginning of the next session, the patient announced that he had decided to move out of his mother's apartment at the end of the coming summer. The decision had been made after a long conversation with his mother in which she had surprised him by agreeing that he needed independence. He acknowledged that he had liked the idea of his mother's dependence on him; he had seen it as his chance to make up to her all she had given him. He was disturbed that she had taken the discussion of his wish to move with such equanimity, and wondered whether his view of her as a rather fragile woman was accurate. Although he had talked to his mother about his father, she had been unwilling or unable to enlarge on the same stereotyped images she had always used. Mr. R. was planning a trip to the South that summer to see his relatives and ask them about his father. He also planned at the end of the summer to take a vacation in the Caribbean Islands, something he had wanted to do for a long time. He and his mother had discussed the fact that she would go back to work when she felt better. He had decided that he could move out and still help his mother financially, and that she was well enough now to go back to work.

As the end of therapy approached, the patient reported becoming more assertive in work and school relationships and showing more initiative in seeking out male and female friends. He felt surprised and relieved about his mother's cooperation in his plans to move out on his own and was already feeling more independent. Although he discussed continued feelings of sadness about the lost relationship with J., and expressed a desire to try to see her, he felt that he might want to become involved in a new relationship in which he felt he had more to give the woman. He had been off medication for several weeks and experienced no return of symptoms. At the end of the last session, he became tearful and thanked the therapist for his help.

Although Bob R. started treatment with a severe depression and had had significant and long-standing problems with interpersonal relationships, he was able to use several aspects of the brief treatment to make substantial gains. In early sessions he had required pharmacotherapy and an active, supportive, structuring stance from the therapist to help him manage day-to-day functioning. With the symptomatic relief that followed this approach, he was able to make several important changes. First, in the interaction with the therapist around the therapist's vacation and his own missed sessions, he was able to acknowledge his desire to form a relationship with a supportive man. More important, he was given the opportunity to discover that angry feelings can be fruitfully discussed in a relationship and do not necessarily spell the end of it. Being able to discuss his anger with the therapist made him feel affirmed and valued and more able to continue the therapeutic work.

Review of the patient's current relationship with his mother revealed appropriate desires for independence, and over the course of subsequent sessions the patient was able to recognize that many of the feelings that kept him living with his mother—such as excessive guilt and fear of being identified with his father—were irrational. In addition, he was surprised to find that his mother supported his moving, having her own life to lead, including beginning to date a new man.

Finally, discussions of the patient's feelings about his father enabled him to recognize that he could be a man without being the same kind of man as his father. He began trying to sort out the myths from the realities concerning his father by questioning relatives about him. This was an important process because he felt that he could not really know who he was without knowing who his father was. Although the patient ended treatment with much work to be done to develop a satisfactory adult life for himself, he felt stronger and more optimistic than he ever had.

The major goals of the early sessions had been to obtain essential background information, form a therapeutic alliance, and help the patient manage his symptoms and reduce his social isolation from his peers. The therapist maintained a warm and supportive stance but remained relatively unintrusive, sensing that Mr. R. needed to "open up" at his own pace, lest he feel threatened. Because of the relative absence of here-and-now "live" relationships, emphasis was placed on an exploration of the patient's feelings about relationships in the past, particularly within the family, with the goal of helping him broaden his social contacts both within the extended family and among peers. Later sessions dealt with termination issues and served to consolidate his understanding of the origins of some of his interpersonal difficulties. He began to resume activities and his social isolation was reduced.

Chapter 10

Termination of Treatment

Since IPT is explicitly short-term and not open-ended, it is important to maintain the initial contract. As in other short-term therapies, termination should be specifically discussed at least two to four sessions before it occurs.

At termination the patient faces the task of giving up a relationship and establishing a sense of competence to deal with further problems without the psychotherapist's help. Failure to accomplish these tasks may lead to a return of depressive symptoms as the end of treatment approaches or shortly after the end of treatment. This symptomatic worsening may in turn bring on a renewed sense of hopelessness.

To facilitate the tasks of termination, the last three to four sessions should contain:

1. explicit discussion of the end of treatment;
2. acknowledgment of the end of treatment as a time of potential grieving; and
3. movement toward the patient's recognition of his independent competence.

Presumably the patient has been trying new ways of coping, so that he is likely by now to have a renewed sense of self-esteem. Despite this, he may feel that his improvement has depended entirely upon the psychotherapist's help and that when this is gone regression is unavoidable.

It must be emphasized to the patient that the goal of the treatment is to help the patient deal successfully with life (work, love, friendship) on the outside. The therapist-patient relationship is meant to enhance the patient's health and competence on the outside and is not a substitute for "real world" relationships.

With at least three or four sessions to go, the therapist should bring up the topic of the end of treatment and elicit reactions to it if the patient has not already volunteered such information. Many patients are unaware of having any feelings about the end of treatment; others may hesitate to acknowledge that they have come to value the relationship with the therapist. If they find themselves already missing the relationship or experiencing a slight recurrence of symptoms as termination approaches, they may interpret their feelings as a relapse. To prevent this misunderstanding, such patients should be told that toward the end it is usual for patients to have feelings of apprehension, anger, or sadness about ending the treatment, but that the appearance of these feelings does not portend a return of depression.

To aid the patient's perception of his own competence to cope with new problems, *the therapist should systematically, throughout treatment, call attention to the patient's independent successes, to the friends, family, church, and other supports that are available on the outside, and to the ways in which the patient has begun to handle his own difficulties.* In the last visit, the therapist may bolster the patient's sense of being able to handle future problems by discussing *areas of future difficulty and guiding the patient through an exploration of how various contingencies could be handled.* Particularly important is the patient's future ability to judge when he needs to seek help. Early warning signals of distress and situations of stress should be identified, and ways of coping—family, friends, and other resources—discussed.

The previously established work pattern of treatment need not be disrupted as termination approaches. Some patients continue to bring up new issues even at the end of treatment. More typically, as the final session approaches the opening of new problem areas ceases, providing opportunities to review the course of treatment and the options that remain open. The patient should be given the opportunity to evaluate the treatment and to assess future needs.

DIFFICULTIES WITH TERMINATION

Because most patients have some discomfort with termination, a decision not to terminate as planned should not be based on the patient's discomfort. A patient who does not want to terminate should be told that further treatment is possible but there should be a waiting period of at least four to eight weeks, to see if it is really needed. Exceptions to this are made for patients who are still severely symptomatic and have shown little or no improvement in the course of therapy. In such cases alternative treatments including use of medications not previously tried, a psychotherapy of a different type, or a psychotherapy with a different therapist should be considered and, if necessary, begun at once.

To the patient who is free of serious symptoms but is uncomfortable or hesitant about termination the psychotherapist might say:

> Many patients have some uneasiness about ending these sessions if they have found them helpful. We have found that a treatment-free period is usually helpful. Let's see how you are doing over the next eight weeks before making any decisions about further treatment. You can, of course, call me if you need to and treatment will be arranged.

INDICATIONS FOR LONG-TERM TREATMENT

For certain patients longer-term treatment is indicated. Such patients may include those with long-standing personality problems, those who can initiate relationships but can't sustain them, those with interpersonal deficits who lack the skills for initiating relationships and thus feel perpetually lonely, those with recurrent depression who require maintenance treatment, and patients who have not responded and are still acutely depressed.

In short-term treatment the initial time contract should be maintained. Patients who require longer-term treatment should be referred elsewhere or should make a different contract, involving a change in focus and techniques, with the same therapist.

Chapter 11

Specific Techniques

Many of the techniques used in IPT are common to dynamic psychotherapy and have been described in part by Bibring (1954) and by Menninger and Holzman (1971). Each technique is used in a specific sequence and with varying frequency, depending on the characteristics of the patient and the particular interpersonal problem the patient brings. These techniques, which will be familiar to clinicians who practice many forms of psychotherapy, are defined here to specify the range of options open to the therapist practicing IPT. Techniques are not the major element of IPT, however. In this mode of treatment, it is the strategies that are distinctive.

Every patient needs a different combination of techniques; for each one some techniques will be emphasized and others not used. The techniques are listed here in order of increasing intrusiveness on the part of the therapist and in general, with the exception of the adjunctive techniques, in the order they are most often used as the therapeutic relationship develops.

Exploratory Techniques

Systematically gathering information about the patient's symptoms and presenting problems using exploratory techniques can be either direct or nondirect.

Nondirective Exploration. Nondirective means using general, open-ended questions or verbalizations. When eliciting information from patients it is best to allow leeway in the style (choice of words, use of detail) of their responses to questions. To facilitate relatively free discussion of material, general, open-ended questions are best, especially in the first phases of a session. The therapist may begin the session with silence or with a highly general opening such as "Where should we begin today?" If material is being discussed in a relatively productive way, nondirective techniques can be used to encourage the patient to continue talking. These techniques include:

Supportive acknowledgment, a nondirective technique that includes such metacommunication as nodding, saying "mmhm," "I see," or "please continue," and other comments designed to encourage the patient to continue talking.

Extension of the topic discussed, one of the nondirective techniques in which the therapist directly encourages the patient to continue on an initiated subject, invites the patient to return to a subject presented earlier, or repeats key or charged words the patient has used.

Receptive silence, one of the nondirective techniques in which the therapist maintains an interested and attentive attitude that encourages the patient to continue talking.

Nondirective exploration is most useful in allowing the patient to bring up new material, to identify problem areas which were not touched on in initial sessions, or to bring in an update of events that have occurred since the previous session. By refraining from structuring parts of a session, the therapist facilitates the patient's sense of responsibility in the treatment (since the patient can choose areas to be concentrated on) and the patient's feelings of being understood and accepted by the therapist (the therapist accepts his choice of concerns as legitimate).

GUIDELINES FOR USING NONDIRECTIVE EXPLORATION

The optimal use of nondirective exploration is with the verbal patient who has a sense of his own problems and is usefully communicating to the therapist. It can also be useful when the therapist feels that the patient is struggling to relate something previously undisclosed or is usefully trying to shift the focus of the treatment. It is a mistake to use this technique when the patient is nonverbal or stuck and groping for direction, or when more active or specific techniques are called for (such as decision analysis or communication analysis).

Direct Elicitation of Material. This technique uses directive questioning or therapist-initiated inquiry into a new topic. Formal questionnaires such as a review of depressive symptoms would be included in this category of therapeutic techniques. Open-ended questions should precede more detailed inquiry; for example, in inquiring about a patient's spouse, the first question, "Tell me about your husband," would be followed by progressively specific questioning. Included in direct elicitation is the *interpersonal inventory,* a systematically detailed exploration of the patient's important relationships with significant others (see Chapter 5).

Direct elicitation is best used for getting a thorough evaluation of a particular problem area and in checking the therapist's interpersonal hypotheses. Specific questions should be asked only with some purpose in mind—such as helping the patient see his role in a situation, or developing a data base—and in some semblance of flow from where the discussion has been. Too much skipping around and specific close-ended questions should be avoided. It is a mistake to ask overspecific questions with nothing in particular in mind, questions that interrupt a patient who is already doing fine discussing an issue, or questions that inhibit expression of affect.

Encouragement of Affect

Encouragement of affect denotes a number of therapeutic techniques that are intended to help the patient express, understand, and manage affect. The relatively free expression of affect in psychotherapy distinguishes it from other relationships, in which affective components are often highly constricted. The learning in therapy is an emotional learning, and dealing with affect is essential in bringing about changes. In developing new interpersonal strategies, the elicitation of affect about others may help patients decide on priorities and strive toward emotionally meaningful goals.

Depending on the nature of the affect and the patient, the IPT therapist may pursue three general strategies:

1. facilitating acknowledgment and acceptance of painful affects that cannot or should not be changed;
2. helping the patient use his affective experiences in bringing about desired interpersonal changes; and
3. encouraging the development of new and unacknowledged desirable affects which, in turn, may facilitate growth and change.

Acceptance of Painful Affects. Many patients have excessive guilt feelings related to strong hostile or sexual feelings about significant others. They may be only partly aware of such emotions. For example, an important aspect of distorted or delayed grief reactions is unacceptable. When the patient gives evidence of painful, unacknowledged or suppressed feelings of this sort, the therapist's job is to encourage the clear expression of the affect. One way to do this is to inquire into sensitive areas, perhaps by eliciting the details of a patient's interactions with significant others or extending discussions of topics to which the patient has shown an emotional response. A second way is to repeatedly inquire about feelings the patient is experiencing while discussing emotionally charged issues in treatment. As the feelings are expressed, it is important for the therapist to help the patient accept them. Direct reassurance, through statements like "Most people would feel like that" or "Of course you're angry," may be helpful. At other times, by simply being silent the therapist conveys his tacit acceptance of the patient's feelings. For patients who are afraid that their hostile or sexual feelings will be acted upon, it is important to make clear the distinction between feelings and actions: the latter is not necessarily the consequence of the former.

Using Affects in Interpersonal Relationships. Some schools of psychotherapy hold the belief that the best way to manage affects is to express them in a cathartic fashion, both in and out of the therapy. In IPT the expression of strong feelings in the therapeutic session is seen as an important starting point for much therapeutic work, but their expression outside the session is not a goal in and of itself. Since the goal is to help the patient act more effectively in interpersonal relationships, this may involve either expressing or suppressing affects, depending on the circumstances. The IPT therapist may help the patient manage his affective experience in several ways. First, the patient and the significant other may negotiate to bring about changes that eliminate the circumstances that evoke painful feelings. For example, a patient who feels repeated disappointment and anger with a spouse's behavior may not feel this way if the behavior changes. Second, the patient may learn to avoid painful situations when appropriate. A third way of managing affect is to delay expressing it or acting on it until one has calmed down. This might include such strategies as planning with a spouse to postpone an argument until a time when both people have some distance on the matter to be discussed. A fourth way of changing painful affects is to help patients revise their thinking about an affect-laden topic so that the affect that arises in response to this thinking is also revised. This strategy is particularly important in the management of anxiety. Patients frequently have high levels of anxiety in relation to irrational thoughts and fears. By exposing the irrational thoughts and helping the patient arrive at alternative ways of understanding a situation, the therapist may help reduce anxiety. Anger can also be mitigated through a revision of the patient's understanding of the situation in which anger arose. Often this revised understanding involves a more mature acceptance of unchangeable circumstances.

Helping the Patient Generate Suppressed Affects. Some patients are emotionally constricted or have a maladaptive lack of emotionality in situations in which strong affects are normally felt. They may be so unassertive that they do not feel anger when their rights are violated by others. Some patients may feel anger but lack the courage to express it in assertive behavior. Others may not feel angry because it has never occurred to them that others should act differently toward them. With these patients it may be useful to point out that they are being abused. Patients who have difficulty feeling and expressing other types of feelings —such as affection, gratitude, or caring—may be helped to discover irrational fears that led to the suppression of these emotions.

GUIDELINES FOR USING ENCOURAGEMENT OF AFFECT

For extremely emotionally constricted individuals this technique cannot be overused, particularly when the patient seems to be unaware of strong feelings such as sadness, anger, or love. The therapist should usually be listening for emotionally important statements and encouraging their expansion.

However, for some patients who are troubled by intense, diffuse, and flooded affective experiences, the strategy may be to help suppress these overwhelming experiences. In addition, mere repetition of angry, hostile, or sad outbursts without an attempt to understand these feelings is probably counterproductive. In such cases the therapist may interrupt an affective display by, for instance, inquiring about the patient's thoughts regarding the strong feelings. Alternatively, the therapist may explore with the patient various strategies for delaying action on impulsive feelings, to allow time to think over the consequences.

It is a mistake to fail to distinguish patients in whom affective responses should be encouraged from those who should not be encouraged. Other mistakes include missing cues from the patient about emotional issues, failure to use the technique when appropriate, and verbal or nonverbal disapproval of the patient's feelings.

Clarification

The therapist uses clarification to restructure and feed back the patient's material. The short-term purpose is to make the patient more aware of what has actually been communicated. In the longer term this may facilitate the patient's discussion of previously suppressed material. Specific techniques for clarification include:

Asking patients to repeat or rephrase what they have said. This is particularly useful if the patient has made a misstatement, said something in a surprising or unusual way, or contradicted previous statements.

The therapist may rephrase what the patient has said and ask the patient if this is what was intended. The rephrasing should be done in a way that places the patient's statement in an interpersonal context. For instance, a patient discussing an incident in which his wife had come home late described his feelings by saying, "There was anger," to which the therapist replied, "You were angry with her?"

The therapist may call attention to the logical extension of a statement that the patient has made or point out the implicit assumptions in what was said.

Calling the patient's attention to contrasts or contradictions in his presentation of material is involved in the most useful clarification techniques. Contradictions may be noted between the patient's affect expression and the verbal discussion of a topic. Discrepancies can be noted over time when the same material is brought up. Contrasts can be seen between a statement of intentions and overt behavior, between the patient's statements of goals and the limitations of reality. In confronting the patient with contradictory statements, it is important to do this in the spirit of inquiry and not in an accusing fashion. Contradictions can be pointed out by a statement such as "Isn't it interesting that you said——— while previously you said———" or "What can we make of the contrast between ———and———?"

Statements that imply a pervasive, unhelpful belief or thought may be restated explicitly, and the patient is then asked if this represents the real belief. Some people, for example, have a habit of thinking in extremes. From a patient's discussion of his work the therapist may note that the patient thinks that he is either a total success or an utter failure, without gradations in between.

GUIDELINES FOR USING CLARIFICATION

The optimal use is at times when the therapist has some hypothesis in mind and can use clarification techniques when the patient is talking about the related subject, or as follow-through to make sure the patient has gotten the point. The point is made at a time when it is likely to be understood, not when the patient is feeling a strong, unrelated affect.

Communication Analysis

Communication analysis is used to examine and identify communication failures in order to help the patient learn to communicate more effectively. Specifically, the therapist seeks out problems in communication by asking for a highly detailed account of an important conversation or argument the patient has had with a significant other.

Faulty communication may be responsible for interpersonal disputes even if those involved have mutually supportive or noncontradictory expectations of one another. When there is a realistic basis for conflict, poor communication can make a relatively minor disagreement insoluble. Communication failures may come about in a number of ways, most of which include failure of one partner to openly correct mistaken assumptions about the other's thoughts, feelings, or intentions. Some common communication difficulties include the following:

Ambiguous, indirect nonverbal communication as a substitute for open confrontation. Verbal communication has many advantages over nonverbal communication in terms of its explicitness and understandability. Many patients who either distrust verbal communication or fear openly expressing their feelings or thoughts rely on nonverbal communication or actions to get their point across to others. They may sulk when angry or make suicidal gestures when they feel lonely or deprived. The person to whom these actions are addressed cannot know what is being asked or how best to respond.

Incorrect assumption that one has communicated.

Many people assume that others will know their needs or feelings without their having to make themselves clear, expecting the other person to anticipate their wants or, in effect, be a mind reader. This often results in anger and frustration, again silent. Other people, having tried to communicate a message, do not bother to make sure that they have been heard or understood.

Incorrect assumption that one has understood.

Many depressed patients fear massive retaliation or criticism from others and are afraid to ask if what was perceived as criticism was actually intended that way.

Unnecessarily indirect verbal communication.

Many depressed patients are highly inhibited about directly expressing quite reasonable expectations or criticisms of others. As a result they may build up resentments about being mistreated by a person who is unaware of having given offense. Instead of direct communication, the patient may use hints or ambiguous messages.

Silence—closing off communication.

Many patients have discovered that silence can be an effective and infuriating way of handling a disagreement with others, but they may be unaware of the destructive potential of closing off communications entirely.

GUIDELINES FOR USING COMMUNICATION ANALYSIS

Communication analysis is aimed at identifying these and other communication failures and at guiding the patient toward learning to communicate more effectively. Identifying faulty communication often involves listening for the *assumptions* that the patient makes about others' thoughts or feelings. The optimal use is when disputes are present, especially if there has been a recent argument (or unsuccessful communication). It is important to try to be as thorough as the patient's memory permits, even if the patient resists or is bored.

Patients should be allowed to draw their own conclusions first before the therapist gives feedback.

It is a mistake not to follow through or pursue a particular conversation, not to let the patient draw his own conclusions, to misunderstand the patient's communications, or to fail to suggest alternatives to poor communication.

Use of the Therapeutic Relationship

In this technique the patient's feelings about the therapist and/or the therapy become the focus of discussion. Thoughts, feelings, expectations, and behavior in the therapeutic relationship are examined insofar as they represent a model of the patient's characteristic way of feeling and/or behaving in other relationships.

In individual therapy, the relationship between the patient and the therapist is the only "live" source of data open to the therapist about the patient's style of interpersonal functioning. On the assumption that people adopt characteristic ways of approaching all personal relationships, the interaction between the therapist and the patient can be used to help the patient learn about other relationships. In IPT the patient-therapist relationship is not the primary focus of treatment and attempts to extrapolate from the therapy relationship the dynamics of others are used only sparingly. However, when the patient begins to think about or act toward the therapist in a way that interferes with the progress of treatment, attention must be paid to the "here-and-now" therapy relationship. Failure to do so will lead to premature termination or unproductive treatment.

To facilitate monitoring of this relationship, the patient should be instructed, at the onset of the treatment, to express to the therapist complaints, apprehensions, and/or other aversive feelings that arise in the course of treatment either about the therapist or about the therapeutic process. More positive feelings (such as, for instance, an exaggerated sense of being helped by a powerful expert) need not be as systematically examined because they probably help rather than hinder the progress of treatment.

Encouraging the patient to express negative feelings about the therapist serves many vital functions. It provides a model for the patient's interactions with others, as patient and therapist negotiate around the patient's legitimate or unrealistic concerns. It allows the therapist to correct distortions or to acknowledge genuine deficiencies or problems in treatment. In addition, analysis of unrealistic negative reactions to treatment may provide convincing data which the patient can use to understand and correct his distorted view of others. For instance, excessive expectations of being attacked, ridiculed, abandoned, punished, and so on are commonly revealed when the patient begins to avoid discussing sensitive material or falls silent for periods of time.

GUIDELINES FOR USING THE THERAPEUTIC RELATIONSHIP

This technique is used optimally in: (1) role disputes, where it gives feedback on how a person comes across to others and helps the patient understand pathological interactions by reexperiencing them with the therapist but going one step further and solving them; (2) grief and loss, when reactions to the therapist may show how the patient has cut off from others or developed relationships that mirror the one with the lost person; (3) interpersonal deficits, as the patient develops a relationship with the therapist as a model for other relationships.

Timing is critical. This technique is especially useful when problems come up (lateness or nothing to say), but it is important not to bring up the problem until some therapeutic alliance is established. The actual constraints of the relationship as well as the actual features of the patient and the therapist must be recognized.

It is a mistake to poorly time this technique, to misunderstand the patient's interactions with the therapist, or to fail to take into account the patient's accurate perceptions about the therapist or the therapeutic relationship.

Behavior Change Techniques

Lasting improvement from depression usually depends on changes in the patient's interpersonal behavior outside therapy. In IPT the therapist can use (1) directive techniques; (2) decision analysis; and (3) role playing to facilitate behavior change.

Directive techniques include interventions such as educating, advising, modeling, or directly helping the patient solve relatively simple, practical problems. In establishing a positive working relationship in the early phases of treatment, the therapist should be alert to the possibility of directly helping the patient solve such practical problems as finding transportation, housing, or public financial assistance. Since the goal of treatment is to help the patient function independently, heavy use of direct assistance or advice is to be avoided. Rather, patients should be taught to analyze new situations for themselves and make their own choices. As an overall strategy, the therapist should move from relatively direct toward relatively indirect helping as treatment progresses. When direct interventions seem warranted, the following techniques may be useful:

Advice and suggestions should be provided only when the therapist thinks the patient is unable to make a relatively successful decision on his own. Patients may ask for advice they do not need or help in an area the therapist cannot be expected to be knowledgeable about (income tax, for example) in order to test the therapist. In such cases the therapist may wish to explore the patient's unrealistic expectations of him. Although crucial at times, giving advice can be detrimental to treatment in that it is contradictory to the general principle that the patient is responsible to himself and for himself even if he *chooses* to follow someone's advice.

Limit setting may be necessary for highly impulsive individuals whose behavior is destructive either to themselves or to the treatment. The therapist may choose to demand that the patient refrain from a given behavior if he is to remain in treatment.

Education is an essential function of IPT generally and specifically. Ultimately all the interventions of IPT are aimed at educating patients about their interactions with others. More specifically, the patient may be simply deficient in knowledge about the range of topics of importance in his life. The therapist may usefully educate the patient about the characteristics of depressive illness and general psychological principles, or about ways to solve practical problems. Education is preferred to advice giving in that it is aimed at providing the patient with the skills with which to make his own choices.

Direct help should be used exclusively for solving practical problems. For interpersonal problems, the patient should receive the message that this is an ongoing matter for which he, with help, is responsible.

Modeling is similar to advice giving, because it involves giving the patient examples of how the therapist has handled problems similar to the patient's. This technique is helpful in conveying to patients that they are not unique in having difficulties and that others have learned to solve their problems.

GUIDELINES FOR USING DIRECTIVE TECHNIQUES

Optimally, with the exception of education, direct techniques should be used sparingly. They are best used in early sessions to create an atmosphere in which the therapist is perceived as a helping person. In addition, when the patient can be clearly helped by obtaining information the therapist possesses, or when the patient is grossly misinformed (for instance, about how to obtain welfare payments), direct advice may be useful. Advice should ideally be in the form of helping the patient consider options not previously entertained rather than direct suggestions. The tone would be: "One thing you might consider is . . ."

Too frequent use is a mistake; so are suggestions that are too specific and direct, or that undermine the patient's sense of autonomy, or that are based on misinformation or incorrect perceptions.

Decision Analysis.

This is a technique by which the patient is helped to consider a wide range of alternative actions (and their consequences) that can be taken to solve a given problem. This is the major action-oriented technique of IPT and should be explicitly taught to the patient for use outside of treatment. Many depressed patients have a history of making self-defeating decisions, partly because they fail to consider all reasonable alternatives and to evaluate the consequences of their actions. The role of the therapist in decision analysis to help the patient recognize a broadening range of options and to insist that action be held off until each option is adequately explored.

Decision analysis may be used whenever the patient has an interpersonal problem to be solved. The therapist should begin by asking generally, "What alternatives do you feel you have now?" or "Why don't we try to consider all the choices you have?" In the ensuing discussion the therapist should be alert to point out useful alternatives the patient has ignored and to direct the patient to explore the probable consequences of each line of behavior. Decision analysis frequently reveals a patient's excessively restricted conceptions of alternatives or unrealistic notions about consequences. Although the therapist is highly active in decision analysis, the choice among alternatives is the patient's.

GUIDELINES FOR USING DECISION ANALYSIS

It is used optimally if the patient has first discussed and analyzed the problem thoroughly and the therapist avoids actually suggesting what to do. There is always an option to continue discussing and thinking about the problem. There is some thoroughness in that the consequences of each action are considered.

It is a mistake if too much activity or pressuring of the patient into decisions occur or if used prematurely before all information is in. If the possibilities are too narrow, there is a failure to consider all opportunities, or to think through the consequences of behavior.

Role Playing.

The therapist using this technique takes the role of some person in the patient's life. Role playing can be used to accomplish two important tasks: 1) exploration of the patient's feelings and style of communication with others, and 2) rehearsal of new ways for the patient to behave with others.

For the first task, role playing can be used when the therapist feels that patients are not adequately conveying a sense of their relationships with others. When the therapist pretends to be the other person, the patient may react in fresh and revealing ways.

For the second task, role playing can be used to train the patient to interact with others in new ways, such as being more assertive. It is a great leap to go from thinking about acting differently to actually doing so. Often the patient has been aware for years of a desire or need to change but has been unable to do so. Role playing allows the patient to practice in a safe setting and thus may provide for a smoother transition from plans to action.

GUIDELINES FOR USING ROLE PLAYING

Optimally this technique may be useful in eliciting the patient's feelings about a subject by providing a structure for the patient's expressions. It may also be useful in helping the patient practice some difficult situations, but it is a technique used sparingly in IPT.

It is a mistake to use it when not necessary, to fail to follow through, or to fail to try it when the patient is not adequately getting into things.

Adjunctive Techniques

Contract Setting. This refers to the sequence of semistructured tasks in the initial session(s) that are aimed at educating the patient about IPT and obtaining the patient's cooperation as a partner in the therapeutic work. Tasks include an individualized explanation of the IPT rationale, and explanation of IPT techniques, some communication to the patient about the therapist's understanding of what brings the patient into therapy, and a discussion of the practical dimensions of treatment—length of sessions, frequency, duration of therapy, appointment time, missed sessions policy, fee, and so on (see Chapter 5).
Administrative Details.

These interventions have to do with the procedural or bookkeeping tasks of therapy—discussion of appointment times, vacation schedules, and so on.

Chapter 12

An Integrative Case Example

A case of grief and loss illustrates the strategies and techniques of IPT and offers a good way to compare them with those used in other psychotherapies. It also illustrates the use of IPT at the levels of chronology, problem areas, techniques, and therapist stance. This detailed presentation includes a description of strategies and sequence of events; a comparison of the IPT approach with that of other approaches in psychotherapy; the levels of intervention; and the techniques used.

Strategies and Sequence of Events

INITIAL PHASE (SESSIONS 1–2)

Ruth C., a sixty-two-year-old woman, came for treatment of a depression that had lasted a year and that she "became aware of" after her husband's death from a progressively debilitating illness caused by diabetes associated with vascular disease. She had no previous history of depression. Her symptoms included unshakable sadness, with little change in mood regardless of events around her; preoccupation with memories of her husband's death and guilty feelings about him; feelings of inadequacy at being unable to get her affairs in order since he died; a tendency to oversleep; retardation and severe difficulty concentrating; social withdrawal so acute that she had restricted her outside contacts to her two grown children and felt that she was a burden on them. The depressive symptoms represented a continuation of her grief reaction and she had thought these feelings were normal. Later, as the symptoms persisted, she became progressively more desperate and hopeless about being able to overcome them, though she denied suicidal feelings.

Mrs. C. had sought treatment at another clinic two months before this first meeting with the psychotherapist. At that time she had been treated with amitriptyline and had begun to experience some improvement in mood. However, the treatment was discontinued when she was hospitalized for treatment of psoriasis. While in the hospital she remained somewhat asymptomatic, but she became as depressed as ever when she returned home. She met the DSM-III criteria for major depression.

Interpersonal Context

Mrs. C. clearly associated her depression with the illness and death of her husband, who had been progressively debilitated from the time they both retired four years ago. Although they had planned to travel during their retirement and held off taking vacations in anticipation of this, she accepted a restricted, isolated life style centered on caring for her husband. She seldom left the house without him and cut off contacts with friends and acquaintances. Most disturbing about her husband's illness was his mental deterioration. Shortly before his death he had to be hospitalized at a state mental hospital, where he developed more severe vascular disease that necessitated a transfer to another hospital and amputation of one leg. From that point until his death, Mrs. C.'s husband was completely mentally incoherent.

Review of the past family life led to Mrs. C.'s assertion that the relationship had been fine and completely satisfying before her husband's illness. They had been married for thirty-five years. Her relationships with the two children, a son of thirty-one and a daughter of twenty-eight, had been characterized by her difficulty giving up control over them. The son was an alcoholic who had been abstinent for over a year and was living at a halfway house. Apparently his progress toward rehabilitation was linked to Mrs. C.'s being able to reduce her attempts to help him with this problem. The relationship with the daughter was less troubled, probably because the daughter was described as more "self-sufficient" and independent of Mrs. C. They had quarreled somewhat in the past because of Mrs. C.'s intrusiveness into her daughter's affairs, but the relationship had improved in recent years.

Although Mrs. C. recognized that she needed to develop new activities and social contacts, she felt pessimistic about ever being able to do so. She described having a "dual personality" about this because there was a marked contrast between what she experienced with other people and her anticipation of it. She had done well in her job as a secretary for many years and had a number of friends from work. She felt that she had no difficulty making friends or meeting them, although she had tended to center her activities in her family. Her husband's illness had led her to cut off contact with friends more or less completely, especially during the last year of his life. Mrs. C. felt she would be unwelcome with her old friends because they would be offended at her neglect of them. Thus she anticipated rejection if she were to attempt to get involved with people.

Her anticipation of rejection and her feeling that she would not enjoy other people's company contrasted sharply with what actually occurred when others asked her to join them in social activities. She reported that she did enjoy herself and that others seemed to appreciate her company. For example, when she was leaving the hospital her roommates had told her they were sad to see her go because they had enjoyed her company. She recognized that she would probably be able to perform adequately in social relations if only she could get over anticipating a bad time and having to force herself to plan activities. But she also brought out long-standing fears of being taken over and exploited by others if she allowed friendships to reach more than a superficial level of interaction.

Comment on Strategy

The therapist conducted the initial information-gathering sessions with the aim of obtaining two general kinds of information: (a) an assessment of the type and severity of the depressive symptoms; and (b) a determination of the interpersonal issues associated with the onset of the current depressive episode. The initial part of the session began with rather general inquiries ("What brought you to the clinic?"), which were followed by a relatively systematic symptom review. This in turn was followed by an assessment of the current social situation (review of social supports and important activities such as work and friends) and of the events preceding and succeeding the onset of the depressive symptoms.

Initial Symptom Management. From the review of the depressive symptoms the therapist determined that they were of moderate severity, not requiring hospitalization, and that they had been somewhat responsive to medication in the past. Given the situational nature of Mrs. C.'s depression, it was decided to hold off initiating pharmacotherapy until there was further evaluation. The thought was that she might have some remission of symptoms as a result of entering psychotherapy. Although the concept of situational depression is controversial, many clinicians interpret the history of patients, like Mrs. C, as indicating that the depression was related to the social circumstances and life events surrounding the onset of her symptoms (Hirschfield, 1981). The issue of symptoms was handled in the first session with education and reassurance such as:

> Therapist: The different ways that you have felt bad—the sadness and crying, being unable to get yourself going, trouble concentrating, not wanting to face other people—are all part of a picture of a depression that seems to have hit you as a result of losing many things over the past several years. As you pointed out, the way you are now is clearly different from the way you were: you've lost your husband; you lost his companionship even before that; you lost the plans you had for a happy retirement. It's very hard to get over these losses. Part of what we will be doing is trying to help you do this . . . confront what you've lost and help you manage it. As we do this I expect that your symptoms will improve.

Initial Formulation of Therapeutic Strategy. From the review of the context of the current depression the therapist tried to determine what it was about and begin to develop an understanding of how changes could be made. Part of the plan was also to develop an alliance with the patient by beginning to work on problems even in the first session; to provide the patient with feedback so that she felt she was being heard and to let her know what to expect from psychotherapy. The patient clearly associated the depression with the death of her husband but was at a loss to determine why she was unable to get it out of her mind. From the review of her husband's last years it became apparent that many aspects of the death were important in preventing Mrs. C. from successfully mourning the loss.

She had responded to his long illness and gradual deterioration with denial, which had led her to expect him to act more responsibly than he was able. Thus his mental deterioration and helplessness led her to become angry with him (and probably to wish for his death). These feelings would be the source of severe guilt after his death. In particular she felt bad about participating in his hospitalization, from which he did not return. Although his illness was out of his control, Mrs. C. also felt angry that her husband's debility had caused them both to give up their plans for a happy retirement.

The first major goal of treatment was defined as helping the patient overcome her guilt surrounding her handling of the illness and death and to develop a more realistic understanding of it. The general strategy was to review the relationship with the husband, the circumstances surrounding the death, and the ways she continued to think about him. While reviewing this material the therapist kept in mind typical feelings associated with pathological grief, including shame over helplessness at not being able to prevent the event; rage at the person who is the source of the event; guilt over aggressive impulses such as destructive fantasies regarding the lost person; survivor guilt, for feeling relieved that the other person died and not oneself; sadness over the loss; and fear of identification or merging with the victim.

When material related to these themes was discussed, the therapist attempted to clarify the feelings to the patient and to point out, where appropriate, their unrealistic nature. This kind of work was begun in the initial session even while taking the history. For example, when the patient discussed how guilty she felt about committing her husband to a state mental hospital during the last few months of his life and expressed sadness at not having been able to talk to him about it, the therapist responded by eliciting information about her husband's condition and found out that he had become unmanageable— wandering around at night; incoherent; violent and threatening. On the basis of this information, as well as her account of what she would have liked to say to her husband, the therapist acknowledged her guilt and sadness at not being able to care for her husband herself toward the end but pointed out that she had no choice.

A second major goal of treatment, helping the patient to resume meaningful activities, was also defined on the basis of initial information gathering. At the onset of treatment her social functioning was restricted to contact with her children and managing household chores. She hesitated to look up old friends not only because she felt guilty about neglecting them but because she was afraid she would not be able to control her depressed mood with them. She was aware of an active senior citizens' center in her neighborhood but was hesitant to become involved in it alone. She had started taking a course at a local community college but was considering dropping it. In addition, her mode of dealing with others often took the form of caretaking and self-sacrifice that was accompanied by fears of being exploited. Despite her current social deficiencies the patient had had relatively active relationships with friends before she retired. Moreover, she acknowledged that once she got involved with other people she tended to enjoy the contact in spite of severe anticipatory anxiety about it.

To help her begin reusing her evident social skills the therapist began a process of reviewing Mrs. C.'s options for getting involved with others and encouraging her to act on them. In this process there was an emphasis on eliciting negative expectations about how various options would turn out and on confronting her about their unrealistic nature. For example, in the first session the patient discussed how her relationship with her former best friend had lapsed because she couldn't visit the friend leaving the husband unattended and had been too embarrassed at her husband's condition to invite the friend to see her. She felt now that she could not bring herself to call the friend because she would be insulted at being neglected. The therapist wondered if the friend would understand her explanation if she offered it and the patient acknowledged that she might.

In reviewing the loss of the husband and the patient's current social functioning the therapist was not only taking the history but helping the patient clarify these situations and beginning to help her develop alternative ways of thinking about them. At the end of the first session, after saying that the depression seemed to be related to the loss of her husband, the therapist gave the patient this introduction to IPT treatment:

> One of the reasons why people sometimes have difficulty starting up again after losing a loved one is because it's been hard to really look the loss straight in the face, and to really think about what it means, and allow yourself to feel the painful feeling. I think one of the things we can do in therapy is try to look at what's happened with you and your husband, to look at what he meant to you. We will go through that in a way that may be painful, but I think it's very necessary to do that if you are going to go back to an active life. The other side of trying to look at what's happened with the loss of your husband is for us to look into the ways you can start enjoying life again. And it seems that in fact you've made a start as far as that kind of thing is concerned. However, it also seems that you have a number of long-term attitudes that to some extent you realize aren't realistic, such as the difference between the way things turn out and the way you anticipate them. Also you have a lot of fears, that somehow people won't like you, that they're avoiding you or perhaps going to exploit you. We will spend some time trying to look at just what makes these things seem so powerful and likely to happen. Also we'll look at ways you can overcome these hesitations. We'll be meeting for twelve sessions and I'd like you to bring in concerns that you have, ways you've been feeling or thinking that you would like to talk over, as well as taking the approach that we will be surveying the important relationships that you've had in the past and in the present.

Evaluation continued in the second session, as the patient discussed two major topics related to the treatment goals: a) her experience of her husband's life and death, and b) her attempts at reestablishing a life of her own without him. Discussion of her family of origin revealed a highly disorganized or disrupted childhood. Her mother had died when she was five and the state split up the family, taking the children away from her alcoholic father when she was seven. From that time until the age of eighteen, she lived for relatively brief periods in a series of foster homes. She described this experience as painful and frustrating because the foster parents tended to look at the foster children as unpaid household help. At eighteen she moved in with an older sister, and she married her husband five years later, after a lengthy courtship. He had been her only serious suitor. Throughout the session Mrs. C. discussed progressively disturbing memories of her husband's final years, particularly his painful inability to care for himself. Toward the end he had become psychotic, and verbally abusive to her. She again described her guilty relief when he was institutionalized and when he died. The therapist tried to be accepting and sympathetic as he drew out details of her memories of this time.

Interwoven with this theme was the topic of her getting involved with new activities. She discussed senior citizens, future college courses, volunteer work, and seeing friends, mostly in terms of her fears about these things. She felt particularly apprehensive because she was single now and could no longer be as selective of others as she had when her husband was there to fall back on. She also felt that married former friends would no longer be interested in her because she was no longer part of a couple. And she thought her depression so obvious that no one could possibly be interested in seeing her. The therapist was gently confronting around these points, inducing her to give counterexamples and pointing out unrealistic aspects. Toward the end of this session the therapist decided to start the patient on a tricyclic antidepressant (100) mgs. This decision was based on the patient's continued high level of depression, which was noticeable throughout the session, and her history of positive response to medication in the past.

INTERMEDIATE PHASE (SESSIONS 3–8)

In Session 3, the patient reported feeling better, and she had passed several minor milestones on the way to a more active life. She had driven at night for the first time (she said her husband had instilled a fear of night driving in her), she had had friends in to dinner for the first time since her husband's death, and she had started to go out more frequently, having made contact with a local senior citizens' center.

Mrs. C. had also begun to think about how much she had restricted herself over the years in response to her husband's inhibited personality. She realized that she was still acting as if her husband were alive, and feeling guilty if she did things he would not have approved of. Moreover, she felt guilty if she spent money both of them had earned, or if she made changes around the house. A discussion of her day-to-day living revealed that she continued to keep space for him around the house, sleeping only on her side of the bed and using only her side of the closet. The session ended with a relatively new realization that she, not he, could choose either to restrict herself or to allow herself to act.

Moreover, coupled with the loss of a valued loved one was a level of freedom that she had not experienced for forty years.

In Session 4 the material from previous sessions was repeated and enlarged on. Mrs. C. discussed her increased social life and her plans for future courses at college and volunteer work. As she talked, she realized that she was not merely regaining her old level of performance but was acting and thinking of herself in entirely new ways. She said she realized that most of her life had been spent in controlling, restricted environments—in foster homes and then with a cautious, controlling husband. She had taken these restrictions and limitations for granted, and was just now starting to sort out how much she wanted to change these things. For example, she followed a household routine in which each day of the week was spent on a specific task—for instance, Monday was wash day. When a desirable activity came up on a Monday she was embarrassed at the degree of conflict she felt if she switched her wash day. However, she felt that the level to which she had routinized her life was excessive.

Session 5 marked a turning point. Two weeks had passed since the previous session, during which time Mrs. C. received the results of her research ratings (various checklists and inventories which provide the patients with ratings on their degree of improvement). She felt that these ratings showed that she had improved considerably. She felt she had nothing more to talk about and was wasting the therapist's time. The therapist took these statements at face value and began to discuss the possibility of terminating after another session or two, encouraging her to review the course of treatment and discuss problems that might remain. In response to this she discussed her fears that her health would deteriorate as she grew older. She was also concerned at not having closed up the file of bills from her husband's treatment, and she feared that her improvement had been due entirely to medications and that she would relapse if they were discontinued. Despite these pessimistic themes, she also discussed her feeling that she had begun to learn new rules to live by. The therapist suggested that therapy did not have to consist simply of discussions of symptoms, which had now been reduced, but could focus on her experience of learning to live differently. Relieved and grateful, she indicated that she would like to remain in treatment after all.

Session 6 focused on the meanings behind a peculiar, persistent "frenzied" feeling she had begun to have, "as if I had to get everything done" before something dreadful happened. She had been feeling better and better, and was becoming more and more involved in new activities, especially in preparation for the Christmas holidays, the first to be celebrated without her husband. In this session she reviewed aspects surrounding her husband's death and was able to relate her frenzied feeling to the fear that she would die too, as a punishment, just when life looked promising again. She also revealed that her two cats had disappeared shortly after her husband's death, and this loss had greatly increased her despair. Discussing the fact that she had not yet gotten a stone for her husband's grave, she realized that in some ways she still could not bring herself to leave her husband in his place, the grave, while she went on to enjoy her life.

The patient began Session 7 with a review of the progress she had made. She said she was feeling better than she had ever felt, that she was experiencing a kind of rebirth, making up for time lost to depression and preoccupation with her husband. She had become acutely aware of how depressed she had been through talking to another widowed woman who was still depressed. She also expressed some embarrassment about how she must have appeared to others when she was depressed. She went on to say that she missed her husband as the holidays approached but these feelings were manageable and even pleasant in a bittersweet way. She said that he had been the only person with whom she could discuss much of her past life and only he had really understood her. Following this was a discussion of how she would continue to manage without him. Asked how she liked her involvement with the senior citizens' center, she replied that her enjoyment of it involved admitting that she was an "old lady" herself. She was somewhat concerned about becoming depressed again after treatment, and this called for a review of different treatment options and of circumstances that might make her depressed again. She had begun to take new things into her life, including listening to new songs, developing confidence in driving, and getting two cats to replace the two she had lost shortly after her husband's death.

In Session 8 the patient brought Christmas cookies, which the therapist accepted and thanked her for without further discussion. Early in this session the patient was reminded that there were only four more visits left after this one. The patient described her successful holidays, which included a Christmas dinner she had prepared for her family, and other social activities. She professed to be "happy, or at least as happy as I get." After a short silence she said that one thought did continue to concern her and came repeatedly to mind. This was her memory of trying to strangle her husband shortly before he was placed in a hospital. The rest of the session was spent in a detailed review of just how bad the last year of her husband's life had been. The incident she recalled had occurred after he had agitatedly accused her of having imaginary lovers. Around this time he had become not merely incompetent and incoherent but also paranoid. He slept at odd hours, and had to be watched lest he damage the house or hurt himself trying to repair something. What made the situation worse was the doctor's refusal to recognize her husband's mental deterioration, so that she felt she must be exaggerating things. The scene she remembered was a breaking point for her, and her husband was hospitalized shortly afterward.

Comment on Therapist's Strategies in Intermediate Sessions

Therapist's Stance. Having identified the probable cause of the depression and the two main interpersonal goals of the treatment during early sessions, the therapist approached each succeeding session with the general plan of listening for material related to the treatment goals and looking for opportunities to make incremental progress toward these goals. In the typical session the topics discussed were those brought in by the patient, who, as her depression improved, was highly articulate and motivated for treatment. The therapist listened to the patient's discussions with the intention of focusing and expanding material related, first, to thoughts and feelings about her husband and his death, and about life without him. In particular the therapist was alert to discussions of the ways she continued to restrict her life based on memories of him and of angry feelings about him, with the plan of helping her to recognize that she was free to run her own life and to accept the angry feelings. Second, the therapist listened for discussion of plans for new or expanded activities. In these discussions the therapist was alert for statements that indicated hesitations based on unrealistic assumptions and took opportunities to help the patient expand her thinking about options open to her.

Thus the therapist entered each session with general strategies in mind and tried to lead the discussion in specific directions. However, the specific topics discussed and the flow of the discussion followed from material the patient brought in. Allowed to take the initiative in choosing topics, the patient indicated in varied and surprising ways the extent to which her life revolved around continuing to grieve for her husband and refusing to give this up enough to allow new things in. The therapy sessions nearly always contained material on the two major themes of the therapy, mourning her husband and taking on new activities. However, as these issues were discussed in each session, new issues arose and progressively deeper revelations were made, culminating in the patient's statement that part of her guilt centered on her having attempted to strangle her husband in a fit of rage. The patient was able to reveal this secret only after developing a trusting relationship with the therapist and after accepting less difficult aspects of her dealing with her husband's illness and death. This repetition of the original version of the current picture with progressively greater revelation of guarded material is typical of a successful therapy and is often arrived at only after a seemingly meandering sequence of sessions in which the patient seems to progress only to move back to a level of discussion that characterized earlier sessions. An aspect of this repetition is the importance of significant detail, represented in this case by the discussion in Session 6 of her lost cats who had disappeared shortly after the husband's death and the follow-up in Session 7 of having acquired two new cats.

TERMINATION PHASE (SESSIONS 9–12)

In Session 9 Mrs. C. again reviewed her progress at school (she had gotten an A+ in her first-semester English course) and her activities with the senior citizens' center and friends. She described accepting the companionship of old people, which she had hesitated to seek at first because she could not accept the fact that she herself was really getting old. She was pleasantly surprised that an anticipated post-holiday slump had not occurred. She then discussed her concern that all this involvement with friends would hamper her independence, which she felt she must always guard fiercely. She recounted how, in foster homes as a teenager, she had received sexual advances from the men of many households. She felt that since that time she had always been cautious about trusting others. Discussion of termination was begun but was limited to her indication that she felt ready to stop and did not anticipate problems.

In Session 10 the patient mainly ran through a list of the areas in which she had made progress. She felt confident that her improvement would continue, although she was still concerned that medications were solely responsible for this. Twenty to thirty minutes into the session, and after a long silence, the patient asked if she could end the session early and the therapist consented.

Session 11 was focused on reviewing the depression and the therapy, and on discussing termination. The husband's decline and the patient's reaction to it were again briefly reviewed, as well as the progress she had made, which included an improved mood, increased comfort and freedom in day-to-day life on her own, improved relationships with her children, a wider range of activities and interests, and many new friends. She discussed her reactions to the therapy: she had been apprehensive at first but had become increasingly positive. She also said she had gotten better too quickly, and could not understand how things could change so much.

The therapist explained that the therapy had not really made her different, but had only allowed her to use the strengths and resources she already possessed. She had gotten depressed largely because she was socially isolated during her husband's long illness. What therapy had done was help her put this loss and her feelings about him in perspective. This had been sufficient to allow her to grow in the direction of her own interests and abilities.

No new material was discussed in Session 12. Mrs. C.'s progress was reviewed again and plans were made for the transfer of her pharmacotherapy to her private internist. The patient expressed her confidence in the future and her gratitude to the therapist.

Comment on Termination Sessions

In this case termination represented a winding down of therapy. The patient had experienced a complete symptomatic improvement and had made much progress toward resuming an active life. In addition, in Session 8 she had revealed an important secret about the degree of rage she had felt toward her husband. After that there were no more detailed reviews of the husband's final years and death and the intensity of the sessions was much reduced. Discussion of termination began and was part of each session after that. The therapist took care to make the ending date explicit and to elicit the patient's reactions to this. The patient was aware of primarily positive feelings about the therapy and the therapist. The patient's progress was frequently reviewed and the therapist emphasized to the patient how much she had contributed to this by active participation in the therapy and by overcoming many obstacles in order to take on new activities. There was also explicit discussion of treatment options should depression recur, with a review of the kinds of symptoms that might indicate that she was becoming depressed again.

CASE SUMMARY

Mrs. C.'s case is an example of a straightforward treatment of pathological grief. The patient had been unable to give up the grieving process because of excessive guilt associated with her anger toward her husband before and after his death. She had responded to his illness with self-denial but secret resentment. As he became progressively more debilitated she was at once horrified at the deterioration of a man on whom she had depended and angry with him for becoming such a burden on her. Her desire for him to die was conscious and even acted upon during a fit of anger. Moreover, she saw her decision to hospitalize him as signing his death warrant. After he died she felt continued resentment at being deprived of his company and his help in handling affairs, including the bills for his illness. Given her anger and her guilt in reaction to it, the patient could not allow herself to pleasurably pursue a life alone. Although she had many personal and social resources, she could not bring herself to take advantage of them.

The focus of the treatment was helping Mrs. C. relieve the guilt while prodding her in her efforts to develop new interests. To help her complete the mourning process, the patient's relationship with the husband, as well as his death and her reactions to it, were exhaustively reviewed, with special attention to painful affects such as sadness and guilty fear that she would be punished for her anger. Her personal resources were such that resolution of the mourning allowed her to improve dramatically.

The IPT Approach Compared with Other Approaches

INTERFACE WITH OTHER TYPES OF THERAPY

The therapist's handling of the case of Mrs. C. illustrates several of IPT's similarities to differences from other short-term psychotherapies.

The types of psychotherapy most like IPT are psychoanalytically oriented psychodynamic therapies such as those described by Malan (1963); Sifneos (1979); and Davenloo (1982). In these therapies the principal hypothesized curative feature is interpretation, which entails the linking of current conflicts, conflicts in childhood, and the transference relationship with the psychotherapist. The IPT conceptualization of the nature of the patient's problem is similar to that of psychodynamic therapists: that the patient was unable to complete the mourning process because of excessive guilt about her rage at her husband before and after his death. Much of Mrs. C.'s behavior can be explained by this guilt. Fearing massive retaliation for her angry thoughts, she needed to deny that her husband was dead to prevent a realization that she had contributed to his death and needed to punish herself to expiate her imagined transgressions against him. Thus she kept her house the way it was when he was alive and continued to feel miserable and deprive herself of opportunities for happiness.

The handling of this issue in an IPT therapy was, however, highly different from that of the other types of therapies. The IPT therapist concentrated exclusively on a review of the patient's experience of life with her husband and his death with an attempt to elicit the affects related to this. There was no attempt to explore childhood events in any detail or to link these with the patient's reactions to her husband's illness and death. Moreover, there was no attempt to explore the relationship with the therapist, despite many opportunities for this. For example, in Session 5 the patient expressed the desire to end the therapy early because she had experienced a symptomatic improvement and felt she was "wasting your time." In response the therapist discussed the possibility matter-of-factly, focusing on what lay ahead of the patient rather than on what had gone on between patient and therapist. As the patient revealed many apprehensions about what might happen next, she realized that she was not ready to stop. Faced with a patient who wants to terminate prematurely, the IPT therapist may choose to discuss aspects of the therapeutic relationship, but discussion of transference issues is reserved for cases in which interventions at other levels have not been successful or appropriate.

Similarly, when the patient brought Christmas cookies to the therapist in Session 8, there was no discussion of the meaning of this because productive work was being done in the discussion of topics more centrally related to the short-term treatment. And in the termination sessions the therapist did not challenge Mrs. C.'s discussion of having only positive feelings about the therapy and handled her apprehensions regarding a possible relapse with a realistic discussion of options rather than an attempt to elicit a discussion of her ambivalent feelings about dependence on others.

Thus one key difference between IPT and other types of psychodynamic short-term psychotherapies is what is *not* focused on, which in this case was the transference and childhood antecedents to current problems.

The way Mrs. C.'s depressive symptoms were addressed illustrates another difference between IPT and other psychodynamic therapies. Here the patient was explicitly reassured about the positive prognosis and treatment with medications begun after the second session, at which it had become apparent that reassurance alone had not resulted in symptomatic improvement.

A third difference is the degree to which the IPT therapist engaged in repeated discussion of specific changes the patient could make to get involved with life again by finding new and more satisfactory roles. In these discussions the therapist was careful not to advocate any specific course of action to the exclusion of others. Rather there was an attempt to discuss options, with the implication that trying these out would be useful.

IPT also differs from psychodynamic therapies in the handling of personality issues. Throughout her life Mrs. C.'s handling of interpersonal relationships showed that she had unresolved feelings of dependency, which she managed through denying the importance of others to her, keeping her distance from others, and taking care of others even when this was an intrusion into their lives, as in her relationship with her alcoholic son. Her surprise at the extent to which the death of her husband affected her is an indication of the counter-dependent attitudes she had adopted. The IPT therapist tried to help the patient formulate treatment goals consistent with her personality style. Since she needed others but had trouble acknowledging it, the therapist encouraged her to think about options for getting involved with others that included offering assistance to them. Hence, many of the options included volunteer jobs and friendships in which she offered something, such as transportation, to the other person. Although in the past this type of functioning had sometimes led to resentful feelings about being "used," these feelings had not usually led to disruption of the relationship. Thus the goal of IPT was to restore the patient to a previous level of functioning which she had considered adequate even though it might not be ideal. In contrast, the goal sought in the other psychodynamic therapies is resolution of key intrapsychic conflicts, which is supposed to lead to personality change.

The IPT therapist's emphasis on unresolved guilt differentiates this approach from a behavioral one, which might focus on the patient's failure to avail herself of reinforcing life experiences, and the cognitive therapist's emphasis on dysfunctional attitudes toward herself and her future. However, in Mrs. C.'s case the most striking differences between IPT and more behavioral treatments are technical. The IPT therapist was far less directive than a behavioral or cognitive therapist would have been. Although therapist and patient defined general areas in which work would be done, there was no explicit discussion of specifically targeted goals. Sessions were loosely structured around key issues, in contrast to the setting of an agenda that is part of cognitive therapy. Attempts to help the patient develop new activities took the form of discussions of options in which the therapist implicitly encouraged the patient to attempt new behaviors. No homework was assigned, progress was assessed in an informal manner, and specific suggestions were given sparingly. In contrast, behaviorist and cognitive therapies frequently involve repeated, explicit discussion of progress made, assignment of homework, and specific planning of actions the patient might take.

Levels of Intervention

The IPT therapist may try to bring about change through interventions at four different levels. In this case three of the levels of change were attempted and effected.

COMBATING DEMORALIZATION/MANAGING DEPRESSIVE SYMPTOMS

In this case the patient's depressive symptoms were elicited, summarized to her, and drawn together as indicative of a depressive episode in which her functioning was clearly different from what preceded it. She was reassured about prognosis. And in view of her good previous response to medications, she was treated with a tricyclic antidepressant.

INCREASING ACCEPTANCE OF SELF/OTHERS

This was a key to the therapy. The patient had not had the opportunity to evaluate the impact of her husband's death nor to get a realistic perspective on her handling of it. She had an exaggerated sense of having been excessively angry and inadequately caring. The therapy focused on helping her acknowledge and accept her angry feelings as natural and normal under the circumstances, and to give up her need to continue punishing herself for them.

TEACHING INTERPERSONAL COPING STRATEGIES

The patient had an adequate repertoire of methods for making friends, getting involved in activities, and keeping occupied with meaningful activities. However, she had temporarily lost her social contact through her exclusive involvement with her husband and she was now prevented from getting involved with others by excessive guilt and the need to deny her husband's death and her own independence. Hence as her symptoms were handled and her guilt abated she was able to use her interpersonal skills more effectively. The therapist's interventions in this area were focused on countering unrealistic or excessive fears of rejection from others through a thorough discussion of options for new activities.

HANDLING OF PSYCHODYNAMICS

As noted in the discussion of the interface between IPT and other psychodynamic therapies, the importance of excessive guilt was recognized by the therapist and focused on in the treatment. However, explicit interpretation of this material with reference to parallels in past and present relationships was not attempted.

Techniques

EXPLORATORY TECHNIQUES

Most of the therapist's activities in this case consisted of using exploratory techniques. The important aim in their use was to formulate a goal that would help the therapist determine what areas of discussion to expand upon. For example, in middle sessions the therapist was likely to elicit further information about the patient's reluctance to visit her husband's grave rather than a discussion of a visit from the son. The general goal of nondirective exploration is to help the patient and the therapist pinpoint what actually goes on in the patient's life, in an attempt to begin assessing where changes need to be made. Thus, there is an interplay between exploration and clarification and feeding back small formulations to the patient. An example of this pattern occurred in Session 1, when the therapist tried to develop an understanding of the things that kept the patient from seeing old friends. In this discussion it became clear that there was a distinction between anticipation of the event and the patient's actual ability to enjoy herself once in it.

Patient: I think I have a fear of . . . rejection so much that I don't institute any kind of a plan for anything. If anybody calls me and says do you want to do so-and-so, I'm glad to go, but I will not . . . initiate any type of activity . . . with anybody.

Therapist: How do you mean, fear of rejection?

Patient: Well, if they say no, I can't do it today, even though they give me a good excuse, it sort of throws me, you know, down into a hole, it's . . . almost like my fault that they can't do it, you know.

Therapist: Um-hm. Or that they're just making it up?

Patient: Yeah.

Therapist: I mean, is that really something that has happened to you a lot that people have sort of found you hard to be with or . . . ?

Patient: I don't think . . . I don't think so. I think that's . . . in my mind.

Therapist: Hm. You've . . . tended to feel like that for some time, or just more recently?

Patient: I probably . . . just . . . maybe more recently . . . Before, I, I think I always [sighs] probably had this feeling that, well, so what if anybody *did* reject me? Whatever . . . I initiated, I always had my husband to fall back on, you know, to, well, so that . . .

Therapist: Um-hm.

Patient: But now it's a little bit different. You just sort of, you hang up the phone, and you can't . . . [unclear] you know, other plans, or something. It's sort—you sort of say, well, what do I do now?

Therapist: Um-hm. When you make plans, it's hard to . . . you don't like to make plans very far in advance, or . . . ?

Patient: No.

Therapist: How come?

Patient: I don't know.

Therapist: So it's like you'll call up someone and want to do something today or tomorrow, that kind of thing?

Patient: Well, if I make a plan for, you know, an event, I can do that all right. But when the time comes, I sort of beat myself for having made that particular plan, because I really don't want to do it, you know, or at least I think I don't want to do it, I . . .

Therapist: And then when you do it?

Patient: Very opposite person or something . . . when I do it, I find I enjoyed it.

Therapist: Um-hm. So it really is, then a marked contrast between that antici . . .

Patient: I have sort of a conflict of some sort.

Therapist: Um-hm, it's like the anticipation of the event is really different from . . . the way it actually turns out.

Patient: Very.

Therapist: Just like . . . your anticipation that people won't or don't like you, and the way it turned out for instance when you were in the hospital, and people didn't want you to leave, that there is somehow . . . those things don't jibe.

Patient: Well . . . I don't have trouble getting along with people, I mean people generally like me. I'm not, you know, I'm not a pushy person, I don't . . . I . . . I'm pleasant enough, when I'm with people. . . . I, uh . . . I'm nervous inside, because I feel like I should be always chattering. And sometimes I come away from a group and think, you know, why, why do I always feel that I have to be always, my mouth always has to be going, and. . . . It's just that I can't stand silence, it's . . .

Therapist: Hm . . .

Patient: I can't stand silence in my house, my radio's going all the time.

Therapist: Um-hm. Do you get the message from people that you . . . talk too much, or that you . . .

Patient: No . . .

Therapist: So once again, I mean it seems . . . that . . . you kind of have a sense . . .

Patient: Like I'm a dual person, you know?

Therapist: How do you mean, a dual person?

Patient: Like part of me can do . . . do things that, uh, you know, I should be doing, and the other part of me just fights against doing them.

MANAGEMENT/ENCOURAGEMENT OF AFFECT

Elicitation of affect was a key aspect of Mrs. C.'s treatment. In reviewing her relationship with her husband there was an explicit attempt to help her experience sadness over the loss, with the plan of helping her realize that she can bear it; to feel anger at her husband, with the plan of helping her realize that it is an acceptable and normal feeling; and to experience loving feelings about her husband, with the plan of helping her see that she need not give these up even if she begins to allow new people and experiences into her life. Encouragement of affect took three primary forms: discussion of significant details in the patient's current and past life; naming her feelings; and encouraging her to accept the feelings as manageable and understandable.

Significant details were elicited throughout the therapy. These included the discussion of how the patient acted as though her husband were still in the house by sleeping on one side of the bed and keeping half of the closet open for him; discussion of what it was like when she attempted to visit the grave; discussion of her reactions to the loss of her cats, and many others.

The following segment from Session 4 illustrates the exploration of significant details.

Patient: The holidays are . . . sort of . . . a sad time for me because . . . [unclear] isn't going to keep me from doing . . . from, you know, decorating a little bit. I like Christmas. I like decorating the house. So . . . I-I just, when my husband isn't there, I still will . . . decorate.

Therapist: Mm-hm, mm-hm.

Patient: Because they're, they're pretty, the red, green—pretty colors.

Therapist: Mm-hm, mm-hm. It's still hard to think about doing things for yourself.

Patient: Well, I think that's where the guilt comes in, that he isn't here, you know. I—don't . . . do that much for myself. I—well, no, I'm picking up, I'm doing—quite a bit—but every once in awhile . . .

Therapist: Mm-hm.

Patient: I get this pang of guilt, thinking, well, gee, you shouldn't be, you shouldn't be so happy about things.

Therapist: Hm, mm-hm. Because if you're enjoying things, that means you can't be thinking about him?

Patient: I think about him less and less, but I don't . . . suddenly, all of a sudden, when I'm doing something that I'm enjoying, the thought intrudes that, you know, you shouldn't be so happy [chuckles].

Therapist: Hm, hm. I guess.

Patient: I'm *sure* he wouldn't want me to be—sad. . . .

Therapist: But in a way, hanging on to those sad thoughts . . . is a little like hanging on to him?

Patient: Probably. Something yesterday that I've been wanting to do for a long time, but yet not being able to, not . . . I guess maybe I didn't admit to myself that—that it had to be done . . . I called about a stone, for the, the grave.

Therapist: Hm.

Patient: And . . . probably will go out next week and pick it out. And maybe that'll help . . . lay things to rest a little bit. I have not been able to do it before.

Therapist: Hm. What, what had happened before, when you . . . tried to do it, or . . . think about it?

Patient: [sighs] I just couldn't think about it, I couldn't deal with it at all. When, in fact, I have been . . . I went to the cemetery once . . .

Therapist: Hm.

Patient: And . . . I was appalled, because . . . I went there, and I couldn't find . . . his grave, because there's no marker, or anything, and I had not . . . looked to see what was on either side of course, so I was . . . Maybe four or five graves there, with nothing on them. I didn't know which one . . . was, *was* his, which one was ours. And I was so appalled to think that . . . I'm *not* a cemetery person, I do *not* go every weekend, I wouldn't, because—that doesn't, I—I, I just—does nothing for me.

Therapist: Mm-hm.

Patient: But occasionally, it doesn't hurt, you know. I wasn't so appalled that I couldn't find him . . . where they are, and everything, where I'm getting the stone is . . . that I got the locks.

Therapist: Mm hm.

Patient: So I've never been back there again, because there's just—no need to go. But I'm not a—I am not one of these people that just goes out and . . . cries, and . . . which would . . .

Therapist: Mm-hm.

Patient: Which would probably make me too sad for a while.

Therapist: What's *too* sad?

Patient: That he's down there and I'm up here, I guess [laughing].

Therapist: How would you be if you're too sad?

Patient: I would, I . . . probably would have a crying fit. Really, probably take me a couple days to get over it, you know . . . that's so—you know —feeling like that is very immobilizing, I don't do anything. I wouldn't do anything. Where now I'm at least accomplishing something.

Therapist: Mm-hm.

Patient: May not sound much like to somebody else, but to me, it's . . . I have been. I'm—I feel like I've sort of . . . grown a little bit.

Therapist: Hm.

Patient: I don't have any fears about my mind going, at all, not at this point.

Therapist: Hm. Mm-hm.

Patient: And I'm not that old yet, either.

Therapist: So if you found a stone for him, though, he would have a place?

Patient: Probably that's the feeling I have, yeah.

Therapist: And that there would be . . .

Patient: And if I went there, it would be sort of . . . that would be sort of comforting, to know that I did, you know, get the things that—the *right* thing, probably.

Therapist: Mm-hm.

Patient: If there's a right and wrong, you know.

Therapist: Mm-hm.

Patient: I feel that would be the right thing to do.

Therapist: Mm-hm. But in a way, if he . . . doesn't really have a place, then . . . ?

Patient: He's just not laid to rest, you know, sort of.

Therapist: Mm-hm.

Patient: It's not, it's not finished, and I, I'd like it, at this point, like everything finished . . .

Therapist: Mm-hm, like with the bills too?

Patient: Right. I've just got about a couple more things, as far as the bills go.

Therapist: Mm-hm.

Patient: And [sighs] that will be settled. And I think that's, I just—I—I mean it'll be a big relief, when I can just put everything aside, and just go on.

Therapist: Mm-hm. But I guess there are two sides to the relief. I mean, one is that you really have settled them, and he's in a place, and, you know, the place is definitely *not* with you, and he is dead.

Patient: Yeah.

Therapist: But on the other hand, I guess, *having* these things still to do, in a way, keeps him around longer. You don't have to give him up.

CLARIFICATION

Naming the patient's feelings or clarifications were done frequently: for example, when the patient discussed having been so angry that she tried to strangle her husband, the therapist commented: "He did things to you that make anyone enraged—his threatening, his suspiciousness, his helplessness were enraging, and you got so angry you temporarily lost control."

In Mrs. C.'s therapy, clarifications usually took the form of tying together the different ways the patient discussed feelings, in an attempt to show her how they related to guilt thoughts and feelings regarding her husband. The intention was to help her recognize that the guilty fantasies were unrealistic and to help her develop an appropriate level of distance from the event. One example of this type of clarification comes from Session 4. The patient had discussed her happy anticipation of Christmas as well as the worrisome fact that her doctor had found a spot on her lung. Her immediate thought was that she had cancer and was going to die quickly, just as she was beginning to enjoy life.

Therapist: Mm-hm, I wonder if through the . . . guilty pang, and the . . . feeling that you're, you know, going to really get sick and die, if those really aren't kind of related in a way, you know, like, almost like you feel . . . that. . .

Patient: I should have died?

Therapist: Yeah . . . or that, you know, that it just, it's fitting that you would get sick, now he's gone.

Patient: I hope not.

Therapist: Mm-hm. But I think that maybe it's *thoughts*, you know.

Patient: Yeah, yeah . . .

Therapist: I mean, they're not realities. But . . . you know, I wonder . . .

Patient: I had them awhile ago, I, I had that type of fear maybe awhile ago but not . . . in the last couple of months.

Therapist: Mm-hm. Mm-hm.

Patient: I mean where, after, after he died, maybe two, three—a couple of months afterward.

Therapist: Mm-hm, Mm-hm.

Patient: I had those . . . types of thinking, but I haven't now.

Therapist: Well, but, you know, I guess the thing is, that as you're enjoying things, you know, and feeling . . .

Patient: Mm-hm.

Therapist: I don't, I don't think that those thoughts, I think you can think other things, you know.

Patient: Yeah . . .

Therapist: It's just that it seems to me that, uh . . .

Patient: They go together.

Therapist: Yeah, that, you know, that as you are starting to enjoy things, and feeling guilty, you know, it would sort of seem like . . . you know . . .

Patient: Just my luck.

Therapist: Yeah, right. I mean that this would be kind of a retribution for . . .

Patient: Yeah . . .

Therapist: For starting to enjoy yourself.

Patient: Well, the mind does a lot of crazy things, I guess.

Therapist: Hm, mm-hm, mm-hm. Well, I guess it's hard, because it—you know, if you do enjoy things, then you really are giving him up.

Patient: Yeah.

Therapist: You know, and you really are . . .

Patient: Maybe I'm not ready, quite ready to let go.

Therapist: Yeah. Entirely, that . . . and I think that, you know, the fact that you sort of stay away from . . . the grave, you know, because it scares you still, how sad you can get.

Patient: Yeah.

Therapist: You know, I, think that uh . . . I think that it's really . . . impressive that you are making the kind of progress that you are, but on the other hand I guess the thing is that, you know, I think you . . . you *don't* have to . . . forget about him. You know, you don't have to be . . . entirely without the memories.

Patient: Yeah . . . well, outside of that little guilty pang, thinking about him doesn't *hurt* quite as much as it had, but . . .

Therapist: Hm, mm-hm.

Patient: The hurt and the guilt—are, I don't know, are they related, sort of? I find that I'm not . . . uh, as lonely in the house at all. In fact, I enjoy being alone now, more . . .

Therapist: Hm.

Patient: And, uh . . . if I, when my daughter asks me to come over, just to sit, or, you know, I don't mean to babysit, but to come over, I don't feel the need that I have to run right over. If I'm tired, I say, I don't think I will tonight, you know.

Therapist: Mm-hm.

Patient: So [sighs] at one point, I just couldn't *wait* to get out of that house, but now it's beginning to take . . . shape . . . for *me*. My things are beginning to be . . . displayed. And, you know . . . little by little, his things are disappearing.

Therapist: Mm-hm.

Patient: Outside of a picture or two, you know.

Therapist: Mm-hm.

Patient: But . . . I have not been able to wholly . . . get rid of all of his clothes, for instance. . . . . I don't know why I'm waiting, I have a couple of bathrobes that are hanging there, and I thought, why did I leave these here? I don't know why I left them here.

Therapist: Mm-hm.

Patient: But I know that I'll get rid of them, you know . . . as soon as I start . . .

Therapist: Mm-hm. You'll get rid of them when you . . .

Patient: When it's time, yeah . . .

Therapist: When it's time. Mm-hm, mm-hm. And it's a little-by-little process.

Patient: Yeah, yeah. . . . Sometimes, after I've gotten . . . think of that, of something like that, I feel real good about it, I don't feel sad at all.

Therapist: Mm-hm.

Patient: In fact, I . . . most of these things, I took off to the thrift shop, where, you know, they're sold to the, for the poor people . . . wearable. My son didn't want anything, so I just thought, well, I would—rather than put, dump them in the Salvation Army, they have a thrift shop where nice . . . you know, the churches have it. . . .

Therapist: Hm.

Patient: And I find my going down to the cellar doesn't bother me quite as much as it did. And that's something else I have to get straightened out, but I'll do that after the holidays. . . .

Therapist: Mm-hm. So you can put some things off.

Patient: I can?

Therapist: You can.

Patient: Yes.

Therapist: Mm-hm.

Patient: My mind gets, my mind gets very . . . [chuckles] mixed up when I think of leaving. If anything happened to me, I think, oh, what a job it's going to be for somebody.

Another clarification occurred in Session 5:

Patient: I deserve staying in bed.

Therapist: Mm-hm. You mentioned before feeling guilty about going out, that you can go out now without feeling guilty. . . .

Patient: Well, it's just . . . I don't know what it is, feeling that—I shouldn't be enjoying myself. I don't know why.

Therapist: Hm.

Patient: But it's . . . I've sort of gotten . . . gotten over that, I think . . . or . . . this past week I didn't allow myself to think about it. I just have this feeling that all . . . [sighs] this is not happening to me, that . . . my house isn't mine, that I, you know . . . It's really—I always felt it, that, you know, the money that was made in that house was always his anyway, and that he never . . . showed that or anything. It was, it *was* just me that, you know, that way, so that I never spent money freely, or . . . unless it was my own money.

Therapist: Mm-hm.

Patient: Uh . . . because . . . you know, we would talk things over, before we bought anything, so it was a ha—a long, long habit, so it's *still* sort of ingrained in me that I shouldn't be doing this, without finding out [chuckles] if I can or not.

Therapist: Hm. Mm-hm. Feeling like you ought to discuss it with him?

Patient: Right.

Therapist: Mm-hm, mm-hm.

Patient: But gradually it's dawning on me that I'm my own person, and I've got to just, you know, stand on my own two feet, do what I want to do.

Therapist: Mm-hm. So, in other words if you want to go out to lunch or . . .

Patient: Just what I did this past week, right.

Therapist: If you want to go to a movie . . .

Patient: Or if I want to stay in bed, see . . .

Therapist: Mm-hm, mm-hm. But it's like you sort of anticipate . . . that something bad will happen if you—

Patient: Not necessarily. I don't think I went that far. It was just . . . something . . . that's just left over from when, from living with another person so long, and always . . . thinking, before I made any plans, whether, you know, he would like to go, or whether he would rather I didn't go. I, I really wasn't . . . as *free* when we were married as I am now. I do have a lot of freedom now, but—that was of my own making too. I think that . . .

Therapist: Hm. He probably would have thought it was OK if you were more independent?

Patient: Yeah. Right. Yeah, I'm sure he would have. I think a lot of my problems were made . . . in my mind.

BEHAVIOR CHANGE TECHNIQUES

As the therapist initiated discussions of different possibilities for developing a more active life, these took the form of reality-oriented considerations of options. Affordability and transportation were discussed, as well as what needs Mrs. C. might satisfy with activities of various sorts. Techniques such as direct advice and role playing were not necessary, since the patient herself took a great deal of initiative. This illustration of a discussion of options comes from Session 3:

Therapist: You know, last week we had discussed, we had talked about the fact that you know, it seems like . . . getting back to what we talked about a little earlier . . . that really, this *is* one of the first times in your life that you've really *been* as free as you are.

Patient: Yeah, in all my life, I think it's my . . .

Therapist: Mm-hm.

Patient: This is the freest I've ever been. And I really sometimes get very annoyed with myself, that I don't put my time to better use.

Therapist: Like . . . ?

Patient: Well, like doing something for somebody else, you know, I still have . . . perhaps doing some, doing some volunteer work somewhere . . .

Therapist: Hm.

Patient: I've been talking to a couple . . . people that I know who are doing some, one of the women . . . working in the convalescent home . . . goes in a couple of times a week and she loves it.

Therapist: Hm.

Patient: And it gives her a feeling of, you know, usefulness.

Therapist: Mm-hm. That seems like a big step to take?

Patient: Yes . . . it's a big step for me to take to call up. I'm . . . not a telephone person. I hate telephones, I've got to be . . . really desperate to pick up a telephone and call somebody . . . or something.

Therapist: Mm-hm. What about dropping by?

Patient: I never thought of that [chuckles]. That to me would be easier than telephoning.

Therapist: Mm-hm, mm-hm. Well, I mean, I . . . I suppose most places where you would volunteer, there must be someone there, you could . . . just go by and see. Or maybe you could go with a friend, or something like that.

Patient: Yeah . . . mm-hm. . . . Well, I-I-I'm still busy trying to get myself . . . in order, that, I'll . . . sort of let that rest a little while.

Therapist: Mm-hm. Well, I guess the thing about, though, having a lot of freedom is that it really, always brings up . . . issues like—you know, what are the things that are satisfying to you? You know, what is it that you want out of life?

Patient: Well, see, I always wanted to go, I'd always . . . I grew up thinking that I never was able to go to college. . . .

Therapist: Hm.

Patient: So . . . now I've got this freedom, and my son said, "Why don't you take a course? That'll keep you occupied and interested . . ."

Therapist: Mm-hm.

Patient: So [sighs] he said, "Why don't you go down to . . ." you know . . . the one down on . . . Anyway, I took South Central, because I thought it was easier for me to get there than it was to go to Southern.

Therapist: Mm-hm, mm-hm. I think South Central also generally does have more . . . community people.

Patient: Yeah . . .

Therapist: Instead of, you know, Southern tends to be more eighteen-year-olds.

Patient: Yeah . . .

Therapist: That kind of thing. Mm-hm.

Patient: Of course, as a senior citizen, there are a lot of things that are open to you, like I don't have to pay for the courses that I take.

Therapist: Hm.

Patient: I pay for my books, but I don't have to pay . . .

Therapist: Mm-hm, mm-hm. Well, have you thought of taking more than one course? Or are you really trying to get a degree?

Patient: Well, I have, I have . . . well, I thought I would like to get an associate degree. I don't know in what, but I always like that, because South Central . . . South Central is . . . a two-year course anyway. So I have to talk to, I have to go down, to get to talk to a counselor there, see what's open for me.

Therapist: Mm-hm, mm-hm.

Patient: Well, this course that I'm taking now, English course, is . . . a lot of writing, I . . . think, my goodness, if I took two courses I'd go crazy.

Therapist: Mm-hm. Well. I guess that's the thing about freedom, is that you have to—decide on what you're . . .

Patient: Yeah.

Therapist: What it is that you want?

Patient: Because I still want some freedom. For myself.

Therapist: Mm-hm.

Patient: To do . . . other things that I like to do.

Therapist: Well, so, so one of the things then, that you want to have in your —as part of your life—picture—the way that you would be organizing your life—would be . . . at least a minimum amount of time at home, or, you know, taking care of the house and I guess being *in* the house that you like.

Patient: Yeah. . . .

Therapist: And . . . you know, just having a sense that it's yours, and relaxation, that sort of thing. And, you know, another aspect of it I guess would be that you'd want to make sure that you *had* time to . . . you know, do some socializing.

Patient: Mm-hm.

Therapist: To, maybe . . . after all, one of the advantages of being retired is that you can . . . spend time doing recreation.

Patient: That's right.

Therapist: That kind of thing.

Patient: As long as you're healthy enough to do that.

Therapist: Mm-hm. But . . . on the other hand, it seems like . . . there are other things . . . that you want to be able to have a sense of building, or of accomplishment.

Patient: Yeah, I've got to, I've got to really sort of pinpoint what I really want to do because my mind whirls around . . . doing this, this, this, this, and . . . uh . . .

Therapist: Well, what . . . ?

Patient: And I don't think that you can . . .

Therapist: Mm-hm.

Patient: You can [sighs] do a good job at everything that you want to do, you know.

Therapist: Mm-hm, mm-hm. Well, what are the things that you've been considering?

Patient: Nothing specific, it's just that my mind is just whirling around. . . .

Therapist: Well, where does it whirl?

Patient: Well, first the volunteer stuff, that, that part . . .

Therapist: Mm-hm. Any particular kind of volunteer?

Patient: No, I hadn't really thought about any kind of volunteer work, and I've been sort of . . . I don't know, I don't know whether I want to work with the elderly or the children . . .

Therapist: Mm-hm.

Patient: Sometimes I think I'd like to work with the elderly, and, you know, then I think maybe I'd rather work with children, so I have to make up my own mind about that.

Therapist: Mm-hm.

Patient: And I think that . . . I haven't really . . . gone into it, I think the senior citizens do have a program . . . for volunteer work too, so that . . .

Therapist: Hm.

Patient: I might be into something there.

Therapist: Mm-hm.

Patient: As I get better acquainted.

Therapist: Mm-hm. So one possibility would be to do some . . . volunteer work, which I guess would be satisfying in the sense that . . .

Patient: Yeah, if it's just one day a week, I think it would sort of satisfy me . . .

Therapist: Mm-hm, mm-hm.

Patient: I think this woman I was talking about, I think she started with one day and decided she had to go two days, because she enjoyed it, and they . . . really looked forward to having her come.

Therapist: Mm-hm.

Patient: So it sort of gives her a sense of being needed, and accomplishing something too.

Therapist: Mm-hm. Then another whole area, though, is the idea of— I guess learning more: I'm going to still be curious about things, and . . .

Patient: Yeah . . .

Therapist: Wanting to . . . ?

Patient: Yeah, I certainly don't want to just sit in a chair and watch television. I don't . . . watch that much television anyway. Nothing much on, you know?

COMMUNICATION ANALYSIS

In this case communication analysis was not used at all, although if, for example, the patient had had difficulty in engaging others in discussion as she tried to get involved in the senior citizens' group, this might have been used.

USE OF THE THERAPEUTIC RELATIONSHIP

If the patient had been more resistant to the work of the psychotherapy, the therapist might well have tried to draw parallels between the patient's interpersonal problems outside of therapy and her behavior in the therapy sessions. As it turned out, this was not necessary.

PART III

SELECTED

ASPECTS OF IPT

A social or interpersonal approach does not deny the
importance of unconscious mental process, of childhood
experience or of biological vulnerability or personality
traits, but they reach their capacity to determine behavior through their ability to influence the patient's definition of the situation in the "here and now."

—Harry Stack Sullivan
The Interpersonal Theory of Psychiatry

Chapter 13

Combining Psychotherapy with Pharmacotherapy

Although the main purpose of this book is to describe the place of interpersonal psychotherapy in the treatment of depression, a discussion of pharmacotherapy is needed because our experience and the research evidence indicate that a considerable proportion of depressed patients benefit from the use of drugs combined with IPT. In this chapter we will deal with some general issues in combining drugs with psychotherapy; describe the drugs most often used in treating depressed patients; suggest guidelines for selecting patients who might benefit from the combination of therapies; and offer specific guidance in the technical aspects of introducing drugs into the psychotherapy, which include explaining the treatment to patients and, when necessary, working with a physician.

The Role of Patient Attitudes and Psychotherapist Attitudes

The major difficulties in combining drugs and psychotherapy do not lie in understanding the pharmacology of drugs or any of the specific problems of treatment. They have to do with patient and therapist attitudes.

American society is deeply divided about the efficacy, as well as the moral and social legitimacy, of drug treatment for emotional and psychiatric disorders. Nationwide surveys (Uhlenhuth, Balter, and Lipman, 1978) indicate that many patients who feel that they have been helped by tranquilizers and antidepressants, nevertheless report that they think drug therapy is less than the ideal way of coping with their emotional and psychological problems. There is a pervasive attitude that the use of medication is a "crutch," that problems should be solved via self-reliance, personal initiative, and "will power." It follows that efforts to get professional help for emotional and psychological problems are viewed as "failure" or "weakness." Although this attitude has decreased dramatically in the past thirty years, it is still widespread.

Even patients who seek professional help for their emotional problems, including depression, tend to think that the most desirable way to deal with them is by psychological means, the gaining of insight and understanding. In this view, drug therapy is a second-class form of psychiatric treatment, reserved for individuals who are not capable of understanding and insight.

These views are mirrored within the mental health professions. Even among psychiatrists—the mental health professionals who by training know most about medication and who are the only ones legally empowered to prescribe medications—there are deep splits over the value of drugs. Surveys indicate that the psychiatric profession is split in a number of different ways, and that one main factor dividing it is disagreement about whether drug therapy is effective and whether, even if it is effective, it is desirable. The psychiatrists who identify themselves as biological psychiatrists are a small but significant minority. Although they make up less than 20 percent of the members of the profession, they have gained considerable scientific and professional status because of advances in the development of new drugs and in the biological sciences in general. These advances have led to better understanding of the pharmacology of drugs and the biochemical and physiological abnormalities that underlie some psychiatric disorders (Wender and Klein, 1981).

For therapists and patients alike, attitudes toward the use of medication not only involve larger social values but affect the meaning that the use of drugs has for the individual. For a patient, a decision to take medication is often related to issues of dependence and independence, control of one's destiny, and sense of responsibility and power.

These issues are illustrated in two contrasting case vignettes. Both involve adults who sought medication because of long-standing emotional problems after many years of psychotherapy of various sorts.

Arnold B., a forty-six-year-old male psychologist, had been very successful in his professional work but had a sense of frustration, low self-esteem, and personal inadequacy that had persisted since boyhood. Because of this he had never been successful in relationships with women and had remained unmarried. He had few friends except professional colleagues. Much of his satisfaction was tied up with his work as a member of a staff of a clinic associated with a university medical center. He and his father had spent many years in a chronic struggle: the son saw his father as intrusive and dominating of all the children but particularly himself. To separate himself from his father he went to graduate school and set up his practice two thousand miles from his family. Chronically frustrated and bitter, he had been in and out of various forms of psychotherapy since graduate school.

Soon after moving to Boston, to join the faculty of a graduate school program, he sought psychiatric help because of the vegetative signs that had begun to accompany his chronic depression. He was also having early morning awakening and had developed a neck pain which was variously diagnosed as coming from cervical disc trouble or muscle tension. Although he himself raised the question whether or not medication would be useful, he was extremely conflicted over the use of medicine, and only when his neck problems exacerbated and he was having progressive early morning awakening did he request the use of a tricyclic. With 150 mg. of amitriptyline there was a rapid decrease in the sleep difficulty and, more strikingly, in his self-depreciation, bitterness, and frustration. His attitude toward his parents, especially his father, improved and he looked forward to visiting them for the Christmas holidays in the hope of working for a better relationship.

His attitude toward the success of the medication was one of a great deal of satisfaction and a sense of having been relieved of a great burden of guilt and self-depreciation that had tormented him for many years. A month after the symptoms had abated, he expressed a great deal of anger toward previous therapists, raising the question whether the use of medication earlier in his life might have produced a happier and better adjustment.

With the subsidence of his symptoms he began to work with his therapist on the question "What am I going to do for myself to make myself happy, now that I'm grownup and successful?"

Barbara W., a twenty-eight-year-old occupational therapist, had been working in the in-patient unit of a psychiatric hospital since her graduation from occupational therapy school and her internship. She had been in psychotherapy ever since her adolescence, when she began to have conflicts with her mother over such matters as choice of dress and selection of boy friends. As long as she could remember she and her mother had been locked in a struggle for control, the patient resisting the mother's attempts to influence her life. The patient saw these efforts as domineering, representing the mother's attempt to live vicariously through her daughter's social, sexual, and occupational achievements.

Mrs. W. had been married for a number of years and had one small child. Although the child was developing well, she was tormented by the feeling that she was not giving enough to the child and that the amount of time she spent in her professional work made her less attentive toward her family. Although the marriage had been turbulent ever since their courtship, her husband, an engineer, had at first refused to consider marital treatment, feeling that if they worked hard enough on their problems they could find some solution themselves. While Barbara was in individual therapy, their sexual adjustment had improved considerably and her husband agreed to couple therapy. She described her husband as very satisfied sexually, although she herself was not always capable of reaching orgasm.

The patient came for possible medication on the suggestion of her psychotherapist, who had been seeing her and her husband in couple therapy for a number of years. Although the quality of the relationship between the patient and her husband had improved considerably, the therapist noted that she still had a low-grade depression, a sense of low self-esteem and self-depreciation out of proportion to her actual life circumstance and to her genuine accomplishments as a professional and as a mother and wife.

The patient was started on imipramine, 125 mg. a day, and within a week reported a decrease in her low self-esteem and a particular sense of increased vitality and activity level. This increased zest for life and activity made her question whether she was having a hypomanic episode and whether she was basically "bipolar."

On the one hand she was extremely pleased with the relief of her distress and the sense of energy, competence, and accomplishment that developed during the weeks after she began medication. On the other, she felt she had lost control over her emotions. She had always prided herself on the hope that if she gained sufficient understanding and insight she could master her emotional state and control her feelings as well as her life circumstances. To her the use of medication represented a challenge to her aspiration for self-mastery. It suggested that some parts of her destiny might be controlled, not by her wishes and understanding but by some biochemical imbalance in her central nervous system.

These two cases illustrate the conflict and ambivalence in our society in general and in the mental health professions in particular about the use of medication in psychotherapy. For the first patient, the medication brought a relief; his feeling was, "Now I don't have to feel responsible for what happened to me." In contrast, the second patient felt the medication took away from her the possibility of determining her own destiny.

The Drugs and Their Utility

A range of effective biological and psychological treatments is available for depression (Paykel, 1982; Klerman and Hirschfeld, 1978). Selecting the most appropriate intervention for each patient requires not only careful assessment of the patient's symptomatology, familial situation, and social resources but also a knowledge of the available therapies.

TRICYCLIC ANTIDEPRESSANTS

The tricyclics are generally the first choice because of their superior efficacy and safety. There are three chemical subseries that share similar pharmacological and clinical actions, but there are differences in dosage and side effects, especially sedative properties. The clinical antidepressant effect of the tricyclic drugs is probably related to their capacity to potentiate the CNS actions of such biochemical neurotransmitters as norepinephrine and serotonin.

The dose range of the tricyclic compounds is wide. It is possible to start patients at a low dosage—for example, 20 to 40 mg. a day of imipramine hydrochloride or its equivalent—and gradually build up to 200 to 300 mg. a day. The therapeutic response may require from two to four weeks of treatment. The adequate dosage is arrived at by gradually increasing the total daily dose until the therapeutically desired response develops or the patient cannot tolerate the side effects. The best recommendation is to proceed with careful regulation of dosage and observation for improvement or adverse effects. If some clinical response has not occurred within four to six weeks at an adequate and individualized dose, continued use of the drug is usually not worthwhile, and an alternate treatment should be considered.

Although the tricyclic drugs are relatively safe, a variety of adverse effects, mostly minor, occur, particularly with dosages larger than 200 to 300 mg. a day. The most common are sedation and atropinic effects—dry mouth, increased sweating, difficulty in visual accommodation, memory difficulty, and urinary retention. The most serious side effects concern the cardiovascular system. Orthostatic hypotension, palpitations, arrhythmias, tachycardia, and ECG abnormalities may occur when tricyclic antidepressants are used.

A history of glaucoma requires consultation with an ophthalmologist before tricyclics are used. Similarly, a history of cardiovascular disease, particularly arrhythmias or previous myocardial infarctions, should prompt a consultation with a cardiologist.

MONOAMINE OXIDASE INHIBITORS (MAO INHIBITORS)

In general, the MAO inhibitors should not be the first choice of drugs to treat most depressed patients, but they may be useful when there is a previous history of positive response by the patient or a family member or when the patient has not responded to tricyclic antidepressants.

Since the observations by West and Dally (1959) of what are called "atypical depressions," further research has documented the value of MAO inhibitors in patients with a clinical syndrome characterized by anxiety, phobias, hysterical features, and the relative absence of vegetative signs such as early morning wakening and weight loss.

The MAO inhibitors are divided into two subgroups based on chemical structure. Both groups inhibit monoamine oxidase activity, which, like the tricyclics, results in the potentiation of the central amine neurotransmitters. In depressed patients, pharmacologically induced reduction in monoamine oxidase activity correlates with improvement in the patient's mood and clinical symptoms.

Although the MAO inhibitors were introduced into therapeutics before the tricyclic antidepressants, two factors limit their clinical usefulness as compared with that of the tricyclics. First, controlled comparisons indicate that the MAO inhibitors are generally less effective than the tricyclics. Second, they are more toxic and have a higher frequency of toxic reactions. Recently, however, research studies have demonstrated their efficacy when a sufficient degree of enzyme inhibition is achieved in selected patients.

Clinical guidelines for dosage are not well established. Starting doses are between 20 and 40 mg. and should be gradually increased over two to three weeks. Response may be delayed. A method exists for measuring platelet MAO enzyme level and this has proven useful.

Minor side effects such as dry mouth and other anticholinergic effects may occur. The main clinical problem is the risk of hypertensive crises resulting from toxic interactions with certain foods or other drugs. The use of MAO inhibitors requires an intelligent, cooperative patient who will adhere to dietary restrictions and who can recognize symptoms of rising blood pressure.

PHENOTHIAZINES AND OTHER NEUROLEPTICS

Phenothiazines are sometimes used in the treatment of acute depressions in patients who have intense agitation, insomnia, and delusions as part of their psychotic depression. The phenothiazines can be readily combined with the tricyclics. The combination of perphenazine and amitriptyline hydrochloride is marketed in several forms and is widely used.

LITHIUM

Lithium carbonate, a simple inorganic substance, interacts with many biological systems and has pharmacologic actions on several biogenic amine processes simultaneously. Presumably lithium acts by altering the electrical conductivity of the CNS. Lithium is of proved efficacy in treating manic-depressive (bipolar) illness, for both short- and long-term therapy. Some patients with recurrent unipolar depression also respond well to lithium maintenance treatment. There is a continuing search to identify a lithium-responsive subgroup of depressed patients. The use of lithium in acute depressions should be limited to those patients who have a bipolar disorder and/or who are unresponsive to other treatments or risk a manic episode precipitated by tricyclics. Lithium administration must be accompanied by conscientious clinical observation and monitoring of blood levels to prevent a toxic reaction.

BLOOD LEVELS

Blood levels of tricyclic drugs or platelet MAO levels are not now considered routine procedures. Although they are still in the research stage, it is likely that in the near future, as the methodology improves, they will be incorporated into routine clinical practice.

MINOR TRANQUILIZERS

Meprobamate and the benzodiazepine derivatives are used for depression because of their capacity to reduce anxiety and insomnia. Their effects are mainly short-term, and they do not lend themselves to use for more than four to six weeks because of possible habituation and the need to increase the dosage. An important distinction must be made regarding types of insomnia. Minor tranquilizers are useful for patients who have trouble falling asleep, but they are less useful for patients who have early morning awakening, one of the cardinal signs of severe depression.

PSYCHOMOTOR STIMULANTS

In clinical practice today, amphetamines (dextroamphetamine sulfate and methylphenidate hydrochloride) have a limited place, if any, in the treatment of most depressions. This limitation is due to their lack of efficacy, their short-lived clinical effect, the development of tolerance, the risk of habituation and dependence, and their adverse side effects.

Methylphenidate may be useful when combined with tricyclics. It has a mood-stimulating effect for patients with neurasthenic and fatigue-like symptoms. In addition, research has shown that a combination of methylphenidate and tricyclics results in an elevated blood level of the tricyclics.

BARBITURATES AND OTHER SEDATIVE-HYPNOTICS

Phenobarbital, pentobarbital sodium, glutethimide, and methaqualone are not recommended for treating depressions. They are generally ineffective, can be toxic, and are best replaced by more efficacious antidepressants.

ELECTROCONVULSIVE THERAPY (ECT)

For severely depressed patients with marked psychomotor retardation or agitation and delusions, ECT is an appropriate treatment, although often controversial. It is also useful for patients who do not respond to other treatments. ECT is of great value for patients with intense suicidal drive and with whom one does not wish to wait five to fifteen days for drug treatment to take effect; for the severely depressed; and for patients whose medical condition contraindicates the use of drugs. The major adverse effect of ECT is memory loss, which, while temporary and rarely severe, is distressing to the patient. Refinements in technology and limitations on the frequency and number of treatments have increased the efficacy of ECT while ameliorating its side effects, especially by reducing memory loss when unilateral ECT is used. ECT can be administered either bilaterally or unilaterally. There is some evidence that unilateral ECT produces less side effects, particularly less reduction of memory. However, there is also evidence that bilateral treatment is more effective for larger percentages of patients.

DURATION OF DRUG TREATMENT

It is important not to stop drug treatment too early, which may precipitate a relapse. Treatment should be continued for at least several weeks after complete symptom relief and then tapered off. In practice, treatment of acute depressive episodes with tricyclic drugs for a period of two to about six months is common.

It is not possible to give firm guidelines about duration of treatment. In practice, the physician is performing a titration—the dose should be gradually lowered to ascertain the lowest feasible dose at which there is not a return of symptoms. This can usually be done in weekly or ten day episodes.

HOSPITALIZATION

Most clinicians prefer to use drug treatment and psychotherapies on an ambulatory basis and thus avoid hospitalization. In current practice, most patients with depressions can be treated effectively on an outpatient basis. However, for severely depressed patients, hospitalization should be considered, especially if suicidal ideation, delusions, or serious medical complications are present.

ECT is usually the most effective treatment for severe depression. Phenothiazines may also be helpful for patients who are experiencing hallucinations or delusions. Difficult, complex, or unresponsive cases of depression may require consultation by psychotherapists, psychologists, and specialists in psychopharmacology.

LONG-TERM DRUG TREATMENT

Problems of relapse, chronicity, and recurrence have brought a recent increase in decisions in favor of long-term drug treatment (Gelenberg and Klerman, 1978; Davis, 1976). Various terms—including "long-term treatment," "continuation treatment," "maintenance treatment," and "prophylaxis"—are used, but the distinctions are trivial.

The decision to begin long-term therapy involves the number, type, and severity of affective episodes; the social consequences of the illness; and the patient's wishes, personality, degree of self-responsibility, medical history, and family situation. Long-term therapy is seldom initiated at the first attack of a mood disorder, especially depression, unless a diagnosis of bipolar disorder is made at once. A questionable diagnosis and/or mild or infrequent episodes of depression are indications that long-term treatment is not warranted, or at least not yet. If the depression is severe and the social consequences of relapse are likely to be great, then long-term treatment should be considered. In general, the more previous episodes there have been, whether treated or hospitalized or not, and the briefer the interval between episodes, the more suitable the patient is for long-term treatment. According to the Prien, Klett, and Caffey (1973) report, patients with two hospitalizations within five years have a 90 percent probability of relapse without maintenance treatment. If long-term treatment is necessary, one or more of the following treatments can be used:

Tricyclic Antidepressants. The current literature suggests that for nonbipolar patients who have responded to tricyclics in previous acute episodes, maintenance tricyclic drugs are effective in decreasing the likelihood and/or severity of future attacks. Since tricyclic drugs often precipitate mania in bipolar patients, accurate diagnosis is essential before long-term tricyclic treatment is prescribed. Average doses are 100 mg. a day for long-term treatment, but variations will depend on the individual patient's response to the drug and tolerance of side effects.

Lithium. For bipolar patients, lithium is the first choice for long-term drug therapy. However, there is a growing body of literature (reported by Davis, 1976) indicating that lithium produces a significant reduction in the number of recurrences and an improvement in social and psychological adjustment in the long-term treatment of many recurrent unipolar patients.

Evidence for Efficacy of Combined Treatments

The efficacy of tricyclic antidepressants for nonbipolar depression has been demonstrated in more than a hundred controlled clinical trials. There is also evidence from twenty-five trials for the efficacy of various psychotherapies for depression (Weissman, 1979, 1984). Until recently, however, empirical evidence for the differential effects of pharmacotherapy compared with or combined with psychotherapy in the treatment of depression has been absent. As a result, the therapist's decision whether to use pharmacotherapy or psychotherapy or a combination in treating depressed patients has been based on ideology rather than data (GAP, 1975).

ANTIDEPRESSANTS COMBINED WITH PSYCHOTHERAPY

Positive Effects. The combination of antidepressants and psychotherapy is probably the treatment most commonly offered for depression, and this trend represents the belief that the two forms of treatment are compatible and complementary. Several studies have suggested that drugs and psychotherapy have an additive effect in the treatment of depression (GAP, 1975; Klerman, 1976). The additive effect may be due to several factors. Psychotherapy may be useful in obtaining compliance with the medication schedule by providing patients with a supportive clinical contact and a relatively consistent access to reassurance about side effects, delayed onset of action, and other things that may cause worry. Alternatively, pharmacotherapy may lead to better attendance and optimism in psychotherapy through a placebo effect, even if the drugs themselves are ineffective. These additive effects might be evidenced if the combined treatment group were found to have a lower dropout rate than the groups with psychotherapy or pharmacotherapy alone. Finally, pharmacotherapy may facilitate the psychotherapy process by keeping symptom levels under control and allowing the patient to make better use of the psychotherapy. For example, patients who are sleeping better and experiencing less confusion and psychomotor retardation or agitation will be more likely to communicate effectively with the psychotherapist in dealing with psychological and interpersonal issues.

Interaction between psychotherapy and pharmacotherapy may be additive, with each producing independent effects, or synergistic, with the two treatments positively interacting, effecting greater improvement when combined than would result from the sum of each treatment alone. In the four completed studies that used a factorial design, evidence for combined treatment effects can be evaluated. In the Klerman et al. (1974) study of interpersonal psychotherapy and/or amitriptyline as maintenance treatment, patients receiving pharmacotherapy had lower relapse rates. Patients receiving psychotherapy had improved social functioning, and there were no negative interactions between treatments. These results suggest that the two treatments together are additive.

In the reports of the effects of interpersonal psychotherapy and amitriptyline as acute treatment for a current depressive episode (Weissman et al., 1979; DiMascio et al., 1979); Weissman et al., 1981) patients in the combined treatment group were more likely to complete treatment than those receiving either treatment alone. A pairwise comparison of rates of symptomatic failure in the treatment groups revealed a trend toward superiority of the combined treatment over either treatment alone. Evaluation of symptom levels over the course of treatment revealed a consistent superiority of combined treatment over either treatment alone, which resulted from psychotherapy and pharmacotherapy exerting effects on different aspects of depression. Pharmacotherapy relieved sleep and other vegetative symptoms, and psychotherapy relieved cognitive symptoms such as apathy and hopelessness. At the one-year follow-up, for patients who received at least eight weeks of treatment the combined treatment proved superior to either treatment alone on self-reported symptom measures and to the pharmacotherapy group on measures of social functioning (Weissman et al., 1981; Rounsaville, Klerman, and Weissman, 1981).

In the Friedman (1975) study of marital psychotherapy and amitriptyline, alone and in combination, there was no difference in early dropout rates across treatment groups. The main effect for marital therapy noted at the end of treatment was strongest on measures of marital satisfaction and family functioning and detectable on symptom measures, while complementary effects were detected for pharmacotherapy, which had stronger effects on symptoms and weaker effects on social functioning. An additive effect can be presumed from this study, although the data are not presented in a way that allows a direct comparison of treatment cells.

In the Covi et al. (1974) study of group psychotherapy and pharmacotherapy, alone and in combination, the only significant treatment effect was for imipramine over diazepam or placebo. A small number of significant drug and psychotherapy interactions was reported in a factorial design, but no more than might be expected by chance. Hence the effect of combining psychotherapy and imipramine in this study was not distinguishable from the use of imipramine alone.

To sum up the findings regarding positive effects of combined psychotherapy and pharmacotherapy in the three studies that found a psychotherapy effect, there appeared to be an additive effect of psychotherapy and pharmacotherapy, which resulted from each treatment's affecting a different aspect of the patient's condition. Pharmacotherapy had a comparatively early effect on depressive symptoms, particularly of the somatic type, and psychotherapy had a later effect on social functioning or the cognitive types of depressive symptoms. In only one study was evidence presented for a positive effect of combined treatment on attendance (Herceg-Baron et al., 1979).

Negative Effects.

A number of ways in which drugs and psychotherapy might interfere with each other have been suggested. Using data derived from a clinical trial evaluating the efficacy of interpersonal psychotherapy as acute treatment for a current depressive episode, Rounsaville, Klerman, and Weissman (1981) described six hypotheses regarding potential negative effects of combined treatment and tested these hypotheses using data from the Weissman et al. study. Four of the six hypotheses concerned possible negative effects of drugs on psychotherapy, and these were evaluated by comparing the combined treatment group with the psychotherapy alone group.

The first hypothesis, the "negative placebo effect," proposed that the use of drugs encourages the therapist's directiveness and the patient's passivity, stifling therapist's efforts to encourage the patient to assume responsibility for self-exploration and change. An evaluation of the process of psychotherapy, in which the combined treatment group and the psychotherapy alone group were compared, revealed no differences in such factors as reflectiveness of the patient, techniques used by the therapist, and topics discussed by the patient. Hence there was no support for this hypothesis.

The second hypothesis was that a drug-induced reduction of symptoms might undermine the patient's motivation for continuing in psychotherapy. The data revealed that the combined treatment group had more rapid symptom reduction and greater retention in treatment than the psychotherapy alone group, which disconfirmed the hypothesis.

The third hypothesis suggested that pharmacotherapy might undercut the patient's defenses, since reduction of symptoms might deprive the patient of dynamically useful behavior and lead to symptom substitution or decompensation. Analysis of symptom levels during treatment and at the one-year posttreatment follow-up revealed no differences in the rate of decompensation or symptom substitution between the combined treatment group and the psychotherapy alone group.

The fourth hypothesis suggested that offering pharmacotherapy to a psychotherapy patient might be perceived as a devaluation of the patient's ability to manage independently. It might be expected, therefore, that the patient would refuse the combined treatment. This was not confirmed, since initial refusal rates were higher for the psychotherapy alone condition than for the combined treatment condition.

The remaining two hypotheses, which concerned possible negative effects of psychotherapy on pharmacotherapy, were evaluated by comparing the combined treatment group with the pharmacotherapy alone group. The first hypothesis was that psychotherapy may be symptomatically disruptive. By encouraging the patient to explore conflictual material the psychotherapist may be working against the beneficial effects of the medication. This hypothesis was notably disconfirmed, since the combined treatment group experienced greater improvement of depressive symptoms than the pharmacotherapy alone group. The second hypothesis was that replacement of hypothetical biochemical deficits is the only rational treatment of depression, and use of psychotherapy thus diverts the patient from seeking effective treatment (pharmacotherapy) by encouraging him to make use of an ineffective treatment (psychotherapy). The study found that patients receiving combined treatment were more likely to remain in treatment and hence to receive drugs. Moreover, follow-up revealed that, in the year following the study, the pharmacotherapy group was equally likely to make use of both psychotherapy and pharmacotherapy as was the combined treatment group. In summary, the Rounsaville, Klerman, and Weissman study found no evidence supporting any of the hypothetical negative effects of combining drugs and psychotherapy.

Friedman, discussing the clinician's impression that marital therapy sessions were characterized by less hostile interactions after the patient began to feel some symptomatic relief, suggested that pharmacotherapy begin several weeks before initiation of marital psychotherapy. In the remaining two completed studies (Klerman et al.; Covi et al.), no negative interactions were reported.
Summary of Positive and Negative Effects.

In reviewing the results from studies that included a combined treatment group, a preponderance of evidence for a positive, additive effect of combined treatment was found, while there was no evidence for negative effects. These results provide guidance in the treatment of ambulatory nonpsychotic, nonbipolar, moderately ill, depressed patients. Drugs and psychotherapy together maximize efficacy and seem to be the treatment of choice. However, in clinical practice, many patients will not or cannot tolerate tricyclic antidepressants, and other patients do not wish to enter psychotherapy. In both cases the patient should not be denied treatment but offered the acceptable alternative.

Selecting Patients for Combined Treatment

In making decisions about the possible value of drug treatment, assessment of severity is often useful (Mandel and Klerman, 1978), in addition to diagnoses of subtypes of depression. In mild depression the indication for antidepressant treatment is often not clear and must be left to the judgment of the therapist. Both no drug treatment and the administration of tricyclics with or without psychotherapy are viable options. Psychotherapy alone is most often used with these patients.

Moderately depressed patients are often helped by antidepressant drugs used conjointly with psychotherapy, and the tricyclics have the greatest efficacy and best relative margin of safety. The clearest indication for tricyclic drugs is an endogenous symptom pattern: sleep disturbance (especially early morning awakening), weight and appetite loss, agitation, psychomotor retardation, and decreased sexual interest. An MAO inhibitor is not recommended as an initial drug, except under the circumstances outlined below. For patients with a history of manic episodes or persistent elation, lithium should be strongly considered in addition to the tricyclics. The reason for this is that tricyclics may precipitate a recurrence of the mania in the midst of a depressive episode.

Severely depressed patients are often incapacitated at work and at home. They may be so severely depressed as to manifest the clinical pattern of "depressive stupor." This syndrome was seen frequently in the past but is relatively uncommon today. Patients with this condition take to their beds and become mute, incontinent, and refuse eating. ECT is often life-saving in this situation. Other manifestations of severe depression are suicidal intent, severe agitation, and severe retardation. In the presence of delusions, recent research has indicated that tricyclic antidepressants are considerably less effective than they are in nondelusional patients. For delusional depressed patients, ECT and/or phenothiazine should be considered.

Technical Suggestions

STARTING THE MEDICATION

When medication is suggested, a preliminary explanation such as the following may be given to the patient:

We see the depressive syndrome you have as being in two main, interrelated parts: 1) the depressed mood accompanied by physical types of symptoms such as low energy, loss of appetite, and poor sleep, and 2) problems in ways of interacting with others and thinking about yourself. Treatment with medications has been shown to be most effective in treating the depressed mood and symptoms of sleep and appetite disturbance, while psychotherapy is intended to help you develop improved ways of dealing with others and solving problems so that you can prevent further depressions. If you feel better and have more energy, you are more likely to be able to settle your problems with [important person in patient's life]. On the other hand, if in psychotherapy you are better able to deal with _____, then you may find yourself with less to be upset about.

If the patient agrees to the combination of pharmacotherapy and psychotherapy, the therapist can then go on to an explanation of the mechanics of pharmacotherapy, such as adjustment of dosage and possibility of side effects and onset of action.

MONITORING MEDICATION DURING IPT

In combining IPT with pharmacotherapy, it is important to explain to the patient the differing rationales for each intervention. The therapist should set aside a separate time, preferably at the beginning of each session, to deal with pharmacotherapy issues—providing prescriptions, discussing side effects, and evaluating effectiveness.

TWO THERAPISTS OR ONE

An important technical issue in combining drugs and psychotherapy is whether there will be one or two therapists.

A therapist who is a psychiatrist may decide to administer both the psychotherapy and the medication. In the clinical practice of psychiatry this is very often the case. However, many psychotherapeutically oriented psychiatrists, particularly psychoanalysts, consider it useful to split the responsibilities by involving a second therapist as a medication therapist. The justification for this is usually based on some combination of three considerations. First, the psychotherapist, even if he or she is a psychiatrist, may not feel sufficiently comfortable and knowledgeable about the technical aspects of medication. This is especially true of many older psychoanalysts and psychotherapists whose training occurred before the new drugs were introduced and before much information about their pharmacology and neurochemistry was available. Second, the therapist may feel there is some advantage to "splitting the transference," in that issues of drug management, side effects, and dosage are often seen as an intrusion into the primary task of working with the patient on psychosocial or intrapsychic issues.

In the majority of instances today, however, psychotherapy is provided by a nonmedical therapist—a social worker, psychologist, counselor, occupational therapist, psychiatric nurse, or family and marriage counselor. In these instances legal and professional requirements necessitate two therapists, a psychotherapist who is nonmedical in background and a drug therapist who is either an internist or a psychiatrist.

When the therapy is split, an effective alliance, with open communication between the professionals, is essential. Efforts should be made to explain the situation carefully to the patient and to seek the patient's cooperation and permission for the two therapists to exchange information and coordinate their decision making. Efforts should also be made to prevent rivalry or competition for the patient's loyalty or support. Some patients may try to manipulate the split relationship and play off one therapist against the other. For example, a patient may complain to the pharmacotherapist that the psychotherapist is uninterested or underactive or doesn't take a direct enough role. The complaint to the psychotherapist may be that the medication therapist is cold, indifferent, and uninterested in the patient's psychological and social problems.

Another common dilemma arises when the patient ascribes improvement or worsening to one treatment or the other. Very frequently patients complain that the side effects of medication are interfering with their lives. The considerations here are the extent to which the pattern of symptoms reported as side effects conform to the known pharmacology of the drugs and the experience of other patients. Also to be considered is the temporal sequence; did the new complaints come after a change in medication or a change in medication dosage? In either event, it is useful for the psychotherapist and the physician prescribing the medication to confer. Conversely, when improvement occurs, some patients attribute it to the drug alone or to the psychotherapy alone and are tempted to make disparaging comments about the other form of therapy.

Chapter 14

Problems Occasionally Encountered in the Therapy

Special problems that often arise in the course of psychotherapy range from those based in social, cultural, or family attitudes to specific reactions to the patient-therapist relationship.

THE PATIENT SUBSTITUTES THE PSYCHOTHERAPIST FOR FRIENDS OR FAMILY

For many patients with poor social support from family, friends, work, or church the psychotherapist can become a substitute for these resources. To allow the nature of the helping relationship to be viewed as a substitute for friends or family is a disservice to the patient. Ethical psychotherapists do not confide in or share social activities with the patient. If a patient begins to use the relationship as a substitute for outside resources, it is important to clarify the matter at once. The therapist might say:

> You can talk quite openly to me about your problems, your hopes, your fears. This shows me that you are capable of an intimate friendship. But we're not friends or family. What is most important for you is what your life is like

outside our relationship. Who can you talk to among your friends or family as you are talking to me? How can we help you find these people? [Or get over your fears of being open with someone?] Who did you have to help you in your life? How can you approach them? Who have you been able to confide in?

THE PATIENT SEES TREATMENT AS A DEFEAT

Many depressed patients see the need for treatment as an additional defeat. In such instances the patient should be reminded not only that seeking treatment is the wisest thing to do in the circumstances, but also that it is somewhat courageous given the patient's negative expectations about treatment. In addition, seeking treatment can be explained as an attempt to take the situation in hand and to actively do something about problems that have previously been allowed to go unresolved. Thus the psychotherapist should foster the patient's understanding that seeking help is in itself doing something active about the problems.

THE PATIENT IS CHRONICALLY DEPRESSED

Some patients have an acute episode of depression superimposed upon a long-standing mild chronic depression, sometimes referred to as "depressive personality." For them, defeat, pessimism, and low self-esteem are a characteristic way of viewing the world and dealing with others. It is difficult to assess the chronic nature of the disorder while the patient is acutely depressed. In the acute phase patients will appear at their worst—dependent, pessimistic, negative, irritable—and they may be quite different when they become asymptomatic. Assumptions about personality of the patient made while the patient is acutely ill can be misleading and lead to therapeutic pessimism. During symptomatic recovery, however, if a chronic depressive personality style is found, the patient may be more difficult to treat than the initial evaluation indicated and may be subject to recurrent acute episodes. Such patients may require long-term treatment.

THE PATIENT SEES DEPRESSION AS INCURABLE

In the early stages of treatment depressed patients often feel that their symptoms will never remit. An initial strategy is to help the patient regain a sense of mastery and hope. In some cases reassurance is sufficient; many patients, once they sense that the depression is manageable, are able to muster their own resources to deal with it. In addition to simply helping patients feel they are working on their problems, various supportive tactics can be useful.

The patient is educated about the syndrome of depression: the sleep and appetite disturbances, the lack of energy, the pessimism that are part of the illness.

THE PATIENT IS SABOTAGING TREATMENT

Since focusing on the therapeutic relationship is not an important part of IPT, the patient's positive feelings for the psychotherapist and high expectations from treatment are not systematically explored except when they interfere with progress (when, for example, patients have such high expectations of being helped by the omnipotent psychotherapist that they make no independent effort to solve problems themselves). The therapist is careful, however, to continuously monitor the treatment for signs that the patient is developing negative or counter-therapeutic feelings about the therapist or the treatment. These may take the form of relatively subtle verbal or nonverbal communication or may be expressed in problematic behavior such as lateness, missed appointments, silence, excessive discussion of tangential material, direct uncooperativeness, or suicidal behavior, among others.

These behaviors are discussed separately later in this chapter. Here we will deal with the principles that underlie the therapist's handling of problematic attitudes and behaviors.

Confronted with such situations the therapist has two goals: 1) to stop or mitigate the behavior, and 2) to relate the patient's disruptive behavior to problems the patient has in interpersonal relationships outside therapy. If the behavior can be brought under control, handling problems within the therapeutic relationship can be a model for the patient's handling of problems in other relationships.

In dealing with disruptive attitudes and behaviors, the general sequence of exploration is to move from matter-of-fact mention of the behavior toward attempting to understand its meaning and interpersonal function. Thus the psychotherapist must first make sure that simple misunderstanding or practical reasons are not responsible, before proceeding to an investigation of the meaning of the behavior. In general, patients' disruptive behavior can be understood as *indirect and inefficient communication* of negative feelings and they should be helped to find more direct and effective alternative ways of expressing themselves.

THE PATIENT FEARS BEING ALONE

If the symptoms worsen when left alone, the therapist may explore with the patient both emergency measures and long-term strategies for reducing social isolation. Alternatively, if the patient becomes depressed when associating with specific other people who are hostile or otherwise unhelpful, ways can be found to have less contact with these individuals.

THE PATIENT FEARS LOSS OF CONTROL

Fear of loss of control may be found in suicidal patients or in patients disturbed by hostile fantasies. For these patients the psychotherapist's extended availability may be particularly useful as treatment begins. Meeting with the patient several times a week, daily phone calls, or assurance of twenty-four-hour availability by phone, may reassure severely disturbed patients. These measures should be reserved for those patients who seem to really need this much support; the offer of extraordinary measures may be perceived with alarm by less disturbed patients, who may get the message that the psychotherapist considers them "really sick."

Many patients are reassured when, in systematically taking the history of the depressive illness, the psychotherapist seems to be anticipating their symptoms. To further normalize the patient's depression, the psychotherapist may discuss the high prevalence of depressive disorders in our society, as well as the good prognosis and responsiveness of depression to treatment. It is particularly helpful to point out that people who are depressed characteristically have a negative outlook and feel that it will never end. For many patients the current episode has been preceded by previous milder or more severe episodes. When appropriate, patients may be told that depression seems to be their way of responding to serious life problems, and when possible, the therapist may demonstrate that on previous occasions the patient has been able to resolve the depression.

THE PATIENT IS INSUFFICIENTLY ACCEPTING OF HIS WISHES

Many depressed patients are insufficiently accepting of their wishes or unwilling to act on them, because they have learned either that their needs were unacceptable or that they were unlikely to be fulfilled anyway. Thus, for instance, a woman may meekly but angrily accept domination by her husband if she does not believe that a different kind of treatment is legitimate or expectable. To counter the tendency to suppress or deny needs or wishes, the psychotherapist may repeatedly guide patients by asking questions such as "What do you want from ———?" and encouraging them to think about this in a freer way. An even more basic intervention is simply to name and implicitly legitimize the needs that are expressed in the patient's behavior.

THE PATIENT AVOIDS POSITIVE EXPERIENCE

Some depressed patients are unable to respond with pleasure to any event while in an acute episode. Others may respond to pleasurable events but have difficulty in anticipating enjoyment. Patients in the latter group may fail to plan or become involved in activities that they would, in fact, enjoy. They can benefit from therapeutic maneuvers in which the psychotherapist reviews their past and current sources of gratification and encourages them to increase these activities. For patients who become depressed over grief and loss, the therapist is especially active in helping the patient "fill the empty space" with new activities and relationships.

THE PATIENT TAKES THE BLAME FOR FAMILY OR GROUP PROBLEMS

Some depressed patients blame themselves for situations over which they have only partial control. Forces growing out of unrecognized family or group dynamics frequently place special pressures on particular individuals, who do not necessarily experience them as coming from the group. In these cases the patient can be taught simple principles of group or family dynamics ("scapegoating," for example), and the way these principles illustrate their role in their group constellation. With this information patients can be guided in changing the nature of their role in their social network.

THE PATIENT MISSES APPOINTMENTS OR IS LATE

The initial approach to this problem is simply to call attention to the behavior and to make sure trivial misunderstandings are cleared up or that realistic problems are not responsible. For instance, patients may think that coming late to an appointment is not a problem because doctors in their previous experience had a large backup in the waiting room. In this case it should be explained that the allotted time is kept open for the patient alone and the psychotherapist has no conflicting appointments. The patient may also be reminded that the missed sessions or lateness means less time to work on problems. Other patients may be habitually late because of practical problems, such as getting baby-sitters. The therapist should make an effort to schedule times when the patient is most likely to be able to attend. When the patients do not readily understand the meaning of their behavior (for example, "I've been coming later because I don't want to talk about . . ."), the psychotherapist may examine the circumstances in which the behavior arose (coming late only after emotional sessions) and the possibly intended interpersonal consequences of the behavior (lateness shortens the sessions or angers the psychotherapist).

If, after the first discussion of lateness, the behavior persists, the psychotherapist may begin to explore the meaning of the event in an interpersonal context by asking such questions as "What do you make of your continued lateness?" or "What effect do you think your lateness has on our work [me]?" The therapist tries to treat the behavior as an indirect and inefficient interpersonal communication, whether or not the patient is aware that the provocative behavior has an effect on others or of feeling any of the things being communicated in this indirect way. For example, patients may feel that therapy is helping and that they want to cooperate, but that for some unknown reason they just cannot remember the time of appointments. Others are quite aware of their mixed feelings and are able to discuss them when asked about missed appointments.

In helping patients discover the meaning of such behavior, it may be helpful to discuss the events connected with the uncooperative actions. For example:

a patient who was punctual in the first phases of treatment, as she discussed her exasperating relationship with her hyperactive son, started missing appointments as the topic began to shift to her long-standing and previously unacknowledged resentment of her aloof, unhelpful husband.

Another technique for exploring uncooperative behavior is to begin with the idea that the patient does recognize the interpersonal consequences of the behavior or that there is at least a partial intention to have them take place. In such a situation the first aim should be to make the patient aware of the effect the behavior has on the therapist. It frequently turns out that the patient affects family or friends the same way. For example:

a patient who came for treatment with a history of short-lived, stormy relationships began early to miss appointments and then place the blame on the psychotherapist. The therapist talked with the patient about the infuriating nature of his behavior. As his behavior was examined, he revealed that he did not believe others could respond to him positively and that when involved in a dispute he felt more comfortable and engaged than when the relationship was quiet.

In applying learning that results from exploring uncooperative behavior, attempts should be made to point out the communicative aspects of this behavior and help the patient discover alternative, more direct methods of getting the point across. The patient's use of nonverbal means of communicating may be due to irrational fears about the outcome of more direct expression of either positive or negative feelings. For instance, a patient's feeling that angry avoidance of direct conflict is preferable to voicing complaints may be based on expectations of massive retaliation from the other person.

THE PATIENT IS SILENT

Some silence occurs in any treatment and in most cases does not call for discussion. In general, IPT is a treatment in which the patient and the psychotherapist share responsibility for bringing up topics to discuss and directing the exploration of an issue. However, there may be times when it is important to allow a prolonged silence, two or three minutes or more. When emotion-laden material has been discussed, or when the psychotherapist feels that the patient may have more to reveal about an issue spontaneously than can be gained by asking questions, silence may be productive. Occasionally patients become concerned about silences, feeling that no work is going on. In such cases they may be told that the therapy involves sharing the experiences of the time, which include silence as well as active discussion.

If silence is a persistent problem, its meaning may be explored by questioning the patient about possible explanations. Improvement may have been so great that the patient feels there is nothing more to talk about. In this case discussion of termination should begin. If the patient does not believe the problems are solved, then the therapist may begin inquiring into what is preventing discussion of the issues at hand. The basic assumption here is that the patient is either avoiding recognition of conflicted thoughts or feelings about an issue or would like to bring up something but is concerned about the therapist's reaction. The therapist may begin by asking silent patients what is on their minds or whether there is something they are refraining from discussing. This inquiry usually leads to discovery of irrational interpersonal fears connected with revealing thoughts and feelings to others. If patients can overcome their hesitation to communicate in the treatment and gain a better understanding of the assumptions they are making about others (that others will disapprove, not care, or let them down), this may lead to improved communication outside.

As with the exploration of lateness, the therapist may choose to point out the effect silence has in an interpersonal context. For example, the patient may use silence in a habitual, pouting way rather than voice legitimate complaints. In this case patients may be helped to see both the annoying effects of silence and the relatively unproductive nature of this communication.

THE PATIENT CHANGES OR AVOIDS SUBJECTS

Avoiding discussion of important material may take place in a variety of ways, such as discussing only childhood events, repeatedly changing the subject, or open refusal to discuss a given problem. As in the case of silence, the psychother apist's initial reaction should be a matter-of-fact mention of the problem. If the therapist notices that the patient changes topics only when a particular issue is brought up, this observation can be shared. In pointing out avoidance of specific topics, it is important to keep in mind the patient's relative autonomy to discuss what is of concern as well as the identified problem that both therapist and patient have agreed will be the focus of treatment. As with silence, after pointing out the problem, the therapist should follow up with an examination of the patient's intentions in repeatedly avoiding issues and the effect this behavior has on others.

THE PATIENT COMPLAINS AND IS UNCOOPERATIVE

Depressed patients often feel that nothing can help them and their depression will go on forever, and such feelings can make them directly uncooperative. It is important to try to instill hope in these patients. They may be honestly told that the prognosis is good, since most depressed patients recover even without treatment in six months to a year. Findings about the utility of IPT in controlled studies can also be shared with the patient. Beyond reassurance, the response to persistent complaints is to use this behavior in an attempt to help patients understand their complaining in an interpersonal context. Excessive complainers may be picking on relatively trivial issues to avoid direct confrontation with central concerns. Others may have expectations of others that can never be fulfilled and may need to learn ways of caring for themselves. Regardless of the meaning of the complaints, patients can be made aware of the effects of their behavior and be provided with alternative ways of handling displeasure.

THE PATIENT IS EXCESSIVELY DEPENDENT

Depressed patients frequently underestimate their own capabilities and feel that others must provide things that they can easily obtain for themselves. In therapy they repeatedly ask for inappropriate advice or try to persuade the psychotherapist to intervene inappropriately in an interpersonal or other problem. Although IPT is a supportive treatment in which the psychotherapist may be realistically helpful, the sort of help offered is focused and limited. If the patient is simply misunderstanding the limitations of the therapeutic relationship, an explanation may suffice to curtail inappropriate demands. If the patient persists, this may provide an opportunity to explore the patient's unwillingness or inability to recognize personal strengths and capabilities.

THE PATIENT ATTEMPTS SUICIDE

Suicide constitutes the most severe danger of depressive illness. For this reason suicide threats or actions must always be taken seriously.

The first task of the psychotherapist is to determine whether hospitalization is necessary for the patient who expresses suicidal ideation. This is a complex judgment that must include consideration of the seriousness of intent, the lethality of previous attempts, and the availability of others in the patient's social network.

If hospitalization is not required, exploration of the meaning of suicide to the patient is in order, beginning with the assumption that suicide represents an attempt at interpersonal communication or problem solving. Attention should be paid to the circumstances in which the suicidal ideation began to develop. Thoughts about the interpersonal intent of suicide can be assessed by reviewing how patients imagine others' reactions to their death, reviewing their ideas of what death is like (there may be reunion fantasies involving deceased loved ones), or assessing what the death would accomplish. Patients can often be helped to imagine a better way to achieve the results intended by the suicide.

A suicidal patient must not feel abandoned by others. The therapist will be as available as possible when a patient feels suicidal—being more reachable by phone or scheduling extra sessions.

THE PSYCHOTHERAPIST DEVELOPS POWERFUL FEELINGS TOWARD THE PATIENT

Psychotherapists occasionally find themselves developing feelings such as anger or sexual attraction toward a patient. These feelings may be an extension of the interpersonal style of the therapist or they may be a response to provocative behavior by the patient. It is important for the therapist to sort out which of the two possibilities is more likely. Response to the patient can be useful because it helps the therapist understand the response the patient elicits in others. This may help in determining the patient's strengths and weaknesses and in guiding inquiries into the patient's problematic relationships outside of treatment. In helping the patient learn about the effects of such behavior on others, the psychotherapist may tell the patient about these reactions. In fact, in instances when it is clear that the patient is acting in a provocative manner, failure to acknowledge it may cause the patient to doubt the psychotherapist's capacity to respond genuinely. For example:

> With a bright, argumentative patient in his early twenties, the therapist found that he was always having disagreements over a range of topics, such as appointment times or remembering what the patient had said earlier in the session. Since this man's chief complaint at the beginning of treatment was his social isolation, the therapist's reaction seemed to be an important clue to the patient's interpersonal difficulties. When the therapist expressed his annoyance, the patient seemed relieved and said he wondered why the therapist had tolerated his baiting behavior so long. Further discussion brought up the patient's long-standing belief that, since others were bound to exploit him if he showed weakness, he must approach them in an offensive, attacking manner.

Showing one's responses, especially negative ones, is a technique the therapist should use carefully and sparingly. In general, a nonjudgmental acknowledgment of the patient's difficulties is the preferred stance. Moreover, when the psychotherapist does express negative feelings to the patient, it is important that the patient's behavior, which can be changed, is what is objected to, and not the patient as a person. In gauging the timing of this kind of intervention, the therapist should be sure that the patient is provoking the response and that learning about the provocation will help the patient understand similar behavior outside of therapy. Properly used, working out conflicts between patient and psychotherapist can be a powerful tool in helping the patient learn about dispute resolution generally.

WHEN THE SIGNIFICANT OTHER IS ASKED TO PARTICIPATE

The inclusion of the patient's significant other(s) in one or more therapy sessions is especially recommended for patients with problems of interpersonal role disputes, such as marital problems. The conjoint session(s) might be used to: 1) obtain additional information; 2) obtain the cooperation of the significant other; or 3) facilitate interpersonal problem solving and improved communication between the patient and the significant other.

Although IPT is conceived of as an individual treatment, the therapist may choose to include significant others in a number of therapy sessions for either of two purposes.

Providing Information. The interpersonal difficulties of depressed patients are often exacerbated by the family's misunderstanding of the characteristics of depressive illness. For instance, one husband had interpreted his wife's apathy as willful resistance to doing housework, and a woman had been seeing her husband's loss of appetite and sexual interest as a direct criticism of her. The explanation that depression is a syndrome with predictable characteristics, a good prognosis, and unknown causes often allays relatives' apprehensions and guilt about the patient's condition. Moreover, the relatives can be told about ways to help the patient recover. They should be warned against either excessively blaming the patient or excessively excusing the patient from responsibility during a depressive illness.

For suicidal patients whose condition is serious but does not require hospitalization, relatives can be adjunctive psychotherapists with the tasks of monitoring the patient's condition and dispensing medications.

Obtaining Information. By either directly asking for information from the relative or observing interactions between the patient and the significant other, the psychotherapist may obtain information that could not be gotten from the patient alone.

THE PATIENT WISHES TO TERMINATE EARLY

The most complete avoidance of the work of therapy is premature termination. In many cases this cannot be prevented because the assumption of psychotherapy that talking things out should precede action runs counter to the beliefs and coping styles of many people. Early termination may also occur when patient and therapist disagree about the therapy contract or the patient feels the continuation of the contract is threatening.

Patients who express a wish to terminate should first be asked if they are satisfied that their problems have been dealt with adequately. This is seldom the case, but the question makes the point that there is still material to be worked on. The therapist should inquire about the patient's possible dissatisfactions with the therapy and try to satisfy reasonable requests or resolve misunderstandings. The tone of this inquiry should imply that the patient's plan to end treatment may be a legitimate and useful course of action. If specific unsolvable problems have arisen between psychotherapist and patient, or if the patient has problems that cannot reasonably be handled with IPT methods, then referral to another psychotherapist or form of treatment is advisable.

If the psychotherapist is convinced that the patient's desire to terminate arises from confrontation of avoided issues or relates to the patient's general interpersonal problems, then the desire to terminate can be treated like any other symptom. In exploring the interpersonal meaning of threats to stop therapy, the patient should be encouraged to think and talk about feelings rather than simply acting on them. If the patient is determined to leave prematurely, it is important to communicate as strongly as possible that return to therapy is open and would not imply defeat or humiliation.

From the interpersonal view, the patient's wish to terminate early is an example of nonshared role expectations. The situation is a particular form of role dispute, in this case between patient and psychotherapist. At dispute is the duration of treatment, and the patient is requesting a renegotiation of the contract.

THE PATIENT HAS PROBLEMS WITH SELF-DISCLOSURE

In eliciting affectively charged material, timing is vital and the therapist must be reasonably certain that the patient can tolerate the feelings without becoming unproductively upset. Establishment of a trusting relationship with the psychotherapist may be necessary before the patient can deal with disclosure of suppressed topics. Moving too quickly in exploring sensitive areas can either stall progress by heightening the patient's defensiveness or lead to premature termination. It is expected that the therapeutic relationship will deepen as the therapy progresses, allowing the patient greater freedom to be open.

To help the patient be more self-revealing, the therapist is guided by the patient's displays of strong affect or, alternatively, by the lack of strong feelings when events or topics that would seem to warrant these feelings are described. If the patient begins to show an emotional response to a topic, further discussion of this material and fuller expression of feelings are encouraged. If the patient seems to be discussing material of little emotional relevance, the therapist may try to bring the focus back to important issues. In eliciting the discussion of highly charged topics, the psychotherapist tacitly or explicitly conveys both acceptance of the affect, which in fact is not under the patient's control, and his confidence that these powerful feelings need not be translated into actions, which are under the patient's control. The psychotherapist may choose to explain this in some such manner as:

> You can't force your feelings to change, and although you find it hard to accept your ———[rage, fear, envy, etc.], we all have feelings like that. On the other hand, the fact that you have these feelings doesn't mean you will act on them, and if we can understand these feelings better, they may become less troubling or even change.

THE PATIENT SEEKS ADDITIONAL, ALTERNATIVE TREATMENT

In rare instances patients may seek additional, alternative treatment while continuing the therapy. The additional treatment may be another kind of psychotherapy and/or psychotropic medication. An open, nonjudgmental, and nonreproachful attitude about these activities should be maintained and they should be discussed in the therapy sessions.

Chapter 15

The IPT Therapist: Professional Background, Role, and Training

---

IPT is designed to be conducted by psychiatrists, psychologists, psychiatric social workers, or nurses who have already achieved specified levels of experience and proficiency in some form of dynamic psychotherapy, such as Rogerian therapy or psychoanalytically oriented therapy. Before attempting IPT, therapists are expected to have a terminal professional degree, such as the M.D., Ph.D., or M.S.W., and at least two years of clinical experience in psychotherapy with ambulatory depressed patients. The therapists are further evaluated by the training therapists to insure that they meet generally accepted standards of clinical competence, including the ability to relate to patients with warmth, interest, and empathy. In addition, therapists should have a positive attitude about short-term treatment and an open-minded attitude about the use of interpersonal techniques. Ideally, the IPT therapist should have no rigid attachment to an alternative therapeutic belief system. Finally, it is assumed on the basis of previous training and experience that the therapist is familiar with personality issues and with his or her own strengths and weaknesses in relating to different kinds of patients.

Therapist's Role and Stance

As Strupp (1969), Frank (1973), and others have pointed out, the types of psychotherapy share many common elements. A particular type of therapy is thus defined by its distinction from other treatments, either a) in using techniques not used in other therapies or b) in refraining from using techniques that are definitive of other therapies.

THE THERAPIST IS A PATIENT ADVOCATE, NOT NEUTRAL

In common with Rogerian practitioners, the IPT therapist is nonjudgmental and communicates warmth and unconditional positive regard. In essence, the therapist is a benign and helpful ally. Confrontation is gentle and timely, and the therapist is careful to foster the patient's positive expectations of the therapeutic relationship. This, of course, does not mean that the therapist accepts all aspects of the patient; rather, the therapist conveys the message that the patient's problems can be resolved and do not necessarily represent permanent features of the patient's personality. In keeping with this stance, the therapist is optimistic and supportive, using such techniques as reassurance and direct advice when they seem useful, usually during the initial sessions when the patient is feeling most symptomatic and helpless. By not taking a withdrawn, neutral role, the therapist avoids allowing the patient to regress in the therapeutic relationship.

THE THERAPEUTIC RELATIONSHIP IS NOT A MANIFESTATION OF TRANSFERENCE

This is a corollary of the role of patient advocate. Since the therapist offers alliance, the patient's expectations of assistance and understanding are seen as realistic, and the relationship between patient and therapist is also realistic. In general, the relationship is not seen as a fantasied reenactment of the patient's (or the therapist's) previous relationships with others. The therapist is sensitive to the patient's pattern of relating. For example, the therapist may try to avoid intellectualized argument with an obsessional patient by focusing instead on feelings and emotional issues.

Positive transference is left alone, and attempts to interrupt, interpret, or specifically explore patient-therapist interactions are made only when the patient's feelings about the therapist are disruptive of progress. This stance is expected to reduce the likelihood of the patient's manifesting angry or hostile feelings toward the therapist. When the patient's feelings about the therapist or therapy do seem to be interfering with progress, as evidenced by problems that get in the way of the therapy, such as lateness or missed sessions (see Chapter 14), then the patient's feelings about the therapist are explored. The overall strategy in this situation is to relate the patient's reactions to the treatment to his ways of handling interpersonal problems outside of treatment, and to help the patient learn alternative ways of handling these reactions both in and out of therapy.

Although IPT therapists offer assistance to patients, it is limited to helping them learn new ways of thinking about themselves in social roles and in solving interpersonal problems. The therapist is careful to keep direct advice and reassurance to a minimum, in order to foster the patient's own sense of competence. The therapist avoids allowing the patient to become too dependent.

THE THERAPEUTIC RELATIONSHIP IS NOT A FRIENDSHIP

Although the therapist is the patient's advocate, there are limitations on this relationship. On the one hand, the therapist can be selectively self-revealing and free in interactions with the patient. When relevant to the issues at hand, therapists may express personal opinions or give examples of problems from their own lives. If the patient asks a personal question, the therapist may feel free to answer. It may, however, be important to explore the patient's reason for asking, if it seems to be related to countertherapeutic attitudes or represent avoidance of self-revelation. If the patient offers a small gift, the therapist may accept it without feeling obligated to explore its meaning. In the pursuit of professional tasks, the therapist may become active in assisting the patient with life problems, perhaps by testifying in court or making arrangements with other medical or psychological professionals for additional care.

On the other hand, the therapist's openness to the patient does not include participation in activities not related to the tasks and goals of therapy. Thus, for example, the therapist would not become involved with the patient socially or in a business relationship.

THE THERAPIST IS ACTIVE, NOT PASSIVE

In structuring the therapeutic hour and focusing sessions, the IPT therapist takes a moderate position between the extremes of being highly active and merely reactive to the patient's productions.

In keeping with the goals of IPT, the therapist is somewhat active in helping the patient focus on bringing about improvement in current interpersonal problem areas. In the initial session the therapist actively elicits the history of the depressive condition, the history of the patient's significant interpersonal relationships, especially current ones, and helps the patient set treatment goals.

In intermediate sessions the therapist is active in guiding the patient to cover the material that is relevant to the treatment goals. If the patient does not bring in material, the therapist may elicit an update or more detailed information in one of the agreed-upon problem areas. If the patient is still unable to discuss the material, it may be advisable to ask if there is something that is difficult to discuss. It is a general rule that if a pressing issue is not discussed, then other issues cannot be fruitfully explored. The therapist may turn the patient's attention to the experience of the session in the here-and-now, and then attempt to uncover thoughts or feelings that are impeding the therapy (see the discussion of silence in Chapter 14). It is not advisable to allow either very long silences or rambling free associations in which topics highly tangential to the goals of treatment are discussed to the exclusion of more central issues.

Although the therapist is active, the ultimate responsibility for change lies with the patient. Even if the therapist could solve the patient's problems, that is not the intention. The intention of the therapy is to help patients learn to solve their own problems and pursue their own goals. Thus therapists limit their interventions relative to the patients' behavior both inside and outside the therapy session. Inside the session patients are told that they will be given the opportunity to discuss their concerns and problems as they see them, because the therapist cannot intuit what is important to the patient. To give the patient an opportunity to change the focus of treatment or to bring up previously unexplored problem areas, each session might begin with the therapist asking (either explicitly or by silence) if there are any concerns, events, or thoughts about either the therapy or significant others that the patient would like to discuss. If the patient brings up material, the session may then be focused through a systematic exploration of the topic the patient chooses. Outside of therapy, patients change their behavior at their own pace. Except in rare circumstances the therapist does not directly intervene on behalf of a patient, and does not assign homework or make direct, specific suggestions.

IPT Training

The IPT approach to depressed patients is most readily learned by fully trained psychotherapists who are already experienced and proficient in a form of insight-oriented, exploratory psychotherapy such as, a Rogerian (1959), a Sullivanian (1953), or a traditional psychoanalytically oriented approach. For psychotherapists with this sort of background, adopting an IPT approach primarily involves refocusing and condensing the type of work they may already be doing with nonpsychotic outpatients. For these therapists, learning the IPT approach requires including a "medical model" approach to education about depression (see Chapter 3); focusing interventions to follow the strategies for identifying and approaching the four types of interpersonal problems (see Chapters 5 through 9);

and increasing the activity level in order to complete the work in a relatively limited number of sessions (twelve to twenty) and a correspondingly brief time period.

Although the general therapeutic stance and techniques of IPT are usually familiar to practitioners of exploratory psychotherapies, psychotherapists who have been trained in a behavioral or cognitive approach may find IPT more difficult to learn. Those who are strong adherents of relatively "pure," long-term and open-ended forms of psychodynamic psychotherapy may also find IPT concepts very different from those they are accustomed to.

Up to now, training in short-term interpersonal psychotherapy has been devised and conducted only for the very specialized purpose of enabling psychotherapists to utilize this form of treatment in research studies contrasting IPT with control conditions, pharmacotherapy, and/or other types of psychotherapy. A major drawback of much research on the efficacy of the different psychotherapies is a failure adequately to insure the specificity of the therapeutic approaches being tested. Although the therapists and therapies evaluated in research studies have been identified as "psychoanalytically oriented" or "behavioral," researchers have rarely specified the actual techniques and strategies the therapists are using.

The IPT Manual, which is the forerunner of this book, as well as the IPT training program, were developed in recognition of the need to improve the precision with which psychotherapies are categorized in clinical trials evaluating their efficacy. Unless every effort is made to see that therapists carrying out different kinds of treatment are using techniques that define their particular approach, researchers cannot know whether the type of treatment being tested is given a fair trial.

Because IPT training was developed for specialized research purposes, it is not broadly available and its use in clinical settings has not been systematically evaluated. However, the IPT training program includes the components of traditional clinical training, and the experience gained from the research setting may be more generally applicable in clinical settings. The three central features of IPT training are: a) the material assembled in this book; b) a didactic seminar; and c) supervised casework based on the supervisor's review of videotapes of psychotherapy sessions.

WRITTEN MATERIAL

Before *Interpersonal Psychotherapy of Depression* was written, the major instrument used to define, specify, and transmit the strategies and techniques of IPT was the training manual. Like most books that describe a type of psychotherapy, ours includes a discussion of the theoretical background and general characteristics of the treatment. However, it differs from other types of books about psychotherapy by providing detailed instructions and guidelines for the actual conduct of the treatment. One way of describing it is to say that it demarcates both the external and the internal boundaries of IPT. Within the IPT approach there is an operationalized list of techniques that may be drawn upon, a detailed outline of four general strategies for approaching the patient's interpersonal problems depending on the type of issues presented, a set of guidelines for handling specific problems (silence, lateness, and so on) that commonly arise in the conduct of psychotherapy, instructions about the sequence of events to be followed in the different phases of therapy, and descriptions of the defining features of the relationship the IPT therapist attempts to form with the patient. Moreover, the external boundaries of IPT are delimited and techniques that are not part of IPT are described, such as assignment of homework. Also outside the boundaries of IPT is the failure to adopt a therapeutic stance consistent with IPT, such as being overactive or directive, or failing to be supportive and active enough.

DIDACTIC SEMINAR

In a two-to-five-day seminar, we attempt to help the therapists identify what they are already doing that is like IPT, what they are doing that is not IPT, and the special skills needed for the IPT approach. This takes the form of an exegesis of the written material with extensive clinical illustration using videotaped case material.

In the didactic seminar, training is focused on clearly emphasizing four definitive aspects of IPT: 1) the recognition of depression as a medical disorder and the strategies of handling depressive symptoms based on this recognition; 2) the focus on helping the patient manage problems in current interpersonal functioning; 3) the exploratory aspect of the treatment process, through which patients come to recognize their own desires and needs and discover new and more productive ways to meet them; and 4) the need to condense the work of therapy into a brief treatment format.

All our training experience is based on work with mental health professionals who have completed their highest degree and have a minimum of two years of psychotherapy experience using an insight-oriented, exploratory approach. These therapists are selected on the basis of a review of their credentials; their having read IPT material and found it compatible with their work; and a trainer's review of videotaped samples of their clinical work. Given this preselection by both the trainers and the trainees, we have found that IPT can be readily learned by most of those who attempt it. In three training courses involving twenty-seven therapists, twenty-three have been certified as competent IPT therapists at the completion of training. However, there have been several areas in which IPT trainees have had difficulty (Weissman, Rounsaville, and Chevron, 1982). These parallel the four areas of IPT emphasized in the training.

First, in regard to the emphasis on depression as a psychiatric disorder, psychotherapists who have not worked in a medical setting are sometimes reluctant to review depressive symptoms systematically, to define their onset as being part of a syndrome, and to direct interventions toward mitigating and managing the symptoms. Rather, they tend to immediately focus on the interpersonal issues without specifically addressing the patient's symptoms. This is a serious mistake, because patients usually seek treatment primarily because of the symptoms; ignoring them may reduce a patient's feeling of being heard and helped.

The second problem area is related to the emphasis on problems in current interpersonal functioning. Highly experienced and psychodynamically trained psychotherapists may fall into lengthy discussions of childhood relationships or of transference without any attempt to relate the patterns discovered to the immediate interpersonal problems. A short-term treatment does not allow time for long explorations of all determinants of current behavior. If past determinants are discussed at all, they should be explicitly related to current patterns.

Third, as to the exploratory aspect of IPT, trainees may err in the direction of following the training manual in a rigid, "cookbook" fashion, failing to pay close attention to nuances of the therapeutic relationship or to subtle shifts in emphasis suggested by the patient. Although one can define the structure and goals of a psychotherapy, the patient-therapist relationship is the central feature without which the treatment cannot work. For example, although many tasks should be defined and accomplished in the initial sessions, it is unwise for the therapist to charge straight through them if the patient is severely symptomatic or manifests doubts and hesitations about the therapist or the treatment. The IPT therapist must recognize that first and foremost there needs to be a working alliance. Those who spend their energy going "by the book" may miss this point.

As to the fourth area, the IPT emphasis on short-term treatment, many experienced psychotherapists have difficulty adjusting to actively focusing the sessions and being quick to offer interpretive feedback to the patient. Many IPT trainees have never explicitly attempted short-term treatment and tend to emphasize long-standing personality issues. These trainees are often surprised and gratified to note the extent to which seemingly intransigent personality traits can be overcome when depressive symptoms are relieved in the course of a brief treatment. Adjustment to the short-term nature of the treatment occurs most readily when the therapist comes to believe the meaningful work can be accomplished in twelve to twenty weeks.

SUPERVISED CASEWORK

After the didactic seminar, therapists are assigned two to four training cases each, on which they receive weekly supervision on a session-by-session basis. This is done on the telephone or in person and follows the supervisor's having reviewed the videotape of the session. Both trainee and supervisor have videotape equipment and tapes available, so that they can watch specific segments as they discuss the session. The primary purpose of the supervision is boundary marking, or helping the therapists learn which techniques are included and which are excluded in IPT. It is also helpful if the supervisor reviews the ratings made by the patient during the session as well as the observer ratings.

A pilot training program in 1978–1980 demonstrated the importance of basing supervision on review of videotapes. In this project, supervision was carried out in the traditional manner, on the basis of review of process notes. After each supervisory session the supervisor rated the therapist's use of IPT techniques and strategies. Videotapes were also made of the supervisory sessions, and several months after the training, the two supervisors reviewed them, making ratings using the same format. What we found was that, while the interrater reliability of the supervisor's ratings of the videotapes was highly significant (Pearson's r = .88), there was no relationship between the videotape ratings of the psychotherapists and those made on the basis of traditional supervision. Therapists were also asked to rate their own performance in sessions based on recall immediately after the sessions, and these ratings did not agree with either the supervisor's ratings or those based on review of the videotapes. Two kinds of discrepancies between traditional supervision and viewing videotapes were noted. Several therapists who on videotape review were thought to be excellent had underrated their own work, while some who could talk IPT theory and technique well, and made a good presentation of their therapies, were rated less highly when actual sessions were viewed. We feel that this independence of impressions gained from supervision and from viewing videotapes is a key issue that needs to be taken into account in other types of clinical training (Chevron and Rounsaville, 1983). It is noteworthy that we dropped a written, multiple-choice examination from the training and evaluation procedures because on this instrument, improvement was found to be negatively correlated with ratings of therapists' skill in actually performing IPT.

EVALUATION METHODS

In keeping with the research orientation of IPT training, we have been careful to evaluate the competence of trainees to perform IPT as defined in this book, and to assess their progress systematically in the course of training. We believe that the best indicator of the therapists' having learned this approach to treatment is their actual performance in psychotherapy sessions with depressed patients. For that reason, certification of psychotherapist competence is now made on the basis of reviewing videotaped psychotherapy sessions. To evaluate the therapist's performance, a rating system has been devised that covers three levels of compliance with the IPT approach: a) broadly defined use of appropriate IPT strategies; b) appropriate use of the specific IPT techniques; and c) the use of techniques that are not part of the IPT approach. In each of these areas, the strategy or technique is rated as having been utilized or not and the quality of the use is also rated. In addition, ratings of general psychotherapeutic skills and of patient cooperation are made.

Two evaluators assess trainee competence: a) the supervisor, who also shares his impressions with the trainee; and b) an independent evaluator who is independent of the training. The use of an independent rater who is not invested in the training process was thought necessary to determine whether aspects of the supervisory relationship have biased the rater in favor of his supervisees. In fact, there has been a high level of agreement between supervisor's and independent evaluator's ratings (Weissman, 1982).

Both evaluators base their ratings on review of entire psychotherapeutic sessions. The reason for viewing the entire hour is that the areas being rated encompass more than the nature of the therapeutic relationship, which could be assessed in a shorter time. Evaluating the appropriateness of the use of specific techniques and strategies requires a knowledge of the context. Moreover, in view of the IPT emphasis on the sequencing of strategies across sessions and focusing on targeted problems, it is actually desirable that ratings be made with knowledge of what has occurred before in the treatment and what the therapist had in mind.

EFFECTS OF SUPERVISED CASEWORK

Because the therapist's competence to conduct IPT was rated on the basis of performance in psychotherapy sessions, the first ratings were made after trainees had already been carefully selected and after the didactic seminar. Thus ratings of change over time could only reflect the effects of supervised casework. In a comparison of therapist ratings for the first training case to those for the final training case, we found that improvement was related to psychotherapist experience. In a training program in which trainees had an average of fourteen years of experience, we noted a ceiling effect; that is, ratings based on review of performance in the first supervised case were already at an average level of "excellent." These therapists had apparently been able to grasp and use IPT techniques on the basis of reading the Manual and attending the didactic seminar. In the course of one to three additional training cases, experienced psychotherapists showed neither significant improvement nor significant deterioration in their performance of IPT. In a similar training program in which trainees had an average of 5.9 years of experience, performance in the first training case was rated as "acceptable" on the average and there was a significant improvement in performance with the second case, although ratings continued to be below the excellent mark. Thus a more extensive course of supervised casework seems to be necessary for less experienced psychotherapists (Chevron, Rounsaville, and Weissman, 1983).

The issue of psychotherapist experience level has been impressive in many aspects of IPT training. Although the psychotherapy research literature contains contradictory evidence about the importance of psychotherapist experience (Parloff, Waskow, and Wolfe, 1978), we have consistently noted experience effects. In evaluating twenty-seven potential IPT trainees on the basis of videotaped samples of their clinical work, we found that the key distinguishing factor was experience. Highly rated therapists had an average of fourteen years of experience and low-rated therapists averaged seven years (Chevron et al.).

In subsequent training efforts we have continued to be impressed with the importance of experience. Even after training, less experienced therapists achieved significantly lower ratings of IPT performance than more experienced ones. We found that inexperienced therapists were likely to be highly skillful at performing the more structured aspects of treatment that are most clearly defined in the training manual. For example, they were rated highly at use of a syndrome approach to depressive symptoms, completion of tasks described for initial sessions and termination sessions, and focusing on a single, defined current interpersonal problem area. However, they were more likely than experienced therapists to try to perform treatment in a stereotyped fashion, being less able to change direction in an exploratory fashion and to form a working therapeutic alliance with difficult or resistant patients. Experienced psychotherapists were excellent at performing IPT in a subtle and flexible way and at maintaining good rapport with patients, although they tended to have difficulty with the more structured aspects of treatment, such as reviewing depressive symptoms and keeping the work focused in order to complete it in a brief treatment. Overall, however, it appeared that the experienced therapists were more readily able to learn the more specific IPT techniques than the less experienced therapists were to gain more general therapeutic skills.

USES OF THIS BOOK

IPT training seems to involve adjusting and refocusing the type of work that many traditionally trained, experienced psychotherapists are doing. For highly experienced and highly selected psychotherapists, participation in a didactic training seminar and careful review of the Manual resulted in their being able to perform IPT adequately in the first supervised training case. For less experienced therapists, more lengthy supervised casework was advisable.

Our experience with training suggests that practitioners not involved with research could well adopt elements of an IPT approach by carefully reviewing the IPT Manual. Thus it is our hope that professional readers of *Interpersonal Psychotherapy of Depression,* which has developed from the Manual, will find its principles, strategies, and techniques useful in their own practice.

Appendix

Interview Format for the Hamilton Rating Scale for Depression

1. Depressed Mood

How have you been feeling? Can you describe what your mood has been? Have you felt blue, down in the dumps, depressed? How would you describe it? How bad has it been?

Have you wanted to cry? Does crying help? Have you felt that you would like to cry but that you were beyond tears?

Have you felt hopeless, unable to control what happens to you, at the mercy of others or unable to do anything for yourself?

How have you felt about the future? Can you see yourself getting better?

(Depressed mood includes gloomy attitude, pessimism about the future, worth-lessness, helplessness, feelings of sadness and the tendency to weep. No diagnosed person will score 0 and few will score 1 or 4.)

The Hamilton Rating Scale for Depression is adapted from the 1967 original version by Max Hamilton, M.D. and is reprinted here courtesy of Dr. Hamilton.

---

0 — Absent
1 — These feeling states indicated only on questioning
2 — These feeling states spontaneously reported verbally
3 — Communicates feeling states non-verbally—i.e., through facial expression, posture, voice and tendency to weep
4 — Patient reports VIRTUALLY ONLY these feeling states in his spontaneous verbal and non-verbal communication

---

2.   Feelings of Guilt

Have you blamed yourself for things you have done? Have you been down on yourself? Do you think that you are a bad person?

Have you let your friends and family down? Do you feel guilty about it?

Have you felt that you are to blame for your illness? In what way? A lot? Do you think about sin?

---

0 — Absent
1 — Self-reproach, feels he has let people down
2 — Ideas of guilt or rumination over past errors or sinful deeds
3 — Present illness is a punishment. Delusions of guilt
4 — Hears accusatory or denunciatory voices and/or experiences threatening visual hallucinations

---

3.   Suicide

Do you think much about death? Have you felt that life was not worth living? Have you wished that you were dead?

Have you had any thoughts of taking your life? Have you made any plans to do so? Have you started to do things to work out that plan?

Have you actually made an attempt on your life?

(An attempt at suicide scores a 4 but such an attempt may sometimes occur suddenly against a background of very little suicidal tendency; in such a case it should be scored as 3. There will be great difficulty sometimes differentiating between a real attempt at suicide and a demonstrative attempt; the rater must use his judgment.)

---

0 — Absent
1 — Feels life is not worth living
2 — Wishes he were dead or any thoughts of possible death to self
3 — Suicide ideas or gesture
4 — Attempts at suicide *(any serious attempt rates 4)*

---

4. Insomnia Early

When you go to sleep at night do you fall asleep easily? Have you been taking sleeping pills?

Do you have difficulty getting off to sleep every night? How long does it take you to fall asleep? What goes through your mind as you lie there?

---

0 — No difficulty falling asleep
1 — Complains of occasional difficulty falling asleep—i.e., more than 1/2 hour
2 — Complains of nightly difficulty

---

5. Insomnia Middle

When you fall asleep, do you sleep well, are you restless or do you keep waking? Do you get up out of bed?

---

0 — No difficulty
1 — Patient complains of being restless and disturbed during the night
2 — Waking during the night—any getting out of bed rates 2 *(except for purposes of voiding)*

---

6.   Insomnia Late

Do you wake early in the morning? Stay awake or fall back to sleep? Is this earlier than you would normally get up?

---

o — No difficulty
1 — Waking in early hours of the morning but goes back to sleep
2 — Unable to fall asleep again if gets out of bed

---

7.   Work and Activities

What have you been doing in work, housework, hobbies, interests and social life? Is this any different than what you used to do?

(Difficulties at work and loss of interest in hobbies and social activities are both included in terms of feelings of incapacity, listlessness, indecision and vascillation, loss of interest in hobbies, decreased social activities, decreased productivity and inability to work. Stopped working solely because of present illness rates 4)

---

o — No difficulty
1 — Thought and feelings of incapacity, fatigue or weakness related to activities, work or hobbies
2 — Loss of interest in activity; hobbies or work—either directly reported by patient or indirect in listlessness, indecision and vascillation *(feels he has to push self to work and activities)*
3 — Decrease in actual time spent in activities or decrease in productivity. In hospital, rate 3 if patient does not spend at least three hours a day in activities *(hospital job or hobbies)* exclusive of ward chores
4 — Stopped working because of present illness. In hospital, rate 4 if patient engages in no activities except ward chores, or if patient fails to perform ward chores unassisted

---

8. Retardation

(Assess solely on basis of observation at interview, not subjective complaint of slowing. Includes slowness of thought and speech, impaired ability to concentrate, decreased motor activity, apathy and stupor. A grade 4 patient is completely mute and is, therefore, unsuitable for rating on the scale. Grade 3 patients need much care and patience to rate, but it can be done.)

0 — Normal speech and thought
1 — Slight retardation at interview
2 — Obvious retardation at interview
3 — Interview difficulty
4 — Complete stupor

9. Agitation

(Rate on basis of behavior throughout the interview. This is defined as restlessness associated with anxiety. It should be differentiated from anxiety; it refers to observable phenomena.)

0 — None
1 — Playing with hands, hair, etc.
2 — Hand-wringing, nail-biting, hair-pulling, biting of lips

10. Anxiety Psychic

Have you been feeling nervous, anxious or frightened? Have you felt tense or found it hard to relax? Have you been worrying about little things?

Have you had a feeling of dread, as though something terrible were about to happen?

Have you tended to become fearful in any special situations such as being alone at home, going out alone, being in crowds, traveling, heights, elevators?

(This includes subjective feelings of tension and irritability, worrying about minor matters, an apprehensive attitude and fears.)

```
0 — No difficulty
1 — Subjective tension and irritability
2 — Worrying about minor matters
3 — Apprehensive attitude apparent in face or speech
4 — Fears expressed without questioning
```

11.   Anxiety Somatic

Have you suffered from any of the following: trembling, shakiness, excessive sweating, feelings of suffocation or choking, attacks of shortness of breath, dizziness, faintness, headaches, pain at the back of the neck, butterflies or tightness in the stomach?

How often? How badly?

(This encompasses a number of somatic complaints common in anxious patients including gastro-intestinal, wind, indigestion, cardiovascular, palpitations, headaches, respiratory, genito-urinary, etc.)

0 — Absent	*Physiological concomitants of anxiety, such as:*
1 — Mild	Gastro-intestinal—dry mouth, wind, indigestion, diarrhea, cramps, belching
2 — Moderate	Cardio-vascular—palpitations, headaches
3 — Severe	Respiratory—hyperventilation, sighing, sweating
4 — Incapacitating	

12. Somatic Symptoms Gastro-Intestinal

How has your appetite been? Have you had a heavy feeling in your stomach?

What is your pattern of bowel movements? Is this different now than your usual pattern?

(Reported changes in appetite over period of recent illness—average as to degree. Where appetite has fluctuated from anorexia to increased appetite, both may be coded. Actual failure to experience normal bowel motion. Distinguish from delusion related to constipation, i.e., bowels being blocked up, although the two may occur together. Average compared with usual pattern.)

```
o — None
1 — Loss of appetite but eating without staff encouragement. Heavy
    feelings in abdomen
2 — Difficulty eating without staff urging. Requests or requires laxatives
    or medication for bowels or medication for C.I. symptoms
```

13. Somatic Symptoms General

Do you feel tired easily? All the time? Is it an effort to do anything? Do you spend a lot of time in bed? Asleep?

Do you have any aches and pains? Feelings of heaviness?

(This includes heaviness in limbs, back or head; diffuse backache; loss of energy and fatiguability—subjective feelings. Consider average in intensity and frequency. In depression these are characteristically vague and ill-defined, and it is extremely difficult to get a satisfactory description of them from the patient.)

```
o — None
1 — Heaviness in limbs, back or head. Backaches, muscle aches. Loss of
    energy and fatiguability
2 — Any clear-cut symptoms rates 2
```

14.   Genital Symptoms

I want to ask you a few questions about your sex life. Have you lost interest in the opposite sex/your spouse/your partner recently? Have you had less sexual drive than usual? Sexual relations less often? Difficulty in obtaining an erection (men) or reaching a climax?

(Degree of reduction in usual sexual interests and activities. Consider only degree to which usual activities or interest have been reduced.)

0 — Absent	
1 — Mild	Symptoms such as: Loss of libido
	Menstrual disturbances
2 — Severe	
3 — Not ascertained	

15.   Hypochondriasis

(This refers to patient's concern with bodily complaints whether or not these are considered to have a realistic basis. The hypochondriacal patient is concerned with and keeps coming back to bodily symptoms rather than psychic complaints. Try to separate from other areas—i.e., somatic anxiety. The two may or may not co-exist. Difficulties can arise with mild hypochondriacal preoccupations. Phobias of specific disease can cause difficulties. A phobia of V.D. or of cancer will sometimes be rated under guilt by the nature of the symptoms, but other cases may give rise to much doubt and judgment requires care. Fortunately, phobias are not common.)

0 — Not present	3 — Frequent complaints, requests
1 — Self-absorption (bodily)	for help, etc.
2 — Preoccupation with health	4 — Hypochondriacal delusions

16. Loss of Weight

Have you lost weight since the trouble started? How much? (Assess *maximum* weight loss from start of illness.)

A. WHEN RATING BY HISTORY:

0 — No weight loss
1 — Probable weight loss associated with present illness
2 — Definite (according to patient) weight loss

B. ON WEEKLY RATINGS BY WARD PSYCHIATRIST, WHEN ACTUAL WEIGHT CHANGES ARE MEASURED

0 — Less than 1 lb. weight loss in week
1 — Greater than 1 lb. weight loss in week
2 — Greater than 2 lb. weight loss in week

---

17. Insight

What would you say is the nature of your trouble? Do you regard yourself as being emotionally or psychologically ill?

What caused this?

(By this is meant patient's awareness that he has a psychological disturbance together with some awareness that it has a depressive component. Degree of self-awareness, understanding of psychodynamics, and psychological causation should not be considered. This must always be considered in relation to the patient's thinking and background of knowledge. It is important to distinguish between a patient who has no insight and one who is reluctant to admit that he is "mental.")

---

0 — Acknowledges being depressed and ill
1 — Acknowledges illness but attributes cause to bad food, climate, overwork, virus, need for rest, etc.
2 — Denies being ill at all

18.   Diurnal Variation

At what time of day do you feel best? Morning? Afternoon? Evening? At what time of day do you feel worst?

(Both items are based on consistent fluctuations of mood and other symptomatology according to first or second half of the day. As a rule one will be absent if the other is present; for occasional patients who are better in the afternoon and worse both in morning and evening, both may be present. Assess difference of degree; if degree varies from day to day, try to average.)

A.M.	P.M.		
0	0 — Absent	If symptoms are worse in the morning or evening,
1	1 — Mild	note which it is and rate severity of variation ·
2	2 — Severe	

19.   Depersonalization

Have you had the feeling at all that everything was unreal, that you were unreal or that the world was distant, remote, strange or changed?

I don't mean just the feeling that you could not really imagine this illness would happen to you.

(Feelings that world and self are unreal, like a dream, remote. Consider intensity and frequency of feeling.)

0 — Absent	3 — Severe	
1 — Mild	4 — Incapacitating	Such as: Feelings of unreality,
2 — Moderate		nihilistic ideas

20. Paranoid Symptoms

Are you suspicious of other people? Do you think people are talking about you or laughing behind your back?

(If patient answers yes, probe for elaborations. Rate ideas of reference and persecution elicited at interview which do not have a depressive element, i.e., are not associated with guilt and a feeling that the persecution is deserved. If paranoid ideas do have such an element, rate instead under the most suitable heading, i.e., guilt or other depressive delusions.)

0 — None	3 — Ideas of reference
1 — Suspicious	4 — Delusions of reference and persecution
2 — Mildly Suspicious	

21. Obsessional and Compulsive Symptoms

Do you find you have to keep checking or repeating things you have already done? Do you have to do things in a special way, special order or a certain number of times?

Do you find unpleasant, frightening or ridiculous thoughts or words come into your head and won't go away, even when you try to get rid of them?

Are you afraid you might commit some terrible act without wanting to?

(Obsessional ruminations and rituals. Thoughts, mental contents, and acts which the patient resists and struggles against and which are felt as alien but originating within rather than externally. Consider intensity and frequency. Symptoms, not personality style.)

0 — Absent	2 — Severe
1 — Mild	

References*

PREFACE

DiMascio, A., Weissman, M. M., Prusoff, B. A., Neu, C., Zwilling, M., and Klerman, G. L. 1979. Differential symptom reduction by drugs and psychotherapy in acute depression. *Arch. Gen. Psychiatry* 36:1450–1456.

Klerman, G. L., DiMascio, A., Weissman, M. M., Prusoff, B., Paykel, E. S. 1974. Treatment of depression by drugs and psychotherapy. *Am. J. Psychiatry* 131:186–191.

Waskow I., and Parloff, M. 1980. *NIMH Treatment of Depression Collaborative Research (Pilot Phase)*, Revised Research Plan, Psychosocial Treatments Research Branch. NIMH, Rockville, Maryland.

Weissman, M. M. 1984. The psychological treatment of depression: an update of clinical trials. In *Psychotherapy Research: Where We Are and Where Should We Go?* eds. R. L. Spitzer and J. B. W. Williams. New York: Guilford Press.

Weissman, M. M., Prusoff, B. A., DiMascio, A., Neu, C., Goklaney, M., and Klerman, G. L. 1979. The efficacy of drugs and psychotherapy in the treatment of acute depressive episodes. *Am. J. Psychiatry* 136:555–558.

Weissman, M. M., Klerman, G. L., Paykel, E. S., Prusoff, B., Hanson, B. 1974. Treatment effects on the social adjustment of depressed patients. *Arch. Gen. Psychiatry* 30:771–778.

OVERVIEW OF IPT

Anchin, J. C., and Kiesler, D. J., eds. 1982. *Handbook of Interpersonal Psychotherapy*. New York: Pergamon Press.

Arieti, S., and Bemporad, J. 1978. *Severe and Mild Depression: The Psychotherapeutic Approach*. New York: Basic Books.

Beck, A. 1976. *Cognitive Therapy and the Emotional Disorders*. New York: International Universities Press.

Becker, J. 1974. *Depression: Theory and Research*. New York: Wiley.

Beier, E. G., and Young, D. M. 1980. Supervision in communications analytic therapy. In *Psychotherapy Supervision*, ed. A. K. Heso. New York: Wiley.

Cashdan, S. 1982. Interactional psychotherapy: using the relationship. In *Handbook of Interpersonal Psychotherapy*, eds. J. Anchin and D. J. Kiesler. New York: Pergamon Press.

Chodoff, P. 1970. The core problem in depression. In *Science and Psychoanalysis*, ed. J. Masserman. Vol. 17. New York: Grune and Stratton.

Cohen, M. B., Baker, G., Cohen, R. A., Fromm-Reichmann, F., and Weigert, E. A. 1954. An intensive study of twelve cases of manic depressive psychoses. *Psychiatry* 17:103–137.

Coyne, J. C., and Segal, L. 1982. A brief strategic interactional approach to psychotherapy. In *Handbook of Interpersonal Psychotherapy*, eds. J. C. Anchin and D. J. Kiesler. New York: Pergamon Press.

Davenloo, H. 1982. *Short-Term Dynamic Psychotherapy*. New York: Jason Aronson.

DiMascio, A., Weissman, M. M., Prusoff, B. A., Neu, C., Zwilling, M. and Klerman, G. L. 1979. Differential symptom reduction by drugs and psychotherapy in acute depression. *Arch. Gen. Psychiatry* 36:1450–1456.

*Preparation by Jacqueline M. Davidson, M.A. and Theresa Falzone-Ross

Frank, J.D. 1973. *Persuasion and Healing: A Comparative Study of Psychotherapy.* Baltimore: Johns Hopkins University Press.

Fromm-Reichmann, F. 1960. *Principles of Intensive Psychotherapy.* Chicago: Phoenix Books.

Glass, G. V., Smith, M. L., and Miller, T. I. 1980. *The Benefits of Psychotherapy.* Baltimore: Johns Hopkins University Press.

Herceg-Baron, R. L., Prusoff, B. A., Weissman, M. M., DiMascio, A., Neu, C., and Klerman, G. L. 1979. Pharmacotherapy and psychotherapy in acutely depressed patients: A study of attrition patterns in a clinical trial. *Compre. Psychiatry* 20:315–325.

Hersen, M. 1976. Pharmacological and Social Skill Treatment for Unipolar (Nonpsychotic) Depression (unpublished protocol; personal communication).

Hirschfeld, R., and Cross, C. Personality, life events and social factors in depression. 1983. In *Psychiatry Update*, vol. II, ed. L. Grinspoon. Washington, D.C.: American Psychiatric Press.

Klerman, G. L. 1981. The pathophysiology of depression. Menninger Prize Award Lecture at the American College of Physicians, Kansas City, Mo. (April 6, 1981).

Klerman, G. L., DiMascio, A., Weissman, M. M., Prusoff, B. A., and Paykel, E. S. 1974. Treatment of depression by drugs and psychotherapy. *Am. J. Psychiatry* 131:186–191.

Lewisohn, P. M., Biglan, A., and Zeiss, A. 1976. Behavioral treatment of depression. In *The Behavioral Management of Anxiety, Depression and Pain*, ed. P. Davidson. New York: Brunner Mazel.

Luborsky, L., Singer, B., and Luborsky, L. 1975. Comparative studies of psychotherapies: Is it true that 'Everybody has won and all must have prizes'? *Arch. Gen. Psychiatry* 32:995–1008.

Malan, D. H. 1963. *A Study of Brief Psychotherapy.* London: Tavistock Publications.

Mann, J. 1973. *Time-Limited Psychotherapy.* Cambridge, Mass.: Harvard University Press.

McLean, P. D., Ogston, K., and Grauer, L. 1973. A behavioral approach to the treatment of depression. *J. Behav. Ther. and Exp. Psychiatry* 4:323–330.

Meyer, A. 1957 *Psychobiology: A Science of Man.* Springfield, Ill.: Charles C. Thomas.

Murphy, J. 1983. A Longitudinal Study of Psychiatric Epidemiology: The Stirling County Study (unpublished).

Parloff, M. B., Wolfe, B., Hadley, S., Waskow, I., and Parloff, G. H. 1978. Assessment of Psychosocial Treatment of Mental Health Disorders: Current Status and Prospects. Report to the National Academy of Sciences. Institute of Medicine, Washington, D.C. Research Branch. NIMH, Rockville, Maryland.

Paykel, E. S., DiMascio, A., Klerman, G. L., Prusoff, B. A., and Weissman, M. M. 1976. Maintenance therapy of depression. *Pharmakopsychiatrie Neuropsychopharmakologie* 9:127–136.

Prusoff, B. A., Weissman, M. M., Klerman, G. L., and Rounsaville, B. J. 1980. Research diagnostic criteria subtypes of depression: their role as predictors of differential response to psychotherapy and drug treatment. *Arch. Gen. Psychiatry* 37:796–803.

Rehm, L. P. 1976. Studies in self-control treatment of depression. Presented at American Psychological Association meeting, NDC, September.

Rounsaville, B. J., Glazer, W., Wilber, C. H., Weissman, M. M., and Kleber, H. D. 1983. Short-term interpersonal psychotherapy in methadone maintained opiate addicts. *Arch. Gen. Psychiatry* 40:629–636.

Rounsaville, B. J., Prusoff, B. A., and Weissman, M. M. 1980. The course of marital disputes in depressed women: a 48-month follow-up study. *Compre. Psychiatry* 21:111–118.

Rounsaville, B. J., Weissman, M. M., Prusoff, B. A., and Herceg-Baron, R. L. 1979. Process of psychotherapy among depressed women with marital disputes. *Am. J. Orthopsychiatry* 49:505–510.

Sifneos, P. E. 1979. *Short-Term Dynamic Psychotherapy: Evaluation and Technique.* New York: Plenum Press.

Strupp, H. 1982. *Time Limited Dynamic Psychotherapy* (TLDP). Center for Psychotherapy Research, Dept. of Psychology, Nashville: Vanderbilt University.

Sullivan, H. S. 1953. *The Interpersonal Theory of Psychiatry.* New York: Norton.

Waskow I., and Parloff, M. 1980. *NIMH Treatment of Depression Collaborative Research (Pilot Phase)*, Revised Research Plan; Psychosocial Treatments Research Branch. NIMH, Rockville, Maryland.

Weissman, M. M., Prusoff, B. A., DiMascio, A., Neu, C., Goklaney, M. and Klerman, G. L. 1979. The efficacy of drugs and psychotherapy in the treatment of acute depressive episodes. *Am. J. Psychiatry* 136:555–558.

Weissman, M. M., Myers, J. K., and Thompson, W. D. 1981. Depression and its treatment in a U.S. urban community, 1975–1976. *Arch. Gen. Psychiatry* 38:417–421.

Weissman, M. M. 1984 The psychological treatment of depression: An update of clinical trials. In *Psychotherapy Research: Where Are We and Where Should We Go?* eds. J. B. Williams and R. L. Spitzer. New York: Guilford Press.

Weissman, M. M., and Klerman, G. L. 1977a. Sex differences and the epidemiology of depression. *Arch. Gen. Psychiatry* 34:98–111.

Weissman, M. M., and Klerman, G. L. 1977b. The chronic depressive in the community: unrecognized and poorly treated. *Compre. Psychiatry* 18:523–532.

Weissman, M. M., Klerman, G. L., Prusoff, B. A., Sholomskas, and D., Padian, N. 1981. Depressed outpatients: results one year after treatment with drugs and/or interpersonal psychotherapy. *Arch. Gen. Psychiatry* 38:51–55.

Weissman, M. M., Klerman, G. L., Paykel, E. S., Prusoff, B. A., and Hanson, B. 1974. Treatment effects on the social adjustment of depressed patients. *Arch. Gen Psychiatry* 30:771–778.

Weissman, M. M., Prusoff, B. A., Klerman, G. L. 1978. Personality and the prediction of long-term outcome of depression. *Am. J. Psychiatry* 135:797–800.

Weissman, M. M., Kasl, S. V., and Klerman, G. L. 1976. Follow-up of depressed women after maintenance treatment. *Am. J. Psychiatry* 133:757–760.

Zuckerman, D. M., Prusoff, B. A., Weissman, M. M., and Padian, N. S. 1980. Personality as a predictor of psychotherapy and pharmacotherapy outcome for depressed outpatients. *J. Consult. Clin. Psychol.* 48:730–735.

Part I

CHAPTER 1

Angst, J. 1966. Etiological and nosological considerations in endogenous depressive psychosis. *Monographien aus dem Gesantgebiete der Neurologie und Psychiatrie.* Berlin: Springer.

Auden, W. H. 1947. *The Age of Anxiety.* New York: Random House.

Beck, A. 1969. Measuring depression: the depression inventory. In *Recent Advances in the Psychology of Depressive Illnesses,* eds. M. M. Katz and J. A. Shields. Washington, D.C.: U. S. Government Printing Office.

Bowlby, J. 1969. *Attachment.* New York: Basic Books.

Bradburn, N. M. 1977. The measurement of psychological well-being. In Elinson, J. et al (eds) *Health goals and health indicators.* Washington: American Association for the Advancement of Science. pp. 84–94.

Darwin, C. 1872. *The Expression of the Emotions in Man and Animals.* London: John Murray.

Eckman, P., ed. 1973. *Darwin and Facial Expression.* New York: Academic Press.

Freud, S. 1917. Mourning and melancholia. In *Standard Edition,* Vol. 14, ed. J. Strachey. London: Hogarth Press.

Goodall, J., and Hamburg, D. 1971. *In the Shadow of Man.* Boston: Houghton Mifflin.

Harlow, H. F., Harlow, M. K., and Suomi, S. J. 1971. From thought to therapy: lessons from a primate laboratory. *Am. Scientist* 59:538–549.

Kaufman, I. C., and Rosenblum, L. A. 1967. The reaction to separation in infant monkeys: anaclitic depression and conservation withdrawal. *Psychosom. Med.* 29:648–675.

Klerman, G. L. 1974. Depression and adaptation. In *The Psychology of Depression: Contemporary Theory and Research,* eds. R. J. Friedman and M. M. Katz, pp. 127–156. Washington, D.C.: Winston-Wiley.

Klerman, G. L. Practical issues in the treatment of depression and mania. In *Handbook of Affective Disorders,* ed. E. Paykel. New York: Guilford Press.

Leonhard, K., Korff, I., and Schulz, H. 1962. Temperament in families with monopolar and bipolar phasic psychoses. *Psychiatr. Neurol.* 143:416.

Lifton, R. J. 1976. *The Life of the Self: Toward a New Psychology.* New York: Simon & Schuster.

Marsella, A. J. 1979. Cross-cultural studies of mental disorder. In *Perspectives on Cross-Cultural Psychology,* eds. A. J. Marsella, R. G. Tharp, and T. J. Ciborowski, New York: Academic Press.

McKinney, W. T., Suomi, S. J., and Harlow, H. F. 1973. New models of separation and depression in rhesus monkeys. In *Separation and Depression,* eds. J. P. Scott and E. C. Senay. Washington, D.C. American Association for the Advancement of Science.

Perris, C. 1966. A study of bipolar (manic-depressive) and unipolar recurrent depressive psychoses. *Acta. Psychiatr. Scand.* Suppl. 42:194.

Robins E., Munoz, R. A., Martin, S., and Gentry, K. A. 1972. Primary and secondary affective disorders. In *Disorders of Mood,* eds. J. Zubin and F. A. Freyhan. Baltimore: Johns Hopkins University Press.

Robins, E., and Guze, S. 1972. Classification of affective disorders. In *Recent Advances in the Psychobiology of Depressive Illness,* eds. T. A. Williams, M. M. Katz, and J. A. Shield. Washington, D.C.: U.S. Government Printing Office.

Schwartz, G. E., Fair, P. L., Salt, P., Mandel, M. R., and Klerman, G. L. 1976. Facial muscle patterning to affective imagery in depressed and nondepressed subjects. *Science* 192:489–491.

Scott, J. P. 1970. Separation in infant dogs: emotional and motivational aspects. Presented at the American Association for the Advancement of Science. Chicago, December 1970.

Weissman, M. M., and Boyd, J. H. 1983. The epidemiology of affective disorders: rates and risk factors. In *Psychiatry Update,* Vol. II, ed. L. Grinspoon. Washington, D.C.: American Psychiatric Press.

Weissman, M. M., Fox, K., and Klerman, G. L. 1973. Hostility and depression associated with suicide attempts. *Am. J. Psychiatry* 130:450–455.

CHAPTER 2

Anchin, J. C., and Kiesler, D. J., eds. 1982. *Handbook of Interpersonal Psychotherapy.* New York: Pergamon Press.

Armor, D., and Klerman, G. 1968. Psychiatric treatment orientations and professional ideology. *J. Health and Soc. Behavior* 9:243.

Bowen, M. 1960. A family concept of schizophrenia. In *The Etiology of Schizophrenia,* ed. D. D. Jackson. New York: Basic Books.

Burdock, E. I., Sudilovsky, A., and Gershon, S., eds. 1982. *The Behavior of Psychiatric Patients.* New York: Marcell Dekker.

Cohen, M. B., Blake, G., Cohen, R., Fromm-Reichmann, F., and Weigert, E. 1954. An intensive study of twelve cases of manic depressive psychosis. *Psychiatry* 17:103–137.

Faris, R. E., and Dunham, H. 1939. *Mental Disorders in Urban Areas: An Ecological Study of Schizophrenia and Other Psychoses.* Chicago: University of Chicago Press.

Fromm-Reichmann, F. 1960. *Principles of Intensive Psychotherapy.* Chicago: Phoenix Books.

Goffman, E. 1961. *Asylums.* New York: Doubleday.

Goldhammer, H., and Marshall, A. 1953. *Psychosis and Civilization: Two Studies in the Frequency of Mental Disease.* New York: The Free Press.

Gruenberg, E. 1966. Evaluating the effectiveness of community mental health services. *Milbank Memorial Fund Quarterly,* Part II, January.

Havens, L. 1973. *Approaches to the Mind.* Boston: Little, Brown.

Hollingshead, A., and Redlich, F. 1958. *Social Class and Mental Illness.* New York: Wiley.

Holmes, T., and Rahe, R. 1967. The social readjustment rating scale. *J. Psychosom. Res.* 2:213.

Klerman, G. 1979. The psychobiology of affective states: the legacy of Adolf Meyer. In *Psychobiology of Human Behavior,* eds. J. Brady and E. Meyer. Baltimore: Johns Hopkins University Press.

Lazare, A. 1979. ed. *Outpatient Psychiatry.* London: Williams and Wilkins.

Leighton, D., Harding, J., Macklin, D. B., Hughes, C. C., and Leighton, A. H. 1963. Psychiatric findings of the Stirling County study. *Am. J. Psychiatry* 119:1021–1026.

Lidz, T., Fleck, S., and Cornelison, A. 1965. *Schizophrenia and the Family.* New York: International Universities Press.

Meyer, A. 1957. *Psychobiology: A Science of Man.* Springfield, Ill. Charles C. Thomas.

Murphy, J. 1976. Psychiatric labeling in cross-cultural perspective. *Science* 191:1019.

Rennie, T. A., and Srole, L. 1956. Social class prevalence and distribution of psychosomatic conditions in an urban population. *Psychosomat. Med.* 18:Nov.–Dec.

Robins, L. N., Helzer, J. E., and Croughan, J. 1981. The development and characteristics of the NIMH diagnostic interview schedule. In *Epidemiologic Community Surveys,* eds. M. M. Weissman, J. Myers, and C. Ross. New York: Neale Watson Academic Publications.

Rothman, D. 1980. *Conscience and Convenience: The Asylum and Its Alternatives in Progressive America.* Boston: Little, Brown.

Srole, L., and Fischer, A. 1980. The midtown-Manhattan longitudinal study vs. the mental illness paradise lost doctrine. *Arch. Gen. Psychiatry* 37:209.

Stanton, A. H., and Schwartz, M. S. 1954. *The Mental Hospital*. New York: Basic Books.

Stouffer, S. 1950. *Measurement and Prediction*. New York: Wiley.

Strauss, A., and Schatzman, L., Bucher, R., Ehrlich, D., and Sabshin, M. 1964. *Psychiatric Ideologies and Institutes*. New York: The Free Press.

Sullivan, H. S. 1956. *Clinical Studies in Psychiatry*. New York: Norton.

Wynne, L., and Singer, M. 1963. Thought disorder and family relations of schizophrenia. *Arch. Gen. Psychiatry* 9:191–198.

CHAPTER 3

Abraham, K. 1927. *Selected Papers of Karl Abraham*. London: Hogarth Press.

Birtchnell, J. 1980. Women whose mothers died in childhood: an outcome study. *Psychol. Med.* 10:699–713.

Bloom, B. L., Asher, S. J., and White, S. W. 1978. Marital disruption as a stressor: a review and analysis. *Psychological Bull.* 85:867–894.

Bowlby, J. 1969. *Attachment and Loss*, Vol I: *Attachment*. London: Hogarth Press.

Bowlby, J. 1977. The making and breaking of affectional bonds: II. Some principles of psychotherapy. *Brit. J. Psychiatry* 130:421–431.

Briscoe, C. W., and Smith, J. B. 1973. Depression and marital turmoil. *Arch. Gen. Psychiatry* 28:811–817.

Brown, G. W., Harris, T., and Copeland, J. R. 1977. Depression and loss. *Brit. J. Psychiat.* 130:1–18.

Brumbach, R. A., Dietz-Schmidt, S., and Weinberg, W. A. 1977. Depression in children referred to an educational diagnostic center—diagnosis and treatment and analysis of criteria and literature review. *Dis. Nerv. Syst.* 38:529–535.

Clayton, P., Desmarais, L., and Winokur, G. 1968. A study of normal bereavement. *Am. J. Psychiatry* 125:168–178.

Collins, J., Kreitman, N., Nelson, B., and Troop, J. 1971. Neurosis and marital interaction: III. Family roles and functions. *Brit. J. Psychiatry* 119:233–242.

Connell, H. M. 1972. Depression in childhood. *Child Psychiatry Human Develop.* 4:71–85.

Coyne, J. C. 1976. Depression and the response of others. *J. Abnorm. Psychol.* 85:186–193.

Evans, J. 1975. Depression in adolescents. *Proc. Roy. Soc. Med.* 68:565–566.

Eysenck, H. *Manual of the Maudsley Personality Inventory*. 1962. San Diego: Educational and Industrial Testing Service.

Foulds, G. A. 1965. *Personality and Personal Illness*. London: Tavistock Publications.

Frank, J. D. 1973. *Persuasion and Healing: A Comparative Study of Psychotherapy*. Baltimore: John Hopkins University Press.

Freud, S. 1917. Mourning and melancholia. In *Standard Edition*, Vol. 14, ed. J. Strachey. London: Hogarth Press.

Gamer, E., Gallant, D., Grunebaum, H. U., and Cohler, B. J. 1977. Children of psychotic mothers. *Arch. Gen. Psychiatry* 34:592–597.

Goodall, J., and Hamburg, D. 1971. *In the Shadow of Man*. Boston: Houghton Mifflin.

Hammen, C. L., and Peters, S. D. 1978. Interpersonal consequences of depression: response to men and women enacting a depressed role. *J. Abnorm. Psychol.* 87:322–332.

Harlow, H. H., and Suomi, S. J. 1974. Induced depression in monkeys. *Behavioral Biology* 12:273–279.

Henderson, S., Byrne, D. G., and Duncan, P. 1982. *Neurosis and the Social Environment*. Sydney: Academic Press.

Henderson, S., Byrne, D. G., Duncan-Jones, P., Adcock, S., Scott, R., and Steele, G. P. 1978b. Social bonds in the epidemiology of neurosis. *Brit. J. Psychiatry* 132:463–466.

Henderson, S., Duncan-Jones, P., McAuley, H., and Ritchie, K. 1978a. The patient's primary group. *Brit. J. Psychiatry* 132:74–86.

Henderson, S., Duncan-Jones, P., Byrne, D. G., Scott, R., and Adcock, S. 1979. Psychiatric disorder in Canberra: a standardized study of prevalence. *Acta Psychiatr. Scand.* 60:355–74.

Henderson, S., Byrne, G., Duncan Jones, P., Scott, R., and Adcock, S. 1980. Social relationships, adversity and neurosis: a study of associations in a general population sample. *Brit. J. Psychiatry* 136:574–583.

Henderson, S. 1980. A development in social psychiatry. The systematic study of social bonds. *J. Nerv. Ment. Dis.* 168:63–69.

Henderson, S. 1974. Care-eliciting behavior in man. *J. Nerv. Ment. Dis.* 159:172–181.

Henderson, S. 1977. The social network, support and neurosis: the function of attachment in adult life. *Brit. J. Psychiatry* 131:185–191.

Hinchliffe, M., Hooper, D., Roberts, F. J., and Vaughan, P. W. 1975. A study of the interactions between depressed patients and their spouses. *Brit. J. Psychiatry* 126:164–172.

Hinchliffe, M., Vaughan, P. W., Hooper, D., and Roberts, F. J. 1977. The melancholy marriage: an inquiry into the interaction of depression, II. Expressiveness. *Brit. J. Med. Psychol.* 50:125–142.

Hinchliffe, M. K., Vaughan, P. W., Hooper, D., and Roberts, F. J. 1978. The melancholy marriage: an inquiry into the interaction of depression. III. Responsiveness. *Brit. J. Med. Psychol.* 51:1–13.

Hinchliffe, M. K., Hooper, D., and Roberts, F. J. 1978. *The Melancholy Marriage.* New York: Wiley.

Hirschfeld, R. M. A., and Klerman, G. L. 1979. Personality attributes and affective disorders. *Am. J. Psychiatry* 136:67–70.

Holmes, T. H., Goodell, H., and Wolf, S. 1950. *The Nose. An Experimental Study of Reactions Within the Nose of Human Subjects During Varying Life Experiences.* Springfield, Ill.: Charles C. Thomas.

Hooper, D. Roberts, F. J., Hinchliffe, M. K., and Vaughan, P. W. 1977. The melancholy marriage: an inquiry into the interaction of depression. I. Introduction. *Brit. J. Med. Psychol.* 50:113–124.

Ilfeld, F. W. 1977. Current social stressors and symptoms of depression. *Am. J. Psychiatry* 134:-161–166.

Kovacs, M., Betof, N. G., Celebre, J. E., Mansheim, P. A., Petty, L. K., and Raynak, J. T. 1977. Childhood depression—myth or clinical syndrome? (unpublished).

Kreitman, N., Collins, J., Nelson, B., and Troop, J. 1971. Neurosis and marital interaction: IV. Manifest psychological interactions. *Brit. J. Psychiatry* 119:243–252.

Lindemann, E. 1944. Symptomatology and management of acute grief. *Am. J. Psychiatry* 101:-141–148.

Maddison, D., and Walker, W. 1967. Factors affecting the outcome of conjugal bereavement. *Brit. J. Psychiatry* 113:1057–1067.

Maddison, D. 1968. The relevance of conjugal bereavement for preventive psychiatry. *Brit. J. Med. Psychol.* 41:223–233.

Malmquist, C. P. 1971. Depression in childhood and adolescence. *New Eng. J. Med.* 284:887–893.

Malmquist, C. P. 1975. Depression in childhood. In *The Nature and Treatment of Depression*, eds. F. F. Flack and S. C. Draghi. New York: Wiley.

Merikangas, K., Ranelli, C., and Kupfer, D. 1979. Marital interaction in hospitalized depressed patients. *J. Nerv. Ment. Dis.* 167:689–695.

Miller, P., and Ingham, J. G. 1976. Friends, confidants and symptoms. *Soc. Psychiat.* 11:51–58.

Myers, J. K., Lindenthal, J. J., and Pepper, M. P. 1975. Life events, social integration and psychiatric symptomatology. *J. Health and Soc. Behavior* 16:421–427.

Orvaschel, H., Weissman, M. M., and Kidd, K. K. 1980. Children and depression: the children of depressed parents; the childhood of depressed patients; depression in children. *J. Affective Disorders* 2:1–16.

Parker, G. 1978. *The Bonds of Depression.* Sydney: Angus and Robertson Publishers.

Parker, G. 1979. Parental characteristics in relation to depressive disorders. *Brit. J. Psychiatry* 134:-138–147.

Paykel, E. 1978. Recent life events in the development of depressive disorders. In *The Psychobiology of Depressive Disorders: Implications for the Effects of Stress*, ed. R. A. Defue. New York: Academic Press.

Paykel, E. S., Myers, J. K., Dienelt, M. N., Klerman, G. L., Lindenthal, J. J., and Pepper, M. P. 1969. Life events and depression: a controlled study. *Arch. Gen. Psychiatry* 21:753–760.

Pearlin, L. I., and Lieberman, M. A. 1977. Social sources of emotional distress. In *Research in Community and Mental Health*, ed. R. Simmons. Greenwich, Conn.: JAI Press.

Poznanski, E., and Zrull, J. P. 1970. Childhood depression. *Arch. Gen. Psychiatry* 23:8–15.

Puig-Antich, J., Perel, J. M., Lupatkin, W., Chambers, W. J., Shea, C., Tabrizi, M. A., and Stiller, R. L. 1979. Plasma levels of imipramine (IMI) and desmethylimipramine (DMI) and clinical response in prepubertal major depressive disorder: a preliminary report. *J. Amer. Acad. Child Psychiatry* 18:616–627.

Rabkin, J. G., and Struening, E. L. 1976. Life events and illness. *Science* 194:1013–1020.

Rado, S. 1968. Psychodynamics of depression from the etiologic point of view. In *The Meaning of Despair,* ed. W. Gaylin. New York: Science House.

Rolf, J. E., and Garmezy, N. 1974. The school performance of children vulnerable to behavior pathology. In *Life History Research in Psychopathology,* eds. D. F. Ricks, T. Alexander, and M. Roff. Vol III. Minneapolis, Minn.: University of Minnesota Press.

Rounsaville, B. J., Weissman, M. M., Prusoff, B. A., and Herceg-Baron, R. L. 1979. Process of psychotherapy among depressed women with marital disputes. *Am. J. Orthopsychiatry* 49:505–510.

Rounsaville, B. J., Weissman, M. M., Prusoff, B. A., and Herceg-Baron, R. L. 1979. Marital disputes and treatment outcome in depressed women. *Compre. Psychiatry* 20:483–490.

Roy, A. 1978. Vulnerability factors and depression in women. *Brit. J. Psychiatry* 133:106–110.

Rutter, M. 1972. *Maternal Deprivation Reassessed.* London: Penguin Books.

Rutter, M., Graham, P., Chadwick, O.F.D., and Yule, W. 1976. Adolescent turmoil—fact or fiction? J. Child. Psychol. 17:35–56.

Schless, A. P., and Mendels, J. 1977. Life events and psychopathology. *Psychiat. Digest* 28:25–35.

Scott, J. P., Stewart, J. M., and DeGhett, V. S. 1970. Separation in infant days: emotional response and motivational consequences. In *Separation and Depression, Clinical and Research Aspects,* eds. J. P. Scott and E. C. Senay. Washington, D.C.: American Association for the Advancement of Science.

Tennant, C., Bebbington, P., and Hurry, J. 1980. Parental death in childhood and risk of adult depressive disorders: a review. *Psychol. Med.* 10(2):289–299.

Uhlenhuth, E. H., and Paykel, E. S. 1973. Symptom intensity and life events. *Arch. Gen. Psychiatry* 28:473–477.

Walker, K., MacBride, A., and Vachon, M. 1977. Social support networks and the crisis of bereavement. *Soc. Sci. Med.* 11:35–41.

Waring, E., McElrath, D., Lefcoe, D., and Weisz, G. 1981. Dimensions of intimacy in marriage. *Psychiatry* 44:169–175.

Weintraub, S., Neale, J. M., and Liebert, D. E. 1975. Teacher ratings of children vulnerable to psychopathology. *Am. J. Orthopsychiatry* 45:839–845.

Weiss, R. S. 1975. *Marital Separation.* New York: Basic Books.

Weissman, M. M., and Paykel, E. S. 1974. *The Depressed Woman: A Study of Social Relationships.* Chicago: University of Chicago Press.

Weissman, M. M., Prusoff, B. A., DiMascio, A., Neu, C., Goklaney, M., and Klerman, G. L. 1979. The efficacy of drugs and psychotherapy in the treatment of acute depressive episodes. *Am. J. Psychiatry* 136 (No. 4B):555–558.

Weissman, M. M., Paykel, E. S., and Klerman, G. L. 1972. The depressed woman as mother. *Soc. Psychiatry* 7:98–108.

Weissman, M. M., Kasl, S. V., and Klerman, G. L. 1976. Follow-up of depressed women after maintenance treatment. *Am. J. Psychiatry* 133:757–760.

Weissman, M. M., and Bothwell, S. 1977. The assessment of social adjustment by patient self-report. *Arch. Gen. Psychiatry* 33:1111–1115.

Welner, Z., Welner, A., McCrary, M. D., and Leonard, M. A. 1977. Psychopathology in children of inpatients with depression—a controlled study. *J. Nerv. Ment. Dis.* 164:408–413.

Zuckerman, D. M., Prusoff, B. A., Weissman, M. M., and Padian, N. 1980. Personality as a predictor of short-term treatment outcome in depressed outpatients. *J. Consult. Clin. Psychol.* 48:730–735.

Part II

CHAPTER 5

Kiresuk, T. J. 1976. Goal attainment scaling of a country mental health service. In *Trends in Mental Health Evaluation,* eds. E. W. Markson and D. F. Allen. Lexington, Mass: D. C. Heath.

Parsons, T. 1951. Illness and the role of the physician: a sociological perspective. *Am. J. Orthopsychiatry* 21:452–460.

Prusoff, B. A., Weissman, M. M., Klerman, G. L., and Rounsaville, B. J. 1980. Research diagnostic criteria subtypes of depression as predictors of differential response to psychotherapy and drug treatments. *Arch. Gen. Psychiatry* 37:796–803.

Rounsaville, B. J., Klerman, G. L., and Weissman, M. M. 1981. Do psychotherapy and pharmacotherapy conflict? *Arch. Gen. Psychiatry* 38:24–29.

Suchman, E. A. 1965a Social patterns of illness and medical care. *J. Health H. Behavior* 6:2–16.

Suchman, E. A. 1965b Stages of illness and medical care. *J. Health H. Behavior* 6:114–28

CHAPTER 6

Horowitz, M. 1976. *Stress Response Syndromes.* New York: Jason Aronson.

Lindemann, E. 1944. Symptomatology and management of acute grief. *Am. J. Psychiatry* 101:-141–148.

Siggins, L. D. 1966. Mourning: a critical survey of the literature. *Int. J. Psychoanal.* 47:14.

CHAPTER 7

Paykel, E. 1982. Life events and early environment. In *Handbook of Affective Disorders,* ed. E. Paykel. New York: Guilford Press.

CHAPTER 8

Erikson, E. H. 1968. *Identity: Youth and Crisis.* New York: W. W. Norton.

Keniston, K. 1968. *Young Radicals.* New York: Harcourt Brace and Co.

Levinson, D. J. 1978. *The Seasons of a Man's Life.* New York: Alfred A. Knopf.

Lidz, T. *The Person.* 1976. New York: Basic Books.

CHAPTER 11

Bibring, E. 1953. Mechanism of Depression. In *Affective Disorders,* ed. P. Greenacre. New York: International Universities Press.

Menninger, K. A., and Holzman, P. S. 1973. *Theory of Psychoanalytic Technique.* New York: Basic Books.

CHAPTER 12

Davenloo, H. 1982. *Short-Term Dynamic Psychotherapy.* New York: Jason Aronson.

Hirschfield, R. M. A. 1981. Situational depression: validity of the concept. *Brit. J. Psychiatry* 139:-297–305.

Malan, D. H. 1963. *A Study of Brief Psychotherapy.* London: Tavistock Publications.

Sifneos, P. E. 1979. *Short-Term Dynamic Psychotherapy: Evaluation and Technique.* New York: Plenum Press.

Part III

CHAPTER 13

Covi, L., Lipman, R., Derogatis, L., Smith, J., and Pattison, J. 1974. Drugs and group psychotherapy in neurotic depression. *Am. J. Psychiatry* 131:191–198.

Davis, J. M. 1976. Overview: maintenance therapy in psychiatry: affective disorders. *Am. J. Psychiatry* 133:1–13.

DiMascio, A., Weissman, M. M., Prusoff, B. A., Neu, C., Zwilling, M., and Klerman, G. L. 1979. Differential symptom reduction by drugs and psychotherapy in acute depression. *Arch. Gen. Psychiatry* 36:1450–1456.

Friedman, A. 1975. Interaction of drug therapy with marital therapy in depressed patients. *Arch. Gen. Psychiatry* 32:619–637.

Gelenberg, A. J., and Klerman, G. L. 1978. The effects of amitriptyline and lithium on a patient with 48-hour recurrent depressions. *J. Nerv. Ment. Dis.* 166:365–368.

Group for the Advancement of Psychiatry. 1975. *Pharmacotherapy and Psychotherapy: Paradoxes, Problems and Progress* 9:261–431. New York: Mental Health Materials, Inc.

Herceg-Baron, R., Prusoff, B. A., Weissman, M. M., DiMascio, A., Neu, C., and Kleeman, G. L. 1979. Pharmacotherapy and psychotherapy in acutely depressed patients: a study of attrition patterns in a clinical trial. *Compre. Psychiatry* 20:315–325.

Klerman, G. L., DiMascio, A., Weissman, M. M., Prusoff, B. A., and Paykel, E. S. 1974. Treatment of depression by drugs and psychotherapy. *Am. J. Psychiatry* 131:186–191.

Klerman, G. L., and Hirschfeld, R. M. 1978. The use of antidepressants in clinical practice. *JAMA* 240:1403–1406.

Klerman, G. L. 1976. Psychoneurosis: integrating pharmacotherapy and psychotherapy. In *Successful Psychotherapy*, ed P. Claghorn. New York: Brunner Mazel.

Mandell, M. M., and Klerman, G. L. 1978. Clinical use of antidepressants, stimulants, tricyclics, and monoamine oxidase inhibitors. In *Principles of Psychopharmacology*, 2nd ed., ed. W. Clark. New York: Academic Press.

Paykel, E., ed. 1982. *Handbook of Affective Disorders*. New York: Guilford Press.

Prien, R. F., Klett, C. J., and Caffey, E. M. 1973. Prepublication Report No. 94. Central Neuropsychiatric Research Laboratory, VA Cooperative Studies in Psychiatry, VA Hospital, Perry Point, Maryland.

Rounsaville, B. J., Klerman, G. L., and Weissman, M. M. 1981. Do psychotherapy and pharmacotherapy of depression conflict? Empirical evidence from a clinical trial. *Arch. Gen. Psychiatry* 38:24–29.

Uhlenhuth, E. H., Balter, M. B., and Lipman, R. S. 1978. Minor tranquilizers: clinical correlates of use in an urban population. *Arch. Gen. Psychiatry* 35:650–655.

Weissman, M. M. 1979. The psychological treatment of depression. *Arch. Gen. Psychiatry* 36:1261–1269.

Weissman, M. M. 1984. The psychological treatment of depression: an update of clinical trials. In *Psychotherapy Research: Where Are We and Where Should We Go?*, eds. J. B. Williams and R. L. Spitzer. New York: Guilford Press.

Weissman, M. M., Klerman, G. L., Prusoff, B. A., Sholomskas, D., and Padian, N. 1981. Depressed outpatients one year after treatment with drugs and/or interpersonal psychotherapy (IPT). *Arch. Gen. Psychiatry* 38:51–55.

Weissman, M. M., Prusoff, B. A., DiMascio, A., Neu, C., Goklaney, M., and Klerman, G. L. 1979. The efficacy of drugs and psychotherapy in the treatment of acute depressive episodes. *Am. J. Psychiatry* 136:555–558.

Wender, P., and Klein, D. 1981. *Mind, Mood and Medicine: Guide to the New Biopsychiatry*. New York: Farrar, Straus and Giroux.

West, E. D., and Dally, P. J. 1959. Effect of iproniazid in depressive syndromes. *Brit. Med. J.* 1:1491–1494.

CHAPTER 15

Chevron, E. S., and Rounsaville, B. J. 1983. Evaluating the clinical skills of psychotherapists: a comparison of techniques. *Arch. Gen. Psychiatry* 40:1129–1137.

Chevron, E. S., Rounsaville, B. J., Rothblum, E., and Weissman, M. M. 1983. Selecting psychotherapists to participate in psychotherapy outcome studies: relationship between psychotherapist characteristics and assessment of clinical skills. *J. Nerv. Ment. Dis.* 171:348–353.

Chevron, E. S., Rounsaville, B. J., and Weissman, M. M. 1983. Training psychotherapists in interpersonal psychotherapy. Presented at SPR meetings. Sheffield, England, July 1983.

Frank, J. D. 1973. *Persuasion and Healing: A Comparative Study of Psychotherapy*. Baltimore: Johns Hopkins University Press.

Parloff, M. B., Waskow, I. E., and Wolfe, B. E. 1978. Research on therapist variables in relation to process and outcome. In *Handbook of Psychotherapy and Behavior Change: An Empirical Analysis*, eds. S. L. Garfield and A. E. Bergin, 2nd ed. New York: John Wiley and Sons.

Rogers, C. R. 1959. Client-centered therapy. In *American Handbook of Psychiatry*, Vol. 3, ed. S. Arieti. New York: Basic Books.

Strupp, H., and Bergin, A. E. 1969. Some empirical and conceptual bases for coordinated research in psychotherapy. *Int. J. Psychiatry* 7:18–19.

Sullivan, H. S. 1953. *The Interpersonal Theory of Psychiatry*. New York: Norton.

Weissman, M. M., Rounsaville, B. J., and Chevron, E. 1982. Training psychotherapists to participate in psychotherapy outcome studies. *Am. J. Psychiatry* 139:1442–1446.

Index